Julie King's Everyday Photoshop® Elements

Julie King's Everyday Photoshop® Elements

JULIE KING

McGraw-Hill/Osborne
New York Chicago San Francisco
Lisbon London Madrid Mexico City
Milan New Delhi San Juan
Seoul Singapore Sydney Toronto

McGraw-Hill/Osborne
2100 Powell Street, 10th Floor
Emeryville, California 94608
U.S.A.

To arrange bulk purchase discounts for sales promotions, premiums, or fund-raisers, please contact **McGraw-Hill**/Osborne at the above address. For information on translations or book distributors outside the U.S.A., please see the International Contact Information page immediately following the index of this book.

Julie King's Everyday Photoshop® Elements

1234567890 WCT WCT 01987654

ISBN 0-07-225681-8

Vice President & Group Publisher	Philip Ruppel
Vice President & Publisher	Jeffrey Krames
Executive Editor	Jane K. Brownlow
Senior Project Editor	LeeAnn Pickrell
Acquisitions Coordinator	Agatha Kim
Technical Editor	Kathy Eyster
Copy Editor	Margaret Berson
Proofreader	Stefany Otis
Indexer	Karin Arrigoni
Creative Director and Series Design	Scott Jackson
Cover Design	Pattie Lee

This book was composed with Adobe InDesign™.

About the Author

Photographer Julie Adair King is the author of several popular books about digital imaging and photography. Her most recent titles include *Julie King's Everyday Photoshop for Photographers, Shoot Like a Pro! Digital Photography Techniques, Digital Photography For Dummies, Photo Retouching and Restoration For Dummies, Adobe PhotoDeluxe For Dummies,* and *Easy Web Graphics.* A graduate of Purdue University, King established her own company, Julie King Creative, in 1988, in Indianapolis, Indiana.

Acknowledgements

This book would not have been possible without the efforts of many talented and dedicated people whose names you don't see on the front of the book—but should. First and foremost, thanks to LeeAnn Pickrell for her editorial insights, great sense of humor, and endless patience. I am also grateful to Jane Brownlow, Roger Stewart, Agatha Kim, Margaret Berson, Scott Jackson, and everyone else on the McGraw-Hill/Osborne team.

In addition, I am indebted to technical editor Kathy Eyster for her valuable input and to my agent, Margot Maley Hutchison at Waterside Productions, for her support through some tough months.

Finally, to my family and friends, I've said it before, but can never do so enough: Thank you for loving me, for listening to me, for laughing with me—and of course, for being my favorite photographic subjects!

CONTENTS AT A GLANCE

CONTENTS

PART IV | Retouching Techniques

PART V | Photographer's Guide to Output

Introduction

When Adobe first introduced Photoshop Elements, most of us in the digital imaging community had the same reaction: "*Wowwwww.*" Elements offered such an impressive array of features at such a low price that it was clear the program would be a huge hit. For less than $100, consumers now had access to sophisticated photo-editing tools that previously were available only in high-priced, professional programs. And with the release of Version 3.0, Elements only gets bigger and better, sporting a new design along with dozens of new features.

Having all this power at your disposal does have a downside, however: Elements offers so *many* tools, palettes, buttons, and commands that figuring out when and how to use each one can be daunting. Add all the techy lingo associated with digital imaging, and you've got a sure-fire recipe for brain overload.

I have good news for you, though, if your encounters with Elements have left you a little overwhelmed or confused. For photo retouching and subtle image enhancement—fixing red eye, adjusting exposure, tweaking colors, and the like—you really need to master only a handful of Elements tools. The rest of the tools are designed for producing original digital art and special effects, and aren't used for the type of digital-darkroom projects that most people do on a regular basis.

It was this realization that led to *Everyday Photoshop Elements.* This book cuts through the maze of Elements menu commands, tools, and filters, and focuses only on the program's primary photo-editing features. So instead of wasting time learning about specialty tools that you might pick up once in a blue moon—if then—you can concentrate on skills that will serve you well every day.

How Is This Book Different?

Most Photoshop Elements books fall into two camps. You can buy thick volumes that provide encyclopedic detail about even the most obscure program features, leaving no room for any practical guidance about how to implement the really useful tools. At the other end of the spectrum, many books are *too* lightweight. They emphasize special-effects filters that you could easily figure out on your own, for example. Or they show you how to do offbeat projects such as giving yourself a nose job, ignoring less-fun but important topics, such as how to safeguard your image files and get better monitor-to-printer color matching.

In fairness, these books are what they are because they're meant to appeal to all Elements users, who have a wide variety of interests. *Everyday Photoshop Elements,* on the other hand, is geared to people who simply want to harness the program's power to solve common picture problems and then prepare the finished product for print or the Web.

Whether you're a professional photographer, a serious hobbyist, or just starting to discover digital imaging, you'll get the step-by-step guidance you need to tackle these and other everyday photo projects:

- Crop to a better composition or specific frame size
- Brighten underexposed images, restore lost shadow detail, and repair blown highlights
- Tweak color balance, saturation, and contrast
- Remove red-eye, cover up other small blemishes, and patch over larger defects
- Fix lens distortion and manipulate focus
- Replace distracting backgrounds
- Convert color photos to stunning black-and-white images
- Set up your digital studio for improved color consistency

Because producing a great photo is pointless if it goes no further than your computer, this book also provides in-depth information about how to output your files, whether you're having them professionally printed, doing the job on your own photo printer, or sharing them via the Internet. Along the way, you'll also find the background information you need to make sense of important digital-imaging concepts, such as resolution, color management, bit depth, and file formats.

Expert Techniques Made Easy

As you explore this book, you'll find that I've opted not to cover simple, automated correction filters. Like most quick fixes in life, these don't produce very good results and can even harm your digital photos. (And if you do want to investigate the one-click filters, you don't need my help.) Instead, I've focused on expert-level techniques, which take a little longer to understand at first but give you much more control and flexibility, making your life easier in the long run.

The point is, don't be intimidated if you encounter unfamiliar jargon or seemingly complex instructions when you first flip through this book. When you try the techniques, you'll find that they're actually fairly simple, and I'll break down all the technical mumbo-jumbo for you.

To make things even easier to digest, each chapter includes sample projects that give you hands-on experience—the best way to learn any new skill. You can download low-resolution copies of the images used in the projects free of charge from the McGraw-Hill/Osborne Publishing web site: www.osborne.com. Find and click the Free Code link, and then navigate to the link for *Everyday Photoshop Elements.* (I probably don't need to mention this since you're a fellow photographer, but do note that the pictures are all copyrighted and not available for any use other than working with this book.)

Version Notes, Operating Systems, and Other Details

Everyday Photoshop Elements covers Version 3.0 of the program. The Version 3.0 program window looks and operates a little differently than in earlier versions; however, many core tools and commands that I cover haven't changed. So if you haven't yet made the move to Version 3.0, you'll find that many of the instructions apply to your software as well.

This book covers both Windows and Macintosh systems, too. Although most illustrations feature the Windows operating system, I provide Mac-specific information when the two versions are significantly different. Keyboard shortcuts— keys you can press to quickly invoke certain functions—are provided for both Windows and Mac as well.

When you see an instruction such as "Choose Filter | Sharpen | Unsharp Mask," it's your cue to click through a series of commands accessible via the program menus. In this case, you would click Filter on the menu bar, click Sharpen to unfurl a submenu, and then click Unsharp Mask to open the Unsharp Mask dialog box.

Finally, although you don't need any experience with Elements to use this book, if you're brand new to computers as well, you may find it helpful to invest in a beginner's book about your operating system. So that I can devote as much space as possible to Elements-related information, I don't go into great detail about basic computer operations.

How to Get the Most from This Book

Many techniques in the second half of this book build on fundamentals presented in the first half, so I recommend that you approach this book as you would a mystery novel: start at the beginning and work your way through to the end. At the least, exploring the chapters on customizing tools (Chapter 2), creating selection outlines (Chapter 5), and using layers (Chapter 6) will enable you to have a much stronger foothold when you tackle projects in later chapters.

However, if you're like some of the fine women in my book club, who can't resist reading the ending first, that's perfectly acceptable, too. I've provided lots of cross-references throughout each chapter so that you can easily flip to the chapter that offers more help should you get hung up on a particular step.

Whichever direction you go, don't try to absorb everything at once. And don't feel stupid if you can't make sense of things on the first, second, or even third, read, either. Even when you whittle down the list of Elements features to the core set covered in this book, some tools and techniques can be pretty darned confusing at first.

I promise, though, that if you spend just a few minutes with *Everyday Photoshop Elements* each week, you'll quickly acquire the skills you need to turn problem pictures into good pictures and make good pictures even better. Before long, tools and techniques that once seemed intimidating will be old friends, and you'll be able to fix any photographic flaw with expert results. So turn the page, fire up your computer, and start taking advantage of all the photo-editing power that Elements has to offer!

PART I INTO THE DIGITAL DARKROOM

Pixels, Bits, and Other Digital Mysteries

When most people begin to pursue photography, they're interested in exploring the creative promise of the medium, not the mechanical and chemical processes that make it possible. But as any good photographer knows, you need to learn the science behind your camera to exploit its artistic capabilities fully. You can't manipulate depth of field and exposure, for example, without understanding aperture and shutter.

In This Chapter:

- [ ] The elements of a digital photo

- [ ] How pixels affect picture quality and size

- [ ] Resolution facts and fiction

- [ ] RGB, HSB, and other color codes

- [ ] Bit-depth decisions

In the same way, familiarizing yourself with the technical aspects of digital imaging enables you to take better advantage of Photoshop Elements. This chapter gives you this background information, explaining such concepts as resolution, color models, and bit depth.

From Tiny Pixels Come Great Pictures

All digital photos, whether from a scanner or digital camera, are made up of tiny colored squares called *pixels*, which are arranged in a rectangular grid. You can see the individual pixels in the inset area of Figure 1.1.

Figure 1.1: When you enlarge a digital image, the pixels become visible, and print quality goes down.

The term *pixel dimensions* refers to the number of horizontal and vertical pixels in the image. If you multiply the two values, you get the total number of pixels. For example, a 1280 × 960–pixel image contains 1,228,800 pixels, or approximately 1.2 *megapixels*. (One megapixel equals one million pixels.)

After opening an image, you can check its pixel supply by choosing Image I Resize I Image Size to open the Image Size dialog box, shown in Figure 1.2. The Pixel Dimensions area at the top of the dialog box lists the pixel count.

Knowing a photo's pixel count is important because it affects print quality, on-screen display size, and file size. The next three sections discuss these issues.

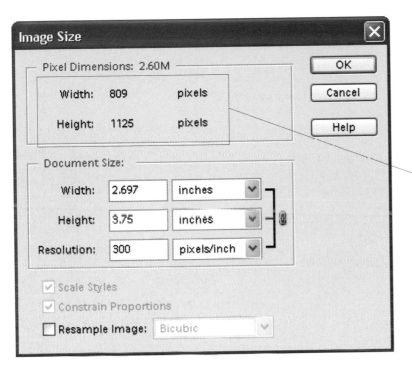

Figure 1.2: The Image Size dialog box reveals the photo's pixel count.

Pixels and Print Quality

Before printing a photo from Photoshop Elements, you specify the image *output resolution*. This value determines how many pixels are spread across each linear inch of your print, which has a major impact on print quality.

For quality prints, you typically need between 200 and 300 pixels per linear inch, or *ppi*. This number varies depending on the printer, so check your manual for the manufacturer's recommendations. A few models ask to be fed more than 300 ppi.

Figures 1.3 and 1.4 illustrate the relationship of ppi to print quality. The first image has pixel dimensions of 750 × 1050, resulting in an output resolution of 300 ppi at this print size, 2.5 × 3.5 inches. (750 pixels divided by 2.5 inches equals 300 pixels per inch; 1050 divided by 3.5 also equals 300.) Compare this image with its 175 × 245–pixel counterpart in Figure 1.4, which has an output resolution of just 70 ppi. The low-resolution image appears blocky due to the larger pixels, and curved and diagonal lines have a stair-stepped appearance. (Photo gurus refer to this stair-stepping as *jaggies.*)

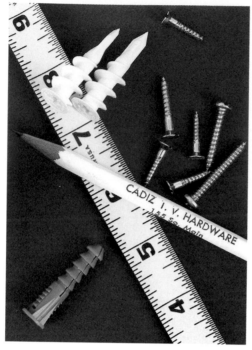

300 ppi,
2.3MB

70 ppi,
137K

Figure 1.3: For good prints, you need between 200 and 300 pixels per inch (ppi).

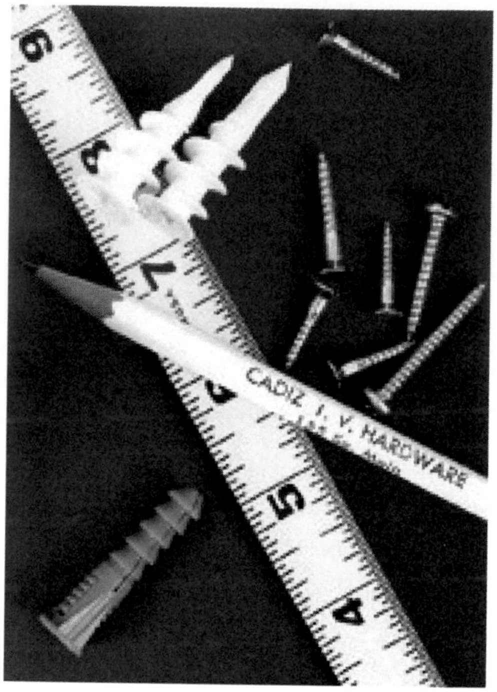

Figure 1.4: A lack of pixels causes lousy print quality.

Photoshop Elements enables you to add pixels to an image—a process called *resampling*—to increase the output resolution. Unfortunately, resampling doesn't improve print quality, as illustrated by Figure 1.5. Starting with the 70-ppi image in Figure 1.4, I increased the pixel count to bring the output resolution up to 300 ppi. The resulting image isn't any better than the low-resolution original, and in fact looks slightly worse.

70 ppi resampled to 300 ppi

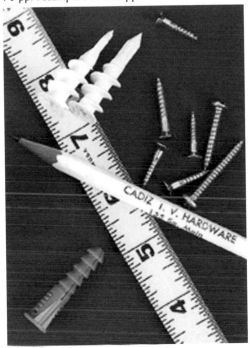

Figure 1.5: Adding pixels to a low-resolution image doesn't improve picture quality.

Watch Out!

The moral of this story is that you should calculate your pixel needs *before* you scan or shoot a picture. To find your pixel sweet spot, divide the desired print size by the desired output resolution. (The following table shows the required pixel dimensions to print an image at traditional frame sizes at 200 ppi.) If possible, capture more pixels than you think you will need to allow yourself the flexibility to crop the photo and print the remaining image area at a decent size. You can always dump excess pixels if necessary; see Chapter 13 for details.

Remember

Don't confuse ppi (pixels per inch) with dpi, which stands for dots per inch and measures how many dots of color a printer can lay down per inch. Although many people use ppi and dpi interchangeably, the two are not the same; many printers use several dots to reproduce one pixel.

Pixel Requirements for 200 PPI Output

Print Size (Inches)	Pixel Dimensions	Megapixels
3.5 x 5	700 x 1000	<1
4 x 6	800 x 1200	1
5 x 7	1000 x 1400	1.5
8 x 10	1600 x 2000	3.2
11 x 14	2200 x 2800	6

Pixels and Screen Display Size

When you display a photo on a computer monitor, television, or other screen device, the pixel dimensions determine how large the photo appears.

Figure 1.6: An 800 × 600–pixel image fills the screen when the monitor resolution is set to 800 × 600.

Like digital images, display devices are pixel-based beasts. The pixels generated by a display vary in size and number depending on the device resolution. For example, you can probably set your computer monitor to several resolution settings: 800 × 600, 1024 × 768, 1280 × 960, and so on. At a resolution of 800 × 600, you get 800 horizontal screen pixels and 600 vertical screen pixels. When you increase the resolution, the computer crams more pixels into the same display area, which means that the pixels get smaller.

To project your photos, the device uses one display pixel to reproduce one image pixel. Therefore, if the number of image pixels and display pixels are the same, your photo fills the screen. In Figure 1.6, for example, I set my monitor resolution to 800 × 600 and then selected an 800 × 600–pixel image to use as my Windows desktop background. At this monitor resolution, the image covers the entire desktop. After changing the monitor resolution to 1600 × 1200, that same 800 × 600–pixel image occupies one quarter of the screen, as shown in Figure 1.7.

As for the quality of an on-screen photo, pixel count is

Figure 1.7: The same image fills just one-fourth of the screen when the monitor resolution is increased to 1600 × 1200.

irrelevant. I know that you've likely heard people referring to screen images in terms of pixels per inch, which may lead you to believe that ppi affects screen quality as it does print quality. But a display device has no way to read the output resolution (ppi) that you establish in Photoshop Elements; the only thing that matters is the total number of pixels.

The bottom line is that you need far fewer pixels for images destined for the screen than you do for pictures you plan to print. For most images, in fact, you need to dump some pixels to properly size them for the screen; Chapter 13 shows you how.

Pixels and File Size

For every image pixel, the computer must store a certain amount of data. More pixels mean more data—and larger image files. As a point of comparison, the 750 × 1050–pixel image featured in Figure 1.3 has a file size of 2.3MB, while the file size of the 175 × 245–pixel version in Figure 1.4 is a mere 137K. (One megabyte (1MB) equals 1024K, or kilobytes.)

Watch Out!

Large file sizes are problematic for several reasons. On a Web page, large image files increase the time needed to download the page. Large files also take longer to transmit via e-mail, slow down Photoshop Elements, and put more strain on your computer's resources. And of course, the larger the file, the more storage space it consumes on your computer's hard drive or removable storage media.

If you're preparing a photo for print output at a large size, you can't do much about file size because you need a hefty pixel supply for good print quality. For Web use, however, always strip files to their minimum pixel requirements to ensure the fastest downloads.

One other important note regarding file size: The file size value shown at the top of the Elements Image Size dialog box (refer to Figure 1.2) does not always reflect file size accurately. For the real file size, check the file data in the Elements File Browser, explained in Chapter 3. You also can view the actual file size using Windows Explorer or, on the Mac, using the Finder's Get Info command.

Remember

Always shoot or scan photos at a resolution appropriate for printing. Then duplicate the image and eliminate pixels as needed to create a screen version.

Color as Math

Computers and digital-imaging devices—scanners, digital cameras, monitors, and printers—can't perceive colors the way we humans do. Unlike our brains, theirs understand numbers only. That means that every color must be translated into numeric code.

Here's an analogy that may help you understand this number-based approach to color. You probably learned in kindergarten that you can mix red, yellow, and blue paint to create other colors. Yellow and blue make green, for example. If you were so inclined, you could describe green in terms of its red-yellow-blue mix. Instead of green, you could say "0 percent red, 50 percent yellow, and 50 percent blue." Digital color works just like that, except that the formulas involve different sets of primary components than red, yellow, and blue.

Imaging scientists have developed several color-coding schemes, known as *color models* or *color spaces*. Each model uses a different set of primary components, and each can represent a specific spectrum, or *gamut*, of colors. Why not one universal code? Because that would be too easy, silly. (Okay, the real reason is that no one model adequately serves all color-production needs.)

The good news is that Photoshop Elements handles all this color coding for you; you don't have to type long strings of numbers to specify the color of each pixel in your image. But you do need a passing familiarity with the major color models to understand some important Photoshop Elements techniques and tools. The next few sections tell you what you need to know.

Color from Light: RGB

Digital cameras, scanners, computer monitors, and other displays are called *RGB* devices because they produce color by mixing red, green, and blue light. This light is measured on a scale of 0 to 255, with 0 representing the complete absence of light and 255 indicating maximum brightness.

To understand RGB, imagine that you are standing in a pitch-black room and you have three colored spotlights at your disposal: one red, one green, and one blue. If you set all three beams to maximum brightness and then position them so that their beams overlap slightly, as illustrated in Figure 1.8, the overlapping area becomes white. Where no light falls, blackness remains. It stands to reason, then, that an equal mix of red, green, and blue at any value other than 0 (black) or 255 (white) produces a shade of gray.

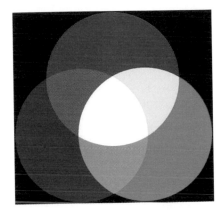

Figure 1.8: In the RGB model, full-strength red, green, and blue produces white.

Variation on the Theme: HSB

Like RGB, the HSB color model is light-based. But with HSB, the primary components are hue, saturation, and brightness.

- Hue values range from 0 to 359, corresponding to a 360-degree *color wheel,* which you can see in Figure 1.9.
- Saturation values can range from 0 to 100 percent. At 100 percent saturation, you get a "pure" color—that is, it contains only a single hue. At 0 saturation, you get white, gray, or black, depending on the Brightness value.

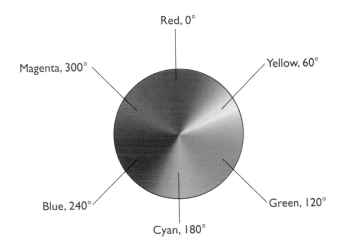

Red, 0°
Magenta, 300°
Yellow, 60°
Blue, 240°
Green, 120°
Cyan, 180°

Figure 1.9: Hue values represent positions on a 360-degree color wheel.

- Brightness values also run from 0 to 100 percent. No matter what the hue or saturation, 0 percent brightness produces black.

You can't create an HSB image; this color model is primarily used to simplify the job of selecting paint colors in image-editing and graphics programs, including Photoshop Elements. Some color-effects filters are also based on the HSB model.

Print Formulas: CMY and CMYK

While scanners, digital cameras, and display devices mix colors using red, green, and blue light, a printer creates colors by mixing cyan, magenta, and yellow inks, which leads us to the CMY color model.

CMY values range from 0 to 100 percent and represent ink coverage on the paper. Figure 1.10 shows the result of blending 100 percent cyan, magenta, and yellow. Blending two colors produces a darker color. When you mix all three colors at full strength, black ensues (well, sort of; more on that momentarily). Zero percent coverage of all three inks produces white, assuming that you're printing on white paper.

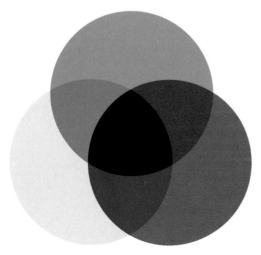

When you compare Figure 1.8 to Figure 1.10, you may notice that both illustrations feature the same eight colors. This fact may lead you to assume that you can create the same colors with either model. Unfortunately, that's not the case. You can't reproduce in CMY the most vivid hues that you can create with RGB because of the inherent differences in the two processes: CMY color is a result of light reflecting off ink-coated paper, and RGB color is pure, projected light. Colors in Figures 1.8 and 1.10 *appear* to be the same because they are both output in the CMY space. On screen, the colors in the RGB illustration are much more vibrant.

Figure 1.10: The print color model, CMY, is based on cyan, magenta, and yellow inks.

Put another way, CMY has a much smaller gamut than RGB, which is the core problem with getting screen and printed colors to match. Chapter 12 discusses ways of getting the two as close as possible, but you should never expect absolute color matching when going from screen to print.

Now for the promised follow-up on the issue of black in the CMY color model: Because inks are impure, it's difficult to achieve true blacks by blending cyan, magenta, and yellow. For that reason, most printers add black ink. Black is called the *key* color, so printers that use the four-ink setup are called CMYK devices. (The illustration in Figure 1.10 was printed on a CMYK printer, which is why the black area appears to be true black.)

Grayscale: Not Just Black and White

The final entry in the color-model hit parade, Grayscale, is childishly simple compared to all the others. This color model incorporates a single component, brightness. Brightness values range from 0 to 255, just as in the RGB model. A value of zero produces black, 255 produces white, and everything else generates gray.

Given that you can produce the same grays in RGB, why the need for Grayscale? Because a Grayscale image file, which needs to store data for only one color component, is much smaller than an RGB file, which must track three color components. Compare the RGB and Grayscale images in Figure 1.11, for example. Both images contain the same number of pixels and yet the Grayscale

2.4MB   814K

Figure 1.11: A full-color image (left) has a much larger file size than a Grayscale image (right).

image is less than one-half the file size of the full-color version. (To find out how to convert an RGB image to the Grayscale model, see Chapter 9.)

Bit Depth: How High Should You Go?

Bit depth refers to how many units of computer data—*bits*—are used to represent each pixel in a digital image. Most scanners enable you to specify bit depth when you scan an image. My scanner, for example, offers 24-bit and 42-bit scanning. Some digital cameras also offer a choice of bit depth.

Scanner and camera bit-depth options usually reflect bits per pixel. But you also can assess bit depth on a per-channel basis. A *channel* is a virtual storage tank within a digital image file; the brightness values for each primary color component go into separate channels. For example, an RGB image has three channels, one each for the red, green, and blue brightness values. And a 24-bit RGB image has 8 bits each for the Red, Green, and Blue channels. (Don't worry, this stuff won't be on the test!)

Elements simplifies things by grouping all images into two bit-depth categories:

- An image with 8 or fewer bits per channel is treated as an 8-bits-per-channel image.

- An image with more than 8 bits per channel is treated as a 16-bits-per-channel image, or a *high-bit image* in Elements lingo.

After opening an image in Elements, you can determine its bit depth by opening the Image | Mode menu. If the Convert to 8 Bits/Channel item is not dimmed, you've got yourself a 16-bit image.

Now, for the important part of the discussion: How many bits are enough? For most images, 8 bits per channel is plenty. Theoretically, more bits provide more editing flexibility because you have more original data to manipulate. When you apply heavy exposure and color corrections to an 8-bit image, you sometimes create breaks in what should be a continuous blend of colors. Figure 1.12 offers an illustration of this defect, known as *banding* or *posterization*. The top image shows how the colors should look; the bottom image shows the defect. Starting with more bits may—I repeat, *may*—alleviate the problem.

Figure 1.12: A defect known as banding produces abrupt shifts in what should be a smooth gradation of colors.

Watch Out!

Before you jump on the high-bit wagon, though, understand that you do so at a price. First, 16-bit images have significantly larger file sizes than 8-bit images. More importantly, some important Elements features aren't available for 16-bit images. Most editing tools are disabled, for example, as are the color-balancing filter, special-effects filters, and layers (a feature explained in Chapter 6).

For every expert who advocates 16-bit editing, an equally qualified person dismisses the idea as overkill. Because Elements becomes so limited in 16-bit mode, I don't recommend going that route unless you're facing a tricky exposure situation. If so, start in 16-bit mode, do your exposure corrections, and then convert to 8-bit mode to do any other needed retouching.

To convert a 16-bit image to an 8-bit image, choose the Image | Mode | Convert to 8 Bits/Channel command.

Photoshop Elements Road Map

2

Many parts of the Elements workspace follow established rules of the computing road: You open an Elements menu just as you do in any program, and the program windows adhere to the standard Windows or Macintosh design. But a few components work in ways that aren't obvious, so this chapter gives you the lowdown, explaining how to access tools and palettes, adjust tool performance, and choose paint colors. You'll also find information that will help you customize your digital studio.

In This Chapter:

- Guide to the Elements 3 workspace

- Recommended program settings

- Tips for customizing palettes

- Brush settings, blending modes, and other tool options

- How to select and store paint colors

Setting Program Preferences

Before you do anything else in Elements, take a few minutes to review the settings in the Preferences dialog box, shown in Figure 2.1. These settings control several aspects of how the program operates. If you're working on a Windows computer, open the dialog box by choosing Edit | Preferences | General. On a Mac, choose Photoshop Elements | Preferences | General.

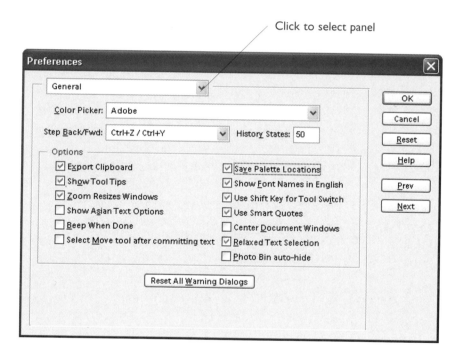

Figure 2.1: Set basic program options via the Preferences dialog box.

The Preferences dialog box is a multi-panel affair, with each panel housing different options. You can select a panel from the drop-down list, labeled in the figure, or cycle through the panels by clicking the Prev and Next buttons.

I could devote a whole chapter to each panel, but frankly, that would not only put us both to sleep, but also be a waste of time and paper. In most cases, the default settings will serve you well, and many options don't come into play at all for everyday photo-editing tasks. So the next several sections discuss just settings that are worthy of checking out before you dig into the program.

Time Saver

To open the Preferences dialog box with the General panel at the forefront, press CTRL-K (Windows) or ⌘-K (Mac).

General Preferences

Figure 2.1 shows my recommended settings for the options on the General panel of the Preferences dialog box. A few items warrant explanation:

- **Color Picker**   A *color picker* is a tool that you use to select paint colors. Stick with the default setting, Adobe; it's more sophisticated than the alternative, which is the color picker provided by your computer's operating system (Windows or Mac).

- **Step Back/Fwd**   This option specifies what keyboard shortcuts invoke the Edit | Undo and Edit | Redo commands, detailed in Chapter 3. While working with this book, use the default option, which sets CTRL-Z (Windows) or ⌘-Z (Mac) as the shortcut for Undo and CTRL-Y (Windows) or ⌘-Y (Mac) for Redo.

- **Use SHIFT Key for Tool Switch**   You can activate the Elements tools by pressing various keyboard shortcuts, which are listed later in this chapter. The Use Shift Key option determines how you cycle through tools that share a keyboard shortcut. If you select the check box, press SHIFT plus the tool shortcut to switch tools; otherwise, every press of the shortcut key by itself toggles the tools. So that we're on the same page, select this option while working with this book.

- **Photo Bin Auto-Hide (Windows only)**   This option relates to the Photo Bin, the area at the bottom of the program window that displays thumbnails of your open photos. If you turn on the option, the bin disappears until you pass your cursor over its border, at which time it pops into view. Move the cursor out of the bin, and it hides itself again. Personally, I think the bin is a waste of screen space—its main function is to allow you to switch back and forth between open images, which you can do just as easily by choosing the file name from the Window menu. And having the thing pop up willy-nilly whenever my mouse strays to the bottom of the workspace is annoying, at best. So leave this option unchecked. You then can hide and display the bin when needed by choosing Window | Photo Bin.

Remember

Your preferences data is stored in a file named Photoshop Elements 3.0 Prefs. If Elements starts behaving strangely, close the program and then locate and delete the file. When you relaunch Elements, it creates a new preferences file. Unfortunately, all preferences settings return to the original defaults, so you need to redo any changes that you made.

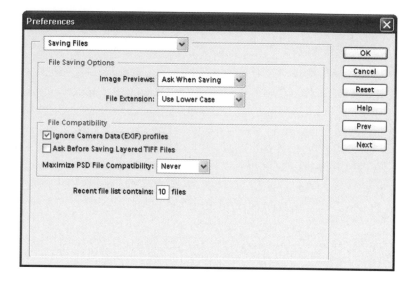

Figure 2.2: These options affect how Elements opens and saves your images.

File-Handling Preferences

Options on the Saving Files panel of the Preferences dialog box, shown in Figure 2.2, affect how Elements saves and opens image files, topics you can explore in Chapter 3. I suggest a couple of changes to the default settings here:

- **Ignore Camera Data (EXIF) Profiles**   Today's digital cameras store certain bits of extra information in picture files. This data, called *EXIF metadata*, includes such details as the model of camera, color profile, shutter speed, and other capture settings. The Ignore Camera Data option relates to the color profile data. Some cameras don't accurately report the color profile, and as a result, you may lose some colors if Elements opens the file according to the EXIF information. Unless you're sure that your camera tags color information correctly, turn this option on. See Chapter 12 for a full explanation of color profiles.

- **Ask Before Saving Layered TIFF Files**   This option comes into play when you save a file in the TIFF format. Turn the option off and follow my instructions in Chapter 13 for saving TIFF files.

- **Maximize PSD File Compatibility**   This option affects files that you save in the program's native format, PSD. If you select the check box, the program saves files with extra data that ensures that they can be opened in programs that recognize only older versions of the format. Because that extra data bloats file sizes, set this option to Never. If you need to open a PSD file in a program that doesn't support the current version, you can turn on the option before saving the file.

- **Image Previews**   This option determines whether Elements saves thumbnail previews with the image file. Enabling the option increases file size, but you may need to include the previews depending on how you plan to use the image. For now, set the option to Ask When Saving so that you can make the call on a case-by-case basis when you save files. See Chapter 3 for details that will help you decide whether to change the setting to Never Save or Always Save. (Note that Mac users get a few preview options not shown in Figure 2.2.)

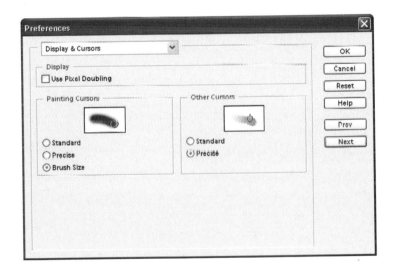

Figure 2.3: Change tool cursor styles here.

Display & Cursors Preferences

Figure 2.3 shows my recommended settings on the Display & Cursors panel of the Preferences dialog box. Two settings deserve comment:

- **Painting Cursors**   When you work with tools that feature customizable brushes, you can choose from three cursor styles: Standard, Precise, and Brush Size, illustrated in Figure 2.4. Brush Size is the best choice. With this option selected, your cursor reflects the size and shape of your brush.

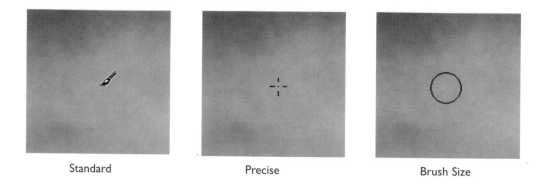

| Standard | Precise | Brush Size |

Figure 2.4: You
can customize the
appearance of
tool cursors.

■ **Other Cursors** These options affect the non-brush tools, such as the
Crop tool. Set this option to Precise, which gives you a crosshair cursor
and provides the best indication of what area your tool is about to alter.

Tool Tricks

While working with a tool that has a customizable brush, press the CAPS LOCK key to
toggle between the Brush Size and Precise cursor styles. (You must select Brush Size
on the Display & Cursors panel of the Preferences dialog box for this trick to work.)
Turn off CAPS LOCK before you use other keyboard shortcuts, though, or the shortcuts may not work correctly.

Plug-Ins & Scratch Disks

To flex its muscles, Elements requires plenty of RAM (system memory). But RAM
alone isn't enough. As you run the program, it uses empty space on your computer's hard drive as a temporary data-storage tank. Computer folk refer to that temporary storage space as the *scratch disk*.

On computers that have a single, nonpartitioned drive, Elements automatically sets
that drive as the primary scratch disk. If your computer has multiple hard drives or
a single hard drive that is partitioned into several virtual drives, visit the Plug-Ins
& Scratch Disks panel of the Preferences dialog box, shown in Figure 2.5. Here,
you can designate the order in which you want Elements to access your drives for
its scratch disk needs. Select the drive that has the greatest amount of free space
from the First drop-down list, select the next-roomiest drive from the Second
drop-down list, and so on.

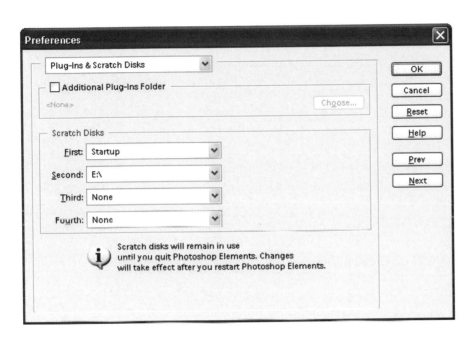

Figure 2.5: Specify which hard drive you want Elements to use as the scratch disk.

Regardless of how many drives your system boasts, make sure that you give Elements substantial scratch disk space. If the program acts squirrelly or displays a message saying that the scratch disk is full, delete unneeded files from your hard drive.

Memory & Image Cache

By default, Elements helps itself to as much as 50 percent of your available RAM. If the program gets bogged down when you work on large image files, you may want to allow it to consume even more memory.

You make this change from inside Elements, using the Memory & Image Cache panel of the Preferences dialog box. Try bumping up the value in the Memory Usage section of the panel by 10 or 20 percent.

Watch Out!

Don't feed Elements *all* your RAM, or the computer won't be able to run the operating system itself or the other programs that normally run in the background. For safety's sake, limit Elements's memory allocation to 75 percent.

Exploring the Workspace

Figure 2.6 shows the Elements 3 program window. (If you're a Windows user, this is the Editor window; if you instead see the Organizer window, click the Edit button on the toolbar to switch to the Editor.)

The window offers a standard menu bar, labeled in the figure. When you see a phrase like "choose Window | Photo Bin" in this book, head for the menus. Click a menu to open it and then click the command you want to use—in the example case, click the Window menu and then click Photo Bin. Below the menu bar, a toolbar—officially called the Shortcuts bar in Adobe lingo—displays icons that offer one-click access to some of those commands.

Menu bar

Figure 2.6: New to Elements 3, the Photo Bin and Palette Bin occupy the bottom and right side of the program window.

Hide/display Palette Bin

Hide/display Photo Bin

In addition, you get the following Elements features:

- **Photo Bin and Palette Bin** The Photo Bin lives at the bottom of the window and displays thumbnails of your open images, as shown in Figure 2.6. The Palette Bin occupies a column on the right side of the window and houses several palettes, which are mini-windows containing additional Elements features. I prefer to hide both bins because they eat up too much of the working space, leaving precious little room for the photo itself. If you concur, choose Window | Photo Bin and Window | Palette Bin to declutter your screen, as shown in Figure 2.7. In Windows, you also can click the hide/display arrows labeled in Figure 2.6. On a Mac, you get the hide/display arrow for the Palette Bin, but the Photo Bin acts as a regular window, so you can close it using the standard Mac window control (the left button at the top of the window). You can redisplay either bin at any time by clicking the arrows or choosing the commands from the Window menu.

- **Toolbox** The toolbox, labeled in Figure 2.7, holds all the Elements tools, plus controls for adjusting the colors applied by those tools and some filters. If you reduce the size of the Elements program window, your toolbox may be a two-column affair instead of the single-column version shown here.

- **Options bar** The options bar, also labeled in Figure 2.7, contains controls for adjusting the performance of the active tool.

Options bar

Toolbox

Figure 2.7: Hiding both bins frees up more space for your photos.

Quick Fix Versus Standard Edit Mode

At the right end of the toolbar, you see two buttons: Quick Fix and Standard Edit. Clicking the Quick Fix button displays a utility that offers controls for making simple adjustments to exposure, color, and focus, as shown in Figure 2.8.

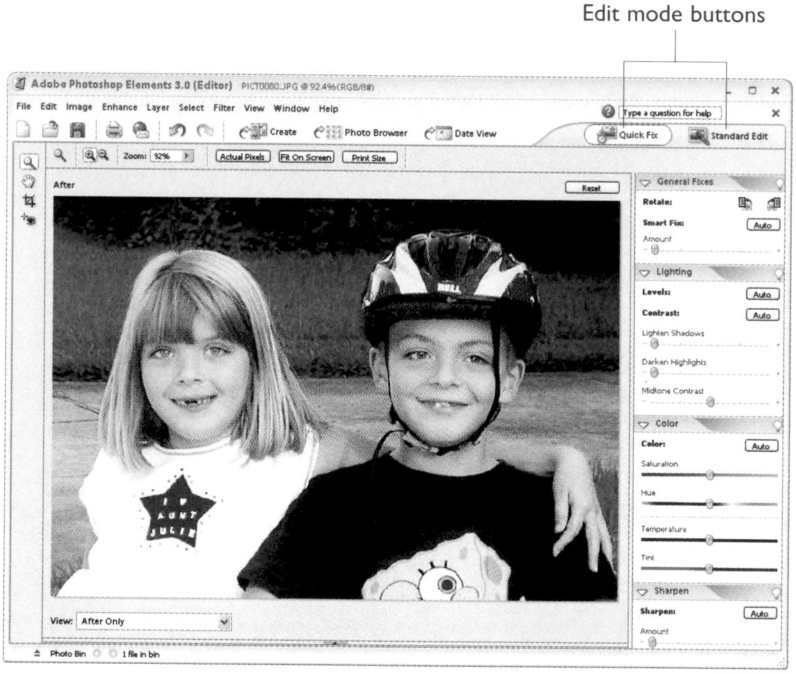

Edit mode buttons

Figure 2.8: The Quick Fix utility offers fast results—but not always the best results.

I've opted not to cover the Quick Fix feature in this book, for three reasons. First, the Quick Fix tools aren't the most sophisticated Elements has to offer. Second, the Quick Fix controls are very intuitive, so I'd probably insult your intelligence by spelling things out for you. Finally, by neglecting Quick Fix, I have more room to explain features that aren't so easy to grasp. So the rest of this book assumes that you're working in Standard Edit mode, where your window appears as shown in Figure 2.7.

Freeing Palettes from the Bin

When you first install Elements, the Palette Bin occupies the right side of the program window, as shown earlier in Figure 2.6. (Don't see the bin? Choose Window | Palette Bin.)

I appreciate that the bin makes it easy for newcomers to find what Adobe probably considers the most important palettes. But I don't appreciate having to make room for a whole column of palettes when I only want to work with one. The Layers palette, specifically, is a regular player in everyday projects, and you can't display it without also getting the How To and Styles and Effects palettes, which aren't big on my play list.

Fortunately, there's a fix. First, drag the Layers palette by its title bar (the bar that runs across the top) out of the bin, as shown in Figure 2.9. The Layers palette transforms into a free-floating window, complete with its own close and minimize buttons, which follow the standard Windows or Mac designs. Click the More button at the top of the palette to display a palette menu. If the Place in Palette Bin item is checked, click it to remove the check mark. Now you can choose Window | Palette Bin to close the bin and regain your screen space. And you can choose Window | Layers to display and hide only your free-floating Layers palette.

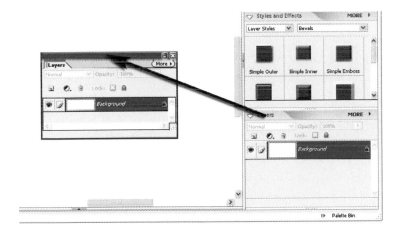

Figure 2.9: Drag the Layers palette out of the bin so that you can view it without giving up much screen space.

If you ever want to restore the original palette organization, choose Window | Reset Palette Locations.

Working with Palettes

You can hide and display any palette by choosing its name from the Window menu or by using the shortcut keys listed in the upcoming Speed Keys table. If the palette is docked in the bin, the entire bin appears; otherwise, the palette appears by its lonesome, in its own window. To relocate a free-floating palette, just drag it by its title bar.

Figure 2.10 shows the Windows version of a free-floating palette. The Mac version is identical, save for the Minimize and Close buttons, which follow the standard OS X design—red button for Close, green button for Minimize. Familiarize yourself with the following palette-window maneuvers:

- **Displaying a palette menu**   Click the More button to display a menu of commands related to the palette, as shown in Figure 2.10.
- **Resizing a palette window**   Drag the lower-right corner of the window to adjust the window size.
- **Collapsing a palette**   When you click the Minimize button in a free-floating palette, the palette remains open, but with just the top part of the window showing. Click the button again to restore the palette to its original size. To collapse a palette that's in the Palette Bin, click the down-pointing triangle that appears to the left of the palette name. Click again to restore the palette.
- **Closing a palette**   Choose the palette name from the Window menu or press the shortcut keys listed in the Speed Keys table. With a free-floating palette, you can also just click the Close button.

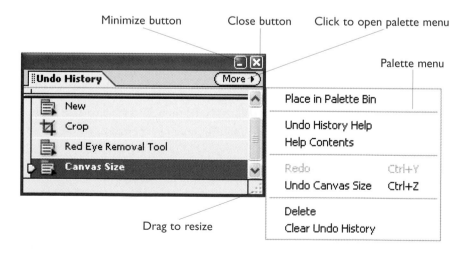

Figure 2.10: Palette menus contain additional commands.

Watch Out!

If you're a Mac user and can't get certain Elements keyboard shortcuts to work, you need to tweak your operating system controls. Otherwise, some shortcuts invoke system-related actions instead of Elements actions. Choose System Preferences from the Apple menu to open the System Preferences window. Click the Show All icon and then the Keyboard and Mouse icon. Click the Keyboard Shortcuts button and disable conflicting shortcuts. Next, click the Show All button again, click the Exposé icon, and disable the Exposé keyboard shortcuts as well.

SPEED KEYS: Hiding and Displaying Palettes

Palette	Shortcut*
How To	F6
Styles & Effects	F7
Info	F8
Histogram	F9
Undo History	F10
Layers	F11
Navigator	F12

*Must disable conflicting Mac OS X system shortcuts. On some keyboards, must also press FN (function) key.

Working with Tools

To select a tool, click its icon in the toolbox. Note, though, that some slots in the toolbox are occupied by more than one tool. For example, the Lasso, Polygonal Lasso, and Magnetic Lasso share the same slot, as illustrated in Figure 2.11. Multi-tool slots are marked with a little black triangle. If you position your cursor over the triangle and then hold down the left mouse button—or your only button, if you use a one-button mouse—you display a flyout menu containing icons for all tools in the slot, as shown in the figure. Click the tool that you want to use. The icon for the selected tool takes center stage in the toolbox, and the flyout menu disappears.

The options bar also displays icons for each tool on the current flyout menu. You can click these icons to switch from one tool to another instead of unfurling the flyout.

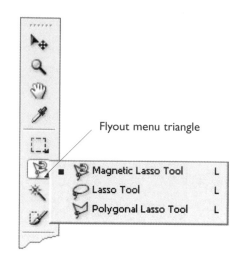

Figure 2.11: The little black triangles access flyout menus containing more tools.

Flyout menu triangle

You also can select tools with the keyboard shortcuts that are shown in the upcoming Speed Keys table. Some tools that share a toolbox slot also share a keyboard shortcut. Your first keypress activates whichever tool is currently visible in the toolbox; press SHIFT plus the shortcut key repeatedly to cycle through the other tools that share the shortcut. If the SHIFT-key thing doesn't work, see the section "General Preferences" earlier in this chapter. Mac users also need to disable conflicting system shortcuts, as explained in the preceding section.

SPEED KEYS: Selecting the Editing Tools from the Keyboard

Tool	Shortcut*	Tool	Shortcut*
Move	V	Zoom	Z
Hand	H	Eyedropper	I
Rectangular and Elliptical Marquees	M	Lasso, Magnetic Lasso, Polygonal Lasso	L
Magic Wand	W	Selection Brush	A
Type, Type Mask	T	Crop	C
Cookie Cutter	Q	Red Eye Removal	Y
Spot Healing Brush, Healing Brush	J	Clone Stamp, Pattern Stamp	S
Pencil	N	Eraser, Background Eraser, Magic Eraser	E
Brush, Impressionist, Color Replacement	B	Paint Bucket	K
Gradient	G	Shape (seven tools)	U
Blur, Sharpen, Smudge	R	Sponge, Dodge, Burn	O

*Press SHIFT plus the shortcut key to cycle through tools that share a shortcut.

Adjusting Tool Brush Tips

When you work with the retouching and painting tools, you can customize the tool brush by using the controls on the options bar. Figure 2.12 shows the options available for the Brush tool.

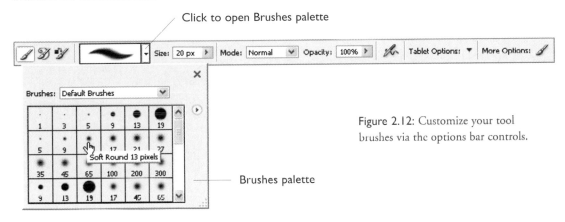

Click to open Brushes palette

Figure 2.12: Customize your tool brushes via the options bar controls.

Brushes palette

As you work through the techniques in this book, you'll find recommendations for specific brush settings. For now, just familiarize yourself with what the various options do and how to access them. (Don't panic if you don't fully understand everything on first read; this stuff will become clearer as you actually begin using the tools.)

Note that not all the brush-based tools offer all these options, and a few tools offer controls unique to their operation. I discuss tool-specific settings in sections of the book that explain techniques involving those tools.

The Big Three: Size, Shape, and Hardness

The top three brush settings to consider are size, shape, and hardness. I won't insult your intelligence by explaining size, except to say that it's measured in pixels. By default, brushes are round, which is appropriate for almost every photo retouching task.

Brush hardness determines whether your tool lays down sharp-edged strokes or *feathered*—fuzzy—strokes. Hardness is measured in percentages, with 100 percent producing the hardest edge and 0 percent the softest. Figure 2.13 gives you a look at a stroke painted at 0, 50, and 100 percent hardness.

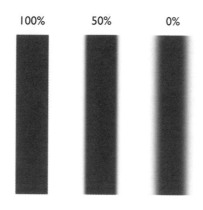

100%   50%   0%

Figure 2.13: Use a low Hardness value to produce fuzzy strokes and a high setting for sharp-edged strokes.

Most brush-based tools offer the version of the Brushes palette shown in Figure 2.12. This palette contains an assortment of brushes, each of which has a different size, shape, and hardness. Click the arrow labeled in the figure to display the palette. (To see more brushes at once, open the palette menu and choose Small Thumbnail, which gives you the display shown in the figure.) Pause your cursor over an icon to see a description of the brush, as shown in the figure, and click an icon to use that brush. You can access additional predefined brushes by opening the palette menu and choosing Load Brushes.

After selecting a brush, you can adjust its size, shape, or hardness as follows:

■ **Adjust brush size**   For most tools, you control this brush characteristic using the Size control on the options bar. For a few tools, the Brushes palette offers a Diameter setting that controls brush size. Regardless of the tool, you can also change brush size by pressing the bracket-key shortcuts listed in the upcoming Speed Keys table.

■ **Adjust brush shape**   Controls for manipulating brush shape also vary depending on the tool. For the Brush tool, for example, you click the More Options button to display the palette shown in Figure 2.14, and adjust the Angle and Roundness values. Don't see a More Options button or the Angle and Roundness controls? Check the Brushes palette; for a few tools, the Angle and Roundness controls live in that palette. However, as I said earlier, using anything but the default round brush is rarely necessary for retouching. On occasion, you may want a square brush; to get one, open the Brushes palette menu, select Load Brushes, and then select the Square Brushes collection.

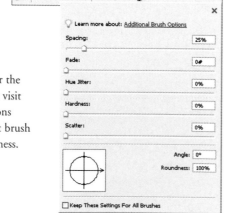

Figure 2.14: For the Brush tool, you visit the More Options palette to adjust brush shape and hardness.

■ **Adjust brush hardness**   Use the Hardness control, found either in the More Options palette, on the options bar, or in the Brushes palette, depending on the tool. You can adjust brush hardness in 25 percent increments by using the bracket-key shortcuts listed in the Speed Keys table. These shortcuts work even for tools that don't offer a specific Hardness control.

SPEED KEYS: Brush Size and Hardness Shortcuts

Action	Shortcut
Increase brush size*	]
Decrease brush size*	[
Increase brush hardness 25%	SHIFT-]
Decrease brush hardness 25%	SHIFT-[

*Adjusts size in 1-pixel increments for brushes up to 10 pixels; for larger brushes, in 10-pixel or 100-pixel increments.

Blending Modes

By changing the tool *blending mode,* you can affect how Elements calculates the new hue, brightness, and saturation of pixels that you alter with a painting tool and some editing tools. You set the blending mode via the Mode menu on the options bar. (The Mode control for the Eraser, Marquee, and Sponge tools adjusts tool-specific behavior and not blending mode, however.) In Figure 2.15, I painted a blue line across the sky image using five different blending modes.

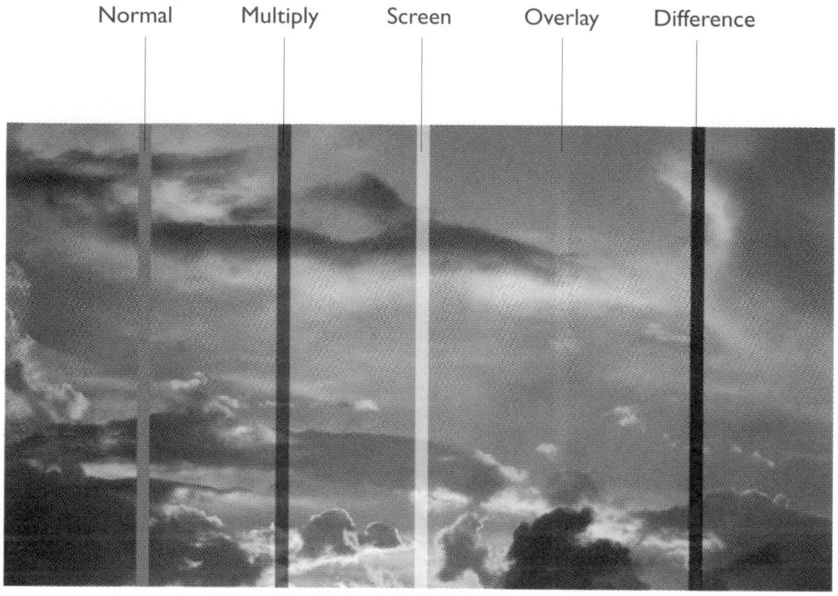

Normal   Multiply   Screen   Overlay   Difference

Figure 2.15: Blending modes determine how your paint or strokes mix with the original pixels.

The math behind the blending modes is pretty complicated, and even if you know the formulas involved, predicting the outcome of a particular blending mode isn't easy. Fortunately, for most retouching work, you use the Normal mode, which is the default setting.

Blending modes are also available for mixing layers in multilayer images, a topic discussed in Chapter 6.

Figure 2.16: At 100 percent opacity, a paint stroke obliterates the underlying pixels.

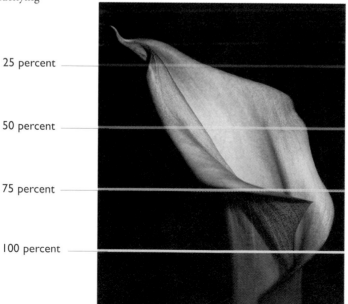

25 percent

50 percent

75 percent

100 percent

Opacity

When you work with any painting tool and some editing tools, the options bar offers an Opacity control. At 100 percent opacity, the altered pixels completely obscure the originals. At anything less than 100 percent opacity, the original pixels remain partially visible. In Figure 2.16, I painted yellow lines across the image using different Opacity values.

You can adjust the Opacity setting quickly by pressing the number keys. For 100 percent opacity, press 0; for 10 percent, press 1; for 20 percent, press 2; and so on. To adjust opacity in smaller increments, type the specific value—for example, for 25 percent opacity, press 25.

However you adjust opacity, the setting remains in force until you change it again (as do all the other brush options). So if a tool isn't providing the coverage you anticipate, revisit the Opacity control.

Airbrush

The Brush tool offers an Airbrush option, which you toggle on and off by clicking the airbrush button, labeled in Figure 2.17. When you enable the option, your tool mimics a traditional airbrush. As long as you hold down the mouse button, the tool pumps out paint.

I suggest that you disable the Airbrush option; otherwise, predicting the impact of your tools is difficult, which is just what you don't need for precision retouching, especially when you're just getting your Elements sea legs.

Tablet Options

Without question, the most valuable addition to any Elements studio is a pressure-sensitive tablet such as the Wacom Graphire, shown in Figure 2.18 (www.wacom.com). With these devices, which start at about $100, you trade in your mouse for a pen-like stylus, which makes precision editing much easier, more intuitive, and less stressful on the wrist. In addition, when you work with some tools, Elements enables you to vary brush size, shape, opacity, or other

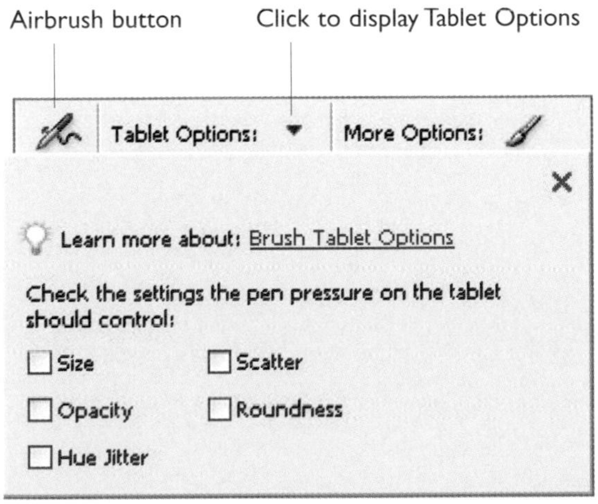

Airbrush button   Click to display Tablet Options

Figure 2.17: Disable the Airbrush option for normal tool operation.

Photo courtesy Wacom Technology Co.

Figure 2.18: A pressure-sensitive tablet such as the Wacom Graphire makes precision editing easier.

characteristics by adjusting stylus pressure. For the Brush tool, you access these options by clicking the arrow next to the Tablet Options control on the options bar, as shown in Figure 2.17. For other tools, you activate tablet control via the Brushes palette or options bar. (The available tablet controls depend on the tool.)

With the Brush tool, the tablet option that I use most often is Opacity. When you select this option, tool opacity depends on how hard you press with the stylus. At full pressure, the tool applies your paint stroke at the Opacity value you set on the options bar.

However, if you want consistent opacity, don't enable the option—it isn't likely that you'll be able to keep the same pressure on the pen for every stroke. Ditto for times when you want full opacity; keeping the maximum pressure on the pen can get tedious.

I also recommend that you stay away from the Hue Jitter, Scatter, and Roundness options until you're very experienced with the Brush tool. It's difficult enough to figure everything out without throwing these advanced options into the mix.

Watch Out!

One more bit of business for tablet users: Adobe enables the Size option by default. The first time you use each tool that offers this control, disable it so that your brush size remains consistent no matter how much stylus pressure you apply.

Tool Tricks

You can force a painting tool to produce a horizontal or vertical line by pressing SHIFT as you drag. You also can paint a straight line at any angle by clicking to set one end of the line and then SHIFT-clicking where you want the line to end. These tricks also work for the editing tools.

Choosing the Foreground
and Background Colors

When working with any tool that applies paint, you need to specify the paint color *before* you click or drag. At the bottom of the toolbox, you see a cluster of controls that indicate the current colors and enable you to select a new color. Figure 2.19 labels these controls.

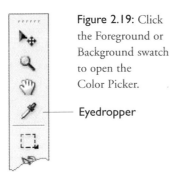

Figure 2.19: Click the Foreground or Background swatch to open the Color Picker.

Eyedropper

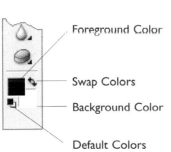

Foreground Color

Swap Colors

Background Color

Default Colors

The toolbox controls work as follows:

■ **Foreground Color**   This swatch indicates the *foreground color*. The Brush and Pencil tools apply this color. Click the swatch to open the Color Picker and choose a new color, as explained in the next section.

■ **Background Color**   This swatch controls the *background color*. The Eraser tool applies the background color when you work on a single-layer image or on the Background layer of a multilayer image. (See Chapter 6 for information about layers.) Again, just click the swatch to open the Color Picker.

■ **Default Colors** Click this icon or press D to return to the default foreground and background colors, which are black and white, respectively.

■ **Swap Colors**   Click this icon or press X to make the foreground color the background color and vice versa.

In addition, you can use the Eyedropper, also labeled in Figure 2.19, to quickly match the foreground or background color to a color in your photo.

■   Click in the image to set the foreground color to the color you click.

■   ALT-click (Windows) or OPTION-click (Mac) to set the background color.

When you select the Eyedropper, the options bar offers a single control, called Sample Size. Choose Point Sample to match the color to the pixel you click. If you choose 3 by 3 Average or 5 by 5 Average, the tool analyzes a 3-by-3-pixel area or 5-by-5-pixel area underneath your cursor and then averages those pixel colors to come up with the new color.

Tool Tricks

When any painting tool is active, you can temporarily switch to the Eyedropper by holding down the ALT key (Windows) or OPTION key (Mac). While pressing the key, click a color in your image to set the foreground color. Release the key to return to the formerly active tool.

SPEED KEYS: Color Shortcuts

Action	Windows	Mac
Restore default colors (foreground, black; background, white)	D	D
Swap foreground/background colors	X	X
Select Eyedropper tool	I	I
Access Eyedropper while a paint tool is active	ALT	OPTION
Match foreground color to image color	Click color with Eyedropper	Click color with Eyedropper
Match background color to image color	ALT-click color with Eyedropper	OPTION-click color with Eyedropper

Selecting Colors via the Color Picker

Clicking either the foreground or background color swatch in the toolbox produces the Adobe Color Picker, shown in Figure 2.20. (If you see the Windows or Mac OS color picker instead, see the first part of this chapter to find out how to switch to the more capable Adobe version.)

The dialog box contains six boxes where you can enter specific color values, using the HSB or RGB color models discussed in Chapter 1. You also can enter an

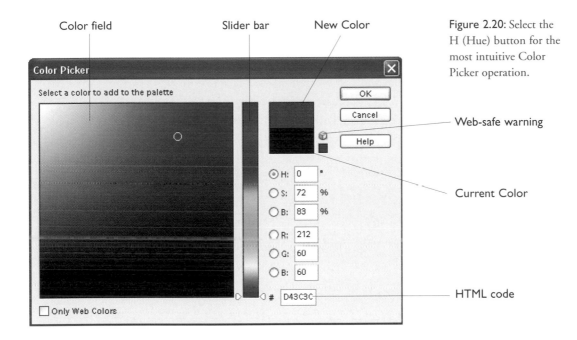

Color field   Slider bar   New Color

Figure 2.20: Select the H (Hue) button for the most intuitive Color Picker operation.

Web-safe warning

Current Color

HTML code

HTML color code, used to specify colors on Web pages in the HTML language. But don't freak out—you don't have to do any number-crunching to select a color.

Instead, use the slider bar and color field, labeled in the figure, to visually choose a color. The slider bar and color field change depending on which of the color-model buttons you select. For the most intuitive way of doing things, click the H button, as shown in the figure. The Color Picker then works as follows:

- To set the hue, drag the triangles on either side of the slider bar or just click in the bar.
- To adjust saturation and brightness, drag or click in the color field. The little circle indicates your current position in the color field.
- As you drag or click in the slider or color field, the values in the color-model boxes update automatically.
- The Current Color swatch shows you the current foreground or background color, depending on which swatch you clicked to open the dialog box. The New Color swatch shows you the new color you've chosen.
- The Web-safe warning, labeled in the figure, appears if you select a color that's outside the so-called *Web-safe color* spectrum. This spectrum includes a limited palette of colors that can be displayed by all Web

browsers and all operating systems. To choose the closest Web-safe color, click the little swatch underneath the alert. You also can select the Only Web Colors check box beneath the color field to restrict the field and slider to the web-safe palette.

Keep in mind that your photo likely contains many colors that are outside the Web-safe gamut. When you're retouching a photo, select the color that produces the best results on your screen and don't worry about the out-of-gamut warning. Otherwise, you may find it impossible to make your corrections invisible. However, if you're adding a border or some other solid-color element, such as text, it makes sense to stay within the Web-safe color gamut.

Storing Colors on the Swatches Palette

Never one to hold back in offering you multiple approaches to the same task, Elements also enables you to set the foreground and background colors via the Swatches palette, shown in Figure 2.21. Choose Window | Color Swatches to open the palette, which contains swatches for a basic set of colors.

- Click a swatch to set the foreground color.
- CTRL-click (Windows) or ⌘-click (Mac) to set the background color.

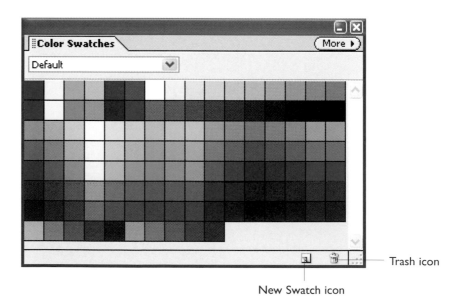

Figure 2.21: Save swatches for colors that you use often.

Trash icon

New Swatch icon

Because it offers such a limited array of colors, the Color Swatches palette isn't that useful for setting the foreground and background colors. Its main benefit is that you can store swatches for colors that you select via the Color Picker or Eyedropper so that you can easily reuse the same color. For example, if you nail down just the right skin color when retouching a portrait, add that color to the Swatches palette so that you don't have to remix the color every time you work on the photo.

To add a swatch, first set the foreground color to the color that you want to save. Then just click the New Swatch icon, labeled in Figure 2.21.

Alternatively, if you want to give the swatch a name—such as "Joe's skin"—click an empty area underneath the existing swatches. (You may need to enlarge the Color Swatches palette to reveal an empty area.) You then see a dialog box where you can name the swatch. After you create the swatch, passing your cursor over it displays the swatch name.

To delete a swatch, drag it to the Trash icon, labeled in the figure.

Watch Out!

Your custom swatches are stored as part of the Elements Preferences file. If that file becomes corrupt, you lose your custom swatches. To ensure the preservation of the swatches, choose Save Color Swatches from the Swatches palette menu. With this command, you create a custom Swatch library that you can load via the Load Color Swatches command on the palette menu. When saving, accept the default storage location for the file.

Picture File Basics

3

In This Chapter:

Before you can process a roll of film, you have to break open the film canister and extract the negatives. Before you can work on a picture in Elements, you have to crack open the digital image file—the virtual canister that holds the picture data.

This chapter explains how to open photo files stored on your computer or removable storage media, scan images into Elements, and access pictures from a digital camera. Just as important, you'll find out how to protect your digital originals and undo the inevitable mistakes that we all make now and then when editing our photos.

Opening Image Files

Elements 3 gives you several ways to get to your photo files. If you know the name and location of the file, the fastest route is as follows:

1. Choose File | Open or click the Open icon on the toolbar, labeled in Figure 3.1, to display the Open dialog box.

The top toolbar in Figure 3.1 is the Windows version; the bottom toolbar has a Mac accent and provides an extra toolbar button.

Figure 3.1: Click the Open button to display the Open dialog box quickly.

You also can display the dialog box by pressing CTRL-O (Windows) or ⌘-O (Mac). And here's a time-saver for Windows users: Just double-click an empty area of the Elements workspace.

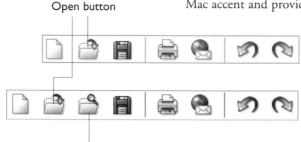

Open button

File Browser button (Mac only)

The dialog box design varies depending on your computer operating system; Figure 3.2 shows the Windows XP version.

2. Track down your file as you do in any program and then click Open.

When you open some types of files, you see a second dialog box containing further options. The next section explains the choices you need to make when opening Camera Raw files, the most common format that involves this second dialog box.

Figure 3.2: The Elements Open dialog box follows the standard Windows design (shown here) or Mac design.

Not sure where you put that picture file? Take advantage of the Elements File Browser, where you can view thumbnails of your images.

1. Choose Window | File Browser or press F5 to display the File Browser window, shown in Figure 3.3.

On a Mac, you also can click the File Browser toolbar button, labeled in Figure 3.1. In Windows, you get a Photo Browser button (not shown in the figure), but this button doesn't open the File Browser. Instead, it opens the Organizer, a separate image-management utility that ships with the Windows version of Elements.

Folder pane

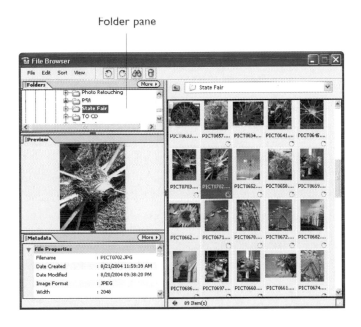

Figure 3.3: Double-click a thumbnail in the File Browser to open the image.

2. Click a folder in the folder pane, labeled in Figure 3.3, to display thumbnails of images contained in that folder.

3. Double-click the thumbnail for the image you want to open.

To open multiple photos, click the first thumbnail and CTRL-click (Windows) or ⌘-click (Mac) the other thumbnails. Then double-click any of the selected thumbnails.

4. **Close the File Browser by choosing Window | File Browser, pressing shift-f5, or using the close button on the window.**

Be sure to add the SHIFT key for the shortcut; F5 by itself simply refreshes the File Browser display.

If you're a Windows user, you can open files from the Organizer as well. I've opted not to cover the Organizer in this book because it is a Windows-only feature that would take several chapters to cover and, frankly, using the File Browser is a quicker and more convenient way to open files. However, if you have a large image collection, the Organizer offers picture-cataloging features that make keeping track of your files easier. You can "tag" files with keywords and then search for files based on those keywords, for example. On the Mac side, these features are provided in the File Browser. And of course, Mac users also can rely on iPhoto, provided free with OS X, for image management (which is one reason why Adobe decided not to include the Organizer in the Mac version of Elements).

Working with Camera Raw Files

If you own a digital camera, it may be able to capture images in the Camera Raw format. In this format, the camera does not apply any white balancing, noise removal, or other processes that occur when you shoot in the JPEG or TIFF format. Instead, you get "uncooked" data straight from the image sensor.

Before you can work with Camera Raw files in most programs, you must use special software to convert the raw data into standard image data that the program can read. Elements offers a built-in converter, but each camera manufacturer uses its own flavor of Camera Raw, and the utility doesn't support all of them. Adobe updates the utility every now and then, so visit the Adobe Web site (www.adobe.com) to make sure that you have the latest version and find out whether your camera is supported.

Assuming that your camera is on the list, the following steps explain how to bring Camera Raw files into Elements:

Zoom tool ———
Hand tool ————

Figure 3.4: You can open Camera Raw files from some digital cameras in Elements 3.

Shadow/Highlight Clipping Preview   Rotate buttons

1. Open the file via the Open dialog box or File Browser, as explained in the preceding section.

You see the Camera Raw converter window, shown in Figure 3.4.

2. Select the Preview check box underneath the image preview.

Now the preview shows you the results of any changes you make inside the dialog box. Use the Zoom tool, labeled in Figure 3.4, to zoom the preview; click with the tool to zoom in, and ALT-click (Windows) or OPTION-click (Mac) to zoom out. To scroll the display, drag with the Hand tool, also labeled in the figure. If the image opens on its side, click the Rotate buttons to set things right.

3. Turn on the Shadows and Highlights options underneath the preview.

When you select these boxes, labeled Shadow/Highlight Clipping Preview in Figure 3.4, Elements displays neon red or blue splotches over areas where the current settings will result in *clipping*—that is, where pixels that were previously different colors will become white (clipped highlights) or black (clipped shadows). Red patches indicate clipped highlights; blue patches, clipped shadows. Either way, you're destroying detail by using the settings that are currently selected in the right side of the dialog box.

4. **Set the image bit depth using the Depth control underneath the image preview.**

Bit depth refers to the amount of color information that the file may contain. Normally, 8 bits is adequate. But if your camera can capture 16-bit files and the image has serious exposure or color problems, you may want to take advantage of that higher bit depth. See Chapter 1 for information that will help you decide.

5. **Select Camera Default from the Settings drop-down list, as shown in Figure 3.4.**

The options underneath the drop-down list, which enable you to tweak the image before you open it in Elements proper, change to show you the settings that Elements thinks are appropriate for your camera. (After you change any setting, the item showing in the drop-down list changes from Camera Default to Custom.)

6. **Use the sliders underneath the Settings drop-down list to adjust color, exposure, and focus—or not.**

You can affect color with the Temperature, Tint, and Saturation sliders; adjust exposure with the Exposure, Shadows, Brightness, and Contrast sliders; and sharpen focus with the Sharpness slider. If the preview indicates a large amount of shadow or highlight clipping, play around with the sliders to reduce the problem. Otherwise, however, I generally advise making color, exposure, and focus adjustments after opening the file. Inside the Camera Raw dialog box, you can't take advantage of selections, which means that you can't change just a portion of the photo. You also don't have access to adjustment layers and other helpful correction features discussed later in this book.

Assuming that you want to make the same correction to the entire photo, however, you may be able to save time by using the Camera Raw options to do a "rough edit." You then can fine-tune after opening the file. If you do fiddle with exposure, keep in mind that you usually can lighten underexposed images with good results in Elements, but bringing back severely overexposed photos isn't always possible.

7. **Soften excess digital noise using the Luminance Smoothing and Color Noise Reduction sliders (optional).**

These controls take different approaches to removing *noise,* a defect that gives images a speckled look. (Chapter 11 shows you other ways to defeat noise.) Zoom in on the preview and monitor image details closely when using these controls; both adjustments have the side effect of softening focus.

8. **Click OK to close the converter and finish opening the picture.**

9. **Save a working copy of your file in the Elements (PSD) format.**

The upcoming section "Protecting Your Picture Files" provides specifics about this critical step. Don't try to save in the Photoshop Raw format, by the way—it's not the same thing as Camera Raw.

Scanning Photos into Elements

If you own a scanner, the software that came in the scanner box should include a scanning utility, which you use to select the scan settings, and may also provide a *driver*. A driver is a bit of code that enables the scanner and computer to communicate. After installing the scan utility and driver (if provided), you can scan images directly into Elements as follows:

1. **Choose File | Import.**

A submenu appears, listing all installed scanners.

2. **Choose your scanner name from the Import submenu.**

Elements launches the scan utility. Every scanner manufacturer offers its own utility, so you'll need to read your scanner manual for specifics.

3. **Select the desired scan settings in your scanner software.**

For help setting the scan resolution and bit depth—the two main options you'll have to consider—see Chapter 1. Bypass scanner-software tools for adjusting exposure, color, and sharpening and instead use the Elements filters for these functions.

4. **After the scan is done, close the scan utility and save the image in the PSD format.**

Watch Out!

Until you save, the file is only temporary. See the section "Protecting Your Picture Files," later in this chapter, for details on saving files.

Importing Files Directly from a Digital Camera

Elements can access files from a digital camera that's connected to your computer. How you get to those files depends on your camera and computer operating system.

- With newer cameras and operating systems, your computer "sees" the camera as a removable drive, just as it does a floppy drive or CD. (You may need to install the driver that shipped with the camera for the computer to recognize the camera.) In this case, you can access files from the File Browser or Open dialog box as outlined earlier in this chapter.

- With older cameras and operating systems, you need to install the driver that came with your camera. Then, to open files, select the camera name from the File | Import submenu. Elements launches your camera's image-transfer software, and you can open files as you normally do using that software. (Sorry, you'll have to read your camera manual for specifics.)

Creating a New Image Canvas

Every image in Elements rests on a virtual *canvas*. Normally, the canvas matches the image size exactly, so you don't see the canvas. The canvas becomes visible only if you delete pixels in the image, as discussed in Chapter 6, or enlarge the canvas, as discussed in the next section.

On occasion, you may want to create a new, blank image canvas. For example, if you're putting together a photo collage, you may want to start with a new canvas and then paste the collage elements into it. To create a new canvas, take these steps:

1. **Choose File | New | Blank File or press CTRL-N (Windows) or ⌘-N (Mac).**

Or click the New button on the toolbar; refer to Figure 3.5. Whichever route you go, you see the New dialog box, also shown in Figure 3.5.

2. **Enter a file name in the Name box.**

3. **Set the canvas size.**

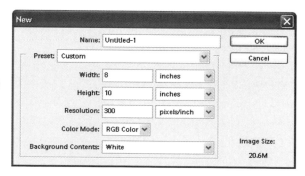

New button

> **Remember**
>
> When you open images that were captured in the JPEG format, create a working copy in the PSD format before you do any editing. See Chapter 13 for details about JPEG and why you don't want to use it to save works in progress.

Figure 3.5: Click the New button on the toolbar to create an empty image canvas.

You can choose a predefined size from the Preset drop-down list or enter custom dimensions in the Width and Height boxes. If you set a custom size, select a unit of measurement from the adjacent drop-down lists. To match the canvas size to a selection that you just copied or moved to the Clipboard via the Edit | Copy or Edit | Cut command, choose Clipboard from the Preset list.

4. Set the Resolution value.

Watch Out!

If you set the Width and Height in any unit of measurement other than pixels, the Resolution value determines the pixel count of your new image. Elements multiplies the Resolution value by the Width and Height values to calculate the number of image pixels. For example, if you set the canvas size to 4 × 6 inches and the Resolution value to 300, you get 1200 × 1800 pixels. If you use pixels as the unit of measurement, ignore the Resolution value. You get however many pixels you specify in the Width and Height boxes. Either way, create enough pixels for your intended final output, as discussed in Chapter 1.

5. Choose a color mode from the Mode menu.

Chapter 1 discusses color modes thoroughly. Select RGB Color for color images.

6. Select a canvas content option.

You can fill the new canvas with white, with the current background color, or with transparent pixels. Make your choice via the Background Contents drop-down list.

7. Click OK to create the new canvas and then save the file in the PSD format.

Until you save, your new canvas—and anything you add to it—are only temporary.

Adjusting the Canvas Size

You can adjust the canvas size at any time by taking the following steps.

1. Choose Image | Resize | Canvas Size to display the Canvas Size dialog box, shown in Figure 3.6.

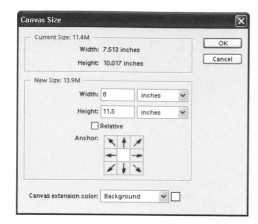

2. **Set the desired canvas dimensions.**

You can go about this in two ways:

- Deselect the Relative box and enter the canvas dimensions in the Width and Height boxes. Specify the unit of measurement using the adjacent drop-down lists.
- Select the Relative box and use the Width and Height boxes to specify how much you want to add or subtract from the existing canvas. If you enter 2 in the Width box, for example, you add 2 inches to the canvas width; if you enter –2, you reduce the width by 2 inches.

Watch Out!

Figure 3.6: Use the Anchor boxes to specify the location of the image with respect to the canvas.

Assuming that your image currently covers the entire canvas, reducing the canvas size crops your photo. See Chapter 4 for other information about cropping.

3. **Use the Anchor control to position the image on the newly sized canvas.**

The empty square represents your image. Click any box to place your image in that position with respect to the new canvas. For example, if you click the center box, your image is centered on the canvas.

4. **If enlarging the canvas, set the canvas color.**

Select an option from the Canvas Extension Color drop-down list or click the adjacent color swatch to open the Color Picker and select a custom color. When the Color Picker is open, you can click a color in your photo to select that color. Chapter 2 explains more about using the Color Picker.

5. **Click OK to close the dialog box.**

Time Saver

When you don't need to enlarge the canvas by a specific amount, try this canvas-stretching trick: Pick up the Crop tool and drag to create a crop boundary. Drag the edges of the crop boundary past the current image borders, and press ENTER. Again, see Chapter 4 for details about the Crop tool. The added canvas area will be the background color.

Rotating the Canvas (and Your Image)

You can rotate the image canvas—and the image on it—by choosing Image | Rotate and choosing an option from the submenu that appears. If you want to rotate the image with respect to the canvas, use the Free Transform command, detailed in Chapter 4.

Viewing Your Photos

Every open image in Elements appears inside its own window, as shown in Figure 3.7. You get the standard Windows or Mac controls for closing, minimizing, and restoring windows, as well as scroll bars for scrolling the image display.

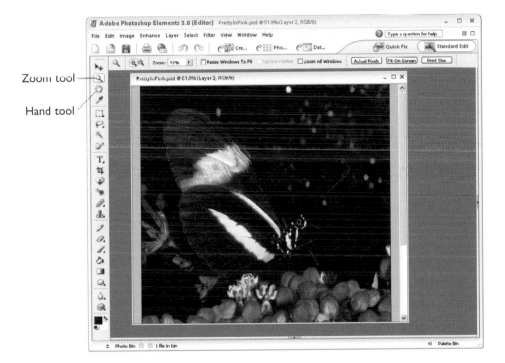

Zoom tool

Hand tool

Figure 3.7: Every open image appears inside its own window.

Use these tactics to get a closer look at your photo or pull out for a wider view:

- Click the Zoom tool, labeled in Figure 3.7, and click the image. Keep clicking to zoom in further. To zoom out, ALT-click (Windows) or OPTION-click (Mac). You can zoom in on a specific area by dragging around it with the Zoom tool.

- Use the keyboard shortcuts listed in the upcoming Speed Keys table.
- Choose Window | Navigator or press F12 to open the Navigator palette, shown in Figure 3.8. Drag the zoom slider to the right to zoom in, and drag the slider left to zoom out. Alternatively, click the zoom-in and zoom-out buttons at each end of the slider.

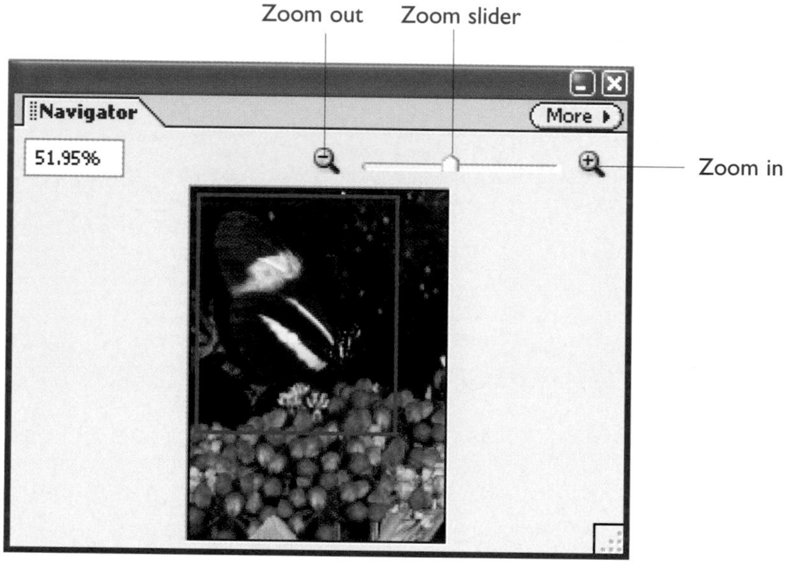

Figure 3.8: The Navigator palette offers one way to scroll and zoom the image.

To scroll the image display, select the Hand tool, labeled in Figure 3.7. Then drag in the image window. If the Navigator palette is open, you can also drag the box that appears on the image thumbnail. Just drag the box over the area you want to see.

Tool Tricks

Press H to select the Hand tool. Or press the spacebar to temporarily switch to the Hand tool while any editing tool is active. Release the spacebar to go back to the editing tool you were using.

SPEED KEYS: Zooming the Image Display

Action	Windows	Mac
Zoom in	CTRL-+ (plus)	⌘-+ (plus)
Zoom out	CTRL-- (minus)	⌘-- (minus)
Fit entire image	CTRL-0 (zero)	⌘-0 (zero)
Display actual pixels*	ALT-CTRL-0 (zero)	OPTION-⌘-0 (zero)

*Matches one image pixel to one screen pixel; see Chapter 1 for details.

Protecting Your Picture Files

A digital image has a potentially unlimited life span—*if* you take a few steps to protect it.

Watch Out!

First, never edit an original image file. Instead, save a copy of the file immediately after you open it and apply any alterations to this working copy. Remember to resave your working copy before you close your image, too; if you don't, all your changes are lost. In fact, you should get in the habit of saving periodically during each editing session because your edits are vulnerable if your system crashes while the image is open.

Elements offers three file-saving commands:

- **File | Save As**   Use this command to create your working copy and to preserve multiple versions of an image—for example, to save copies at various print sizes or in different file formats. Choosing the command produces the Save As dialog box, which varies depending on your operating system. Figure 3.9 shows the Windows XP version. Regardless of your system, you find the standard controls for selecting the folder where you want to store the image, naming the file, and specifying the file format. In addition, you get a few Elements-specific options. The next two sections offer advice about file formats and discuss the Elements options.

Figure 3.9: Choose
File | Save As to save a
working copy of your
original image.

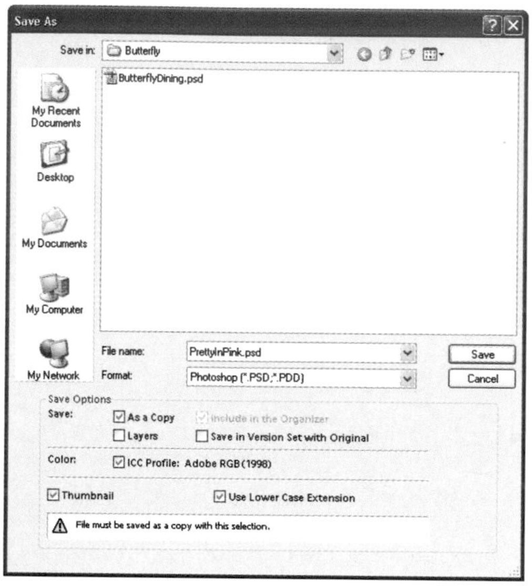

■ **File | Save** Use this command to safeguard edits as you work and
before closing the file. No dialog box appears; Elements simply overwrites
the current file with the version of the image on-
screen, using the settings you established when
saving the file for the first time. Clicking the Save
button on the toolbar, labeled in Figure 13.10,
applies this command. (If you haven't yet saved
the file for the first time, you get the Save As dialog box.)

Save button

Figure 3.10: Click the Save button often as you work
to safeguard changes to the image.

■ **Save for Web** Choose this command only for making JPEG copies of
your photos to use on the Web. Chapter 13 explains Save for Web.

SPEED KEYS: Save Command Shortcuts

Command	Windows	Mac
Save	CTRL-S	⌘-S
Save As	SHIFT-CTRL-S	SHIFT-⌘-S
Save for Web	ALT-SHIFT-CTRL-S	OPTION-SHIFT-⌘-S

File Format Options

The Format drop-down list in the Save As dialog box offers more than a dozen
choices. But for everyday photography projects, you need just three.

- **Photoshop (.PSD)** This is Elements' own format, or native format. Well, technically speaking, PSD is the native format of Elements' higher-priced sibling, Photoshop, carried into Elements, but let's not pick nits, okay? Whatever its origin, PSD is designed to preserve special Elements features, such as layers, and also allows the fastest processing of your edits. Always save your working copies in this format. In fact, there's no reason to save in any other format unless you want to use an image on the Web or in a program that can't open PSD files.
- **TIFF (.TIF)** TIFF, pronounced *tiff,* as in spat, is a print format. You may need to create a TIFF version of your image to import it into a page-layout program or have it printed at a commercial imaging lab. Chapter 13 explains the TIFF options that appear when you save in this format.
- **JPEG (.JPG)** Pronounced *jay-peg,* JPEG is a screen-display format used for Web, e-mail, and multimedia images. After finalizing a photo, create a JPEG copy using the Save for Web command, explored in Chapter 13.

Remember

To save a 16-bit image, select PSD or TIFF as the file format.

Elements-Only Save Options

In the lower portion of the Save As dialog box, shown in magnified view in Figure 3.11, you find a handful of options specific to Elements. A few items become available only when you save in the PSD or TIFF format, and some options are Mac-only or Windows-only features.

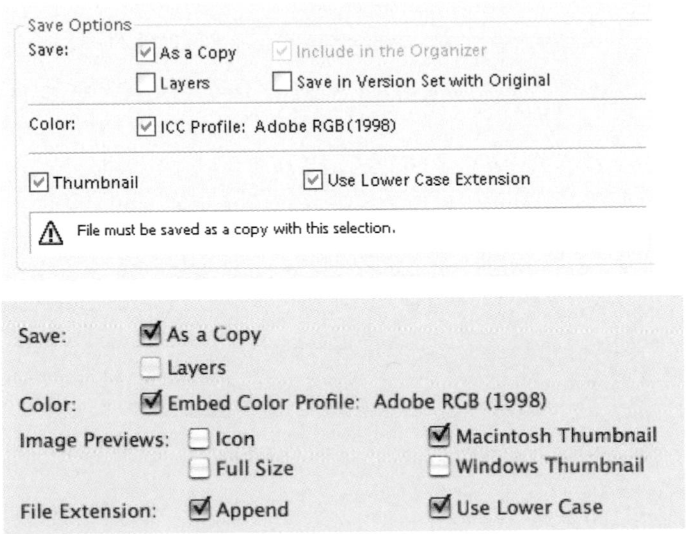

Figure 3.11: The Elements-only file-saving options vary depending on whether you're running the program under Windows XP (top) or OS X (bottom).

Here's the rundown on these options:

- **As a Copy**   If you turn this option on, Elements doesn't save the open image but instead creates a copy of the image at its present state. However, you must give the copy a new name, or you overwrite the open image. Also be sure to save your open image before you close it, using File | Save, or any changes made during the current editing session won't be retained in that file.

- **Layers (PSD or TIFF only)**   Select the Layers check box to preserve individual layers, discussed in Chapter 6. If you deselect the box, all layers are merged into one.

- **Include in the Organizer (Windows)**   This option relates to the Organizer, the file-management tool provided with the Windows version of Elements 3. Selected by default, this feature automatically adds a thumbnail for the image to your current Organizer image catalog.

- **Save in Version Set with Original (Windows)**   Another Organizer feature, this option allows you to create file "sets" that contain different versions of the same image. The option is available only for images already included in the Organizer. When you select the check box, Elements adds a tag to the file name—Edited-1, Edited-2, and so on—to let you know that you're saving an updated version of the open image. Then it saves a copy of the image, leaving the open image unsaved. In the Organizer, you see the thumbnail only for the original image until you choose Edit | Version Set | Reveal Photos in Version Set. The idea is to save screen space in the Organizer, but you have to remember that those additional version files are available. Personally, I have enough problems remembering my own name, so I don't take advantage of this feature. Instead, when I want to make a copy of a file, I just use the As a Copy option and alter the file name myself.

- **ICC Profile (Windows) and Embed Color Profile (Mac)**   Part of the Elements color-management system, this option enables you to include—*embed*—the current color profile. Profiles provide data that specify how the computer should interpret the color values in the file. Embedding profiles is especially helpful when you're sharing files with other people who also use color-managed software. But embedded profiles cause problems in some scenarios; you shouldn't embed profiles in Web images, for example. For the full story on color management, see Chapter 12.

- **Image Previews (Mac)**   These options enable you to save tiny previews with a file. You get four choices, as shown in Figure 3.11. Macintosh Thumbnail creates a preview that appears in the Macintosh Open dialog box; Windows Thumbnail creates a preview that appears on Windows systems; Icon turns the desktop file icon into a tiny thumbnail; Full Size creates a low-resolution image that can be used in programs that can't open high-resolution images. Each preview adds to the file size, so turn these options off unless you absolutely need them.

Time Saver

To avoid dealing with this issue each time you save, open the Saving Files panel of the Preferences dialog box, introduced in Chapter 2 and shown again in Figure 3.12. Select Always Save or Never Save from the Image Previews pop-up menu, depending on your feelings about previews. If you choose Always Save, select the boxes for the previews you want to create. Now Elements implements your preview choices automatically; the options disappear from the Save As dialog box. To regain the opportunity to specify the preview options each time you save, return to the Preferences dialog box and set the Image Previews option to Ask When Saving.

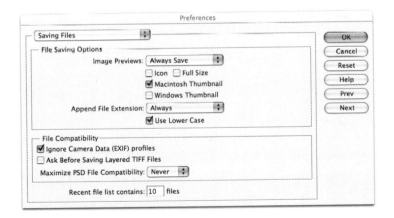

Figure 3.12: Don't enable all four previews; each one increases file size.

- **Thumbnail (Windows)**   This option saves a thumbnail preview with the image file. In Windows, the Elements Open dialog box displays thumbnails regardless of whether you save the preview, however. In fact, most newer Windows programs offer this capability. Again, because the preview increases the size of the image file, turn this feature off. Better yet, open the Saving Files panel of the Preferences dialog box and select Never Save from the Image Previews pop-up menu. Now you don't have to bother unchecking that Thumbnail box every time you save.

- **File Extension: Append/Use Lower Case (Mac) and Use Lower Case Extension (Windows)**   If you're a Mac user who needs to share images with a Windows user, your file names must include the three-letter Windows file extensions (.psd, .tif, .jpg). You can tell Elements to add the extension automatically: Open the Saving Files panel of the Preferences dialog box and select Always from the Append File Extension pop-up menu, as shown in Figure 3.12. If you instead select Ask When Saving, the Save As dialog box offers an Append check box, as shown in Figure 3.11, so that you can make the call on a case-by-case basis.

The Use Lower Case (Mac) or Use Lower Case Extension (Windows) option tells Elements whether to add the extension in lowercase or capital letters. It doesn't make a difference unless you're preparing photos for a use that demands that file names follow strict rules about case.

Elements Safety Nets

Elements gives you a number of safety nets that enable you to undo bad editing decisions.

Reversing Changes with Undo and Redo

Found on the Edit menu, the Undo command takes you back one step in time, reversing your last edit. Undo then morphs into the Redo command, which enables you to undo your undo.

By default, you can undo and restore as many as 50 edits. This value is controlled by the History States option in the Preferences dialog box, explained in Chapter 2.

Time Saver

To apply the Undo command, press CTRL-Z (Windows) or ⌘-Z (Mac). For Redo, press CTRL-Y (Windows) or ⌘-Y (Mac). (These shortcuts assume that you set the Step Back/ Fwd setting in the Preferences dialog box as discussed in Chapter 2.) You also can click the Undo and Redo toolbar buttons, labeled in Figure 3.13.

Using the Undo History Palette

Shown in Figure 3.13, the Undo History palette offers a quick way to undo and redo a long sequence of edits. Choose Window | Undo History or press F10 to display the palette.

Each time you apply an alteration to an image, Elements creates a *history state,* which logs the change in the palette. In Figure 3.13, the palette contains five states. By accessing different states, you can move between current and previous versions of your image, as follows:

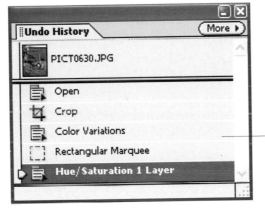

Undo button   Redo button

Figure 3.13: You can go back in time by using the Undo button or the Undo History palette.

History state

- ■ Click a state in the palette to return to the Image as it existed at that point.
- ■ All states following the one you click appear dimmed. If you apply a new edit, the dimmed edits disappear from the palette.
- ■ To restore a dimmed state and the edit it represents, click the state. All states above the one you click also get restored.

As with the Undo command, the number of states the Undo History palette tracks depends on the History States option on the General panel of the Preferences dialog box. The default limit is 50.

Watch Out!

Raising the History States value sounds appealing, but every edit that Elements tracks taxes your computer resources more. In fact, I think that the default value is much too high, especially if you're working with large images, a wimpy computer, or both. Try reducing the value to 20 or even lower if Elements behaves sluggishly.

Remember

Undo can't reverse one critical action: saving a file. However, while the file remains open, you can reverse edits after saving by using the Undo History palette.

Restoring the Last-Saved Version

Edit | Revert to Saved undoes all changes made since you last saved the file. Of course, you also can undo all your changes by closing the file without saving it.

First Steps: Straighten and Crop

4

After saving a backup copy of your original image, put the photo fixes discussed in this chapter at the top of your to-do list. First, use the Free Transform command to straighten tilting horizon lines and correct convergence, the lens distortion that makes vertical structures appear to be leaning. Then crop the image to eliminate any excess background. Because cropping reduces file size, it enables Elements to process your other changes more quickly, saving you time in the editing room.

In This Chapter:

- ☐ A simple fix for tilted horizon lines

- ☐ Convergence correction with Free Transform

- ☐ Quick cropping with the Crop tool

- ☐ How to crop to a specific frame size

- ☐ Non-rectangular cropping with the Cookie Cutter

Straightening the Horizon Line

Unless you're trying to convey the idea that the world is off balance, a tilting horizon line like the one shown in the top half of Figure 4.1 is problematic. Fortunately, correcting the problem takes less than five minutes.

Elements offers an automated straightening command—Image | Rotate | Straighten Image—but unless your photo has very strong vertical lines, the feature usually doesn't do the job. Don't fret; the "manual" fix is almost as easy, and far more reliable. Try it using the sample photo Bridge.jpg.

These steps assume that you're working with a single-layer image. If your photo contains multiple layers, open the Layers palette and click the name of the layer you want to alter before moving forward. (Chapter 6 discusses layers in detail.)

Figure 4.1: A tilting horizon line calls for an application of the Free Transform command.

1. **Choose View | Grid to display gridlines over your image, as shown in Figure 4.2.**

The grid will help you determine when the horizon line is level.

Figure 4.2: The grid serves as an alignment aid.

2. **Select any tool but the Cookie Cutter or Custom Shape tool.**
When these tools are active, you lose access to the command you'll use in Step 4 (Free Transform).

3. **Choose Select | All or press CTRL-A (Windows) or ⌘-A (Mac).**
This step tells Elements that you want to manipulate the entire image (or current layer, in a multilayer photo).

4. **Choose Image | Transform | Free Transform.**

Time Saver

Press CTRL-T (Windows) or ⌘-T (Mac) to choose the Free Transform command without messing with menus.

A solid outline called a *bounding box* surrounds your image, as shown in Figure 4.3. Little squares known as *handles* appear around the perimeter. Don't see the handles? Zoom out or drag a corner of the image window to enlarge it, and they should become more apparent.

Rotate cursor   Rotate box   Cancel button   Apply button   Handle

Figure 4.3: Drag
a corner handle to
rotate the image.

5. **Move your cursor outside a corner handle to display the curved rotate cursor, as shown in Figure 4.3.**

6. **Drag up or down to rotate the image and level the horizon line.**
As you drag, the image updates to preview the rotated photo, as shown in Figure 4.3. In addition, the value in the Rotate box on the options bar changes to reflect the degree of rotation. Figure 4.3 labels this control.

For precision rotating, try this trick: Click inside the Rotate box and then press the up and down arrow keys to change the rotation angle one-tenth degree. Press SHIFT plus an arrow key to increase or decrease the value one degree.

7. **Press ENTER or click the Apply button on the options bar, labeled in Figure 4.3.**
(Press ENTER twice if the Rotate box is active.) Photoshop applies the rotation, and the bounding box and related options bar controls disappear. To get rid of the selection outline, choose Select | Deselect or press CTRL-D (Windows) or ⌘-D (Mac). To lose the grid, choose View | Grid.

8. **Crop the image as needed.**
Rotating the image moves some parts of the photo off the canvas and exposes empty areas of canvas, as shown in Figure 4.3. Crop the image to eliminate the empty canvas, using the techniques explained later in this chapter.

The bottom image in Figure 4.1 shows the final rotated and cropped sample photo. I cropped the rotated photo a little more than necessary purely for compositional reasons, opting to lop off the benches at the bottom of the picture.

Watch Out!

Try to make this repair with one application of the Free Transform command. Each time you rotate, Photoshop rebuilds the image, which can cause a slight loss of picture quality.

Should you want to cancel out of Free Transform mode before applying the rotation, click the Cancel button, labeled in Figure 4.3, or just press the ESC key.

Correcting Convergence

Convergence is a photographic phenomenon that creates the illusion that vertical structures lean either away from each other or toward each other, as shown in Figure 4.4. Also known as *keystoning,* the problem occurs when the camera lens isn't level with the horizon line.

Once again, the Free Transform command is the solution. In addition to its rotation function, this command enables you to distort the image in a way that alters perspective. Experiment with the sample image ChinaHues.jpg, featured in Figure 4.4.

Watch Out!

As with rotating, try to perform the entire correction with one application of the Free Transform command to retain as much picture quality as possible.

Figure 4.4: When you shoot with the lens pointing up, vertical structures may appear to lean together, or converge.

1. **Choose View | Grid to display gridlines over your image.**

The grid, visible in Figure 4.5, enables you to easily monitor the vertical alignment of structures throughout the image.

Handle

2. **Choose Image | Resize | Canvas Size and enlarge the image canvas by 50 percent.**

When the Canvas Size dialog box opens, select the Relative check box and set the unit of measurement to Percent. Enter 50 into the Width and Height boxes, and click OK. You'll need the extra canvas when you distort the photo.

3. **Select any tool but the Cookie Cutter or Custom Shape tool.**

Otherwise, you can't perform the transformation.

4. **Choose Select | All or press CTRL-A (Windows) or ⌘-A (Mac) to select the entire image.**

This instruction assumes that you're working with a single-layer image. To transform one layer in a multi-layer image, click the layer name in the Layers palette instead of choosing Select | All. To transform multiple layers, link them first. And if you haven't a clue what I mean by any of these layer references, visit Chapter 6.

Figure 4.5: To adjust perspective, press CTRL-ALT-SHIFT (Windows) or ⌘-OPTION-SHIFT (Mac) as you drag a corner handle.

5. **Choose Image | Transform | Free Transform or press CTRL-T (Windows) or ⌘-T (Mac).**

As shown in Figure 4.5, you see the transformation bounding box and handles, introduced in the preceding section. If you don't see the handles, enlarge the image window or zoom out.

6. **Hold down the CTRL-ALT-SHIFT keys (Windows) or the ⌘-OPTION-SHIFT keys (Mac) as you drag a corner handle horizontally.**

When you drag, you apply a perspective change. As you move one handle, the opposite handle moves in tandem.

Drag outward to tilt vertical structures away from each other. Go this direction for the sample image, tugging one of the top corner handles as shown in Figure 4.5. Drag inward to tilt structures toward the center of the image.

You may not be able to fix all structures with this one transformation, so release the mouse button when the most visually dominant structures no longer lean. In the sample image, focus on the right column.

7. Apply further distortions as needed to complete the correction.
Depending on your photo, you may need to make further adjustments. For the sample image, drag the top center handle up to increase the height, as shown in Figure 4.6. (This step is often necessary after a large perspective shift.) Then CTRL-drag (Windows) or ⌘-drag (Mac) the top-left corner handle outward until the left column in the photo also appears straight. By CTRL- or ⌘-dragging, you can move one handle without shifting the others, enabling you to distort the image freely. To limit a corner handle to a perfectly horizontal or vertical move, press SHIFT as you CTRL- or ⌘-drag.

For other adjustments, use the handle-dragging techniques listed in the upcoming Speed Keys table. Note that you can limit the transform handles to rotating, scaling, or skewing (slanting) by clicking the corresponding options bar buttons, labeled in Figure 4.7. (Refer to the table to find out what handles to drag with which buttons.) You also can enter values into the Width (W), Height (H), or Rotate box (labeled in Figure 4.7).

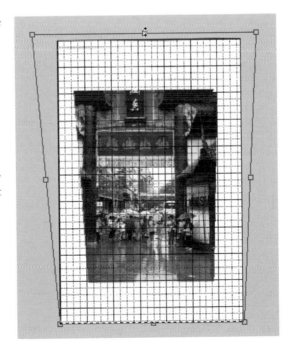

Figure 4.6: Dragging the handles to the positions shown here squared up the rest of the image.

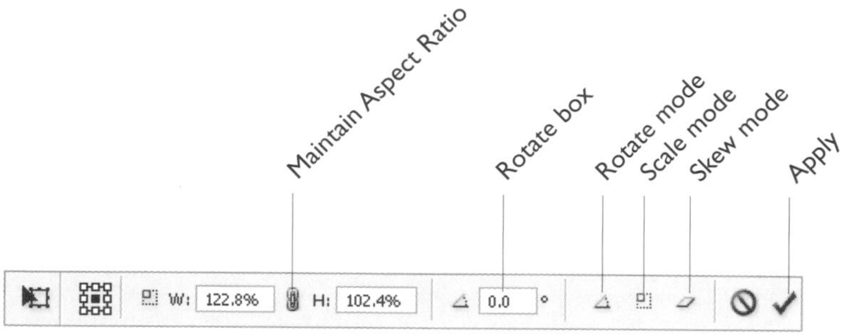

Maintain Aspect Ratio / Rotate box / Rotate mode / Scale mode / Skew mode / Apply

Figure 4.7: You can also distort the image by using the options bar controls.

If you don't like the results of your handle-dragging and want to start over, press ESC or click the Cancel button, located to the left of the Apply button.

8. Do a final alignment check.

When you think you have things squared up, choose View | Grid to hide the grid so that you can see your image more clearly.

Watch Out!

If critical areas of the photo have moved off the canvas, drag inside the bounding box to reposition the image on the canvas. Or cancel out of the transformation (press ESC) and enlarge the canvas more. Any pixels off the canvas will be lost after you apply the transformation in the next step.

9. When you're happy with the image, press ENTER or click the Apply button, labeled in Figure 4.7, and then choose Select | Deselect to get rid of your selection outline.

10. Crop away any excess canvas.

Your corrected photo will have an irregular shape that no longer fills the entire canvas. Crop the image as explained in the next section. Figure 4.8 shows the final sample image.

Figure 4.8: Expect to lose some original image area as the result of the transformation.

SPEED KEYS: Free Transform Shortcuts and Techniques

Action	Windows	Mac
Select the entire image	CTRL-A	⌘-A
Display the transformation handles	CTRL-T	⌘-T
Rotate the horizon line	Drag outside a corner handle or click the Rotate button and drag any handle	Drag outside a corner handle or click the Rotate button and drag any handle
Adjust perspective	CTRL-ALT-SHIFT-drag a corner handle	⌘-OPTION-SHIFT-drag a corner handle
Adjust height	Drag a top or bottom center handle	Drag a top or bottom center handle
Adjust width	Drag a side center handle	Drag a side center handle
Adjust size proportionately	SHIFT-drag a corner handle or click the Maintain Aspect Ratio button and just drag	SHIFT-drag a corner handle or click the Maintain Aspect Ratio button and just drag
Skew the image	CTRL-SHIFT-drag a center handle or click the Skew icon and just drag	⌘-SHIFT-drag a center handle or click the Skew icon and just drag
Distort the image freely	CTRL-drag any handle	⌘-drag any handle
Distort relative to the center point of the bounding box	ALT-drag a handle	OPTION-drag a handle
Move the image around the canvas	Drag inside the bounding box	Drag inside the bounding box

Cropping Your Pictures

The smaller the image file size, the faster Photoshop can process your alterations. Because every pixel adds to file size, always crop your photo loosely after you create your working copy. After editing your photo, you can crop more closely if needed.

Watch Out!

One exception applies: If you need to fix a tilting horizon line or convergence, don't apply the crop before making the correction. Both corrections cause part of your image to be lost, so you should start with as much original image area as possible.

With that caveat in mind, the rest of this chapter explains four ways to crop.

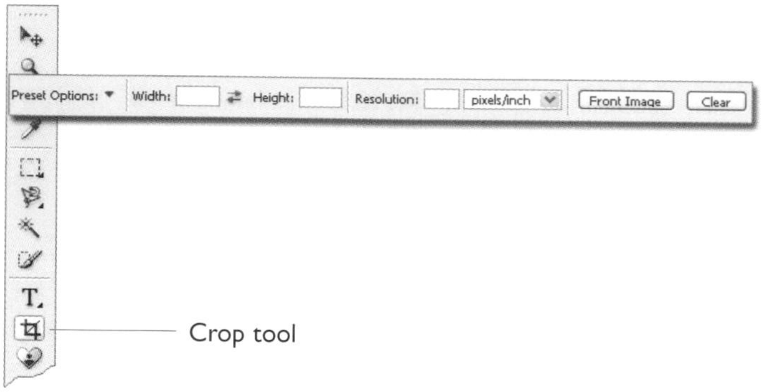

Figure 4.9: For safe cropping, set your tool options as shown here.

Crop tool

Using the Crop Tool

For loose cropping, the Crop tool provides the quickest solution. Crop this way:

1. **If a selection outline is active, choose Select | Deselect or press CTRL-D (Windows) or ⌘-D (Mac) to get rid of it.**

2. **Press c or click the Crop tool icon in the toolbox, labeled in Figure 4.9.**

3. **Set the tool options as shown in Figure 4.9.**

The Crop tool options enable you to specify a specific size and output resolution (ppi) for your cropped photo. However, this approach is dangerous. If you specify a resolution, the image is resampled, which may degrade image quality. And if you don't, you may not wind up with enough pixels to produce a decent print or the right screen display size. See the next section for a better solution. And click the Clear button on the options bar if the Width, Height, or Resolution boxes contain values.

Figure 4.10: Drag to create the initial crop boundary.

Crop boundary

4. **Drag to create a crop boundary, as shown in Figure 4.10.**

Anything inside the dotted outline will be retained when you apply the crop. Don't worry about getting the boundary perfect; you can modify it in the next step.

When you release the mouse button, handles appear around the perimeter of the outline, and anything outside the outline is covered with a dark tint, as shown in Figure 4.11. You can adjust the tint color and opacity using the options bar controls. To lose the tint altogether, deselect the Shield Color box.

5. Adjust the crop boundary as needed.

Figure 4.11: Drag a handle to adjust the crop boundary.

To resize the boundary, drag any handle. To move the boundary, drag inside it. Or, for precision moves, press the arrow keys to nudge the boundary one pixel in the direction of the arrow. Press SHIFT plus an arrow key to nudge the boundary 10 pixels.

If you have trouble positioning the edges of the crop boundary, the problem may be related to a feature known as Snap to Grid. When enabled, this feature causes crop boundaries and selection boundaries to cling to points on the grid, introduced earlier in this chapter, even when the grid isn't displayed. Open the View menu; if a checkmark appears next to the Snap to Grid command, the feature is enabled. Click the command to turn it off.

6. **Press ENTER or click the Apply button on the options bar.**

To instead cancel out of the crop operation, press ESC or click the Cancel button, next to the Apply button.

Watch Out!

If you move your cursor outside the crop boundary in Step 4, the cursor turns into a double-headed arrow, which is Elements signal for "rotation possible." By dragging, you can rotate the crop boundary. This feature enables you to rotate an image and crop it in one action. However, I suggest that instead you use the Free Transform command to rotate the image so that you can see a live preview of the rotation. See the first section in this chapter for details.

Cropping to a Specific Size or Aspect Ratio

In addition to the Crop tool, Elements offers a Crop command. Use this command to crop to specific dimensions. Follow these steps:

1. **Choose the Rectangular Marquee tool, shown in Figure 4.12.**

2. **Choose Fixed Size from the Mode pop-up menu on the options bar.**

Figure 4.12: Specify the size of the crop boundary on the options bar.

Rectangular Marquee tool

3. **Set the other options as shown in Figure 4.12.**

4. **Type the desired image dimensions in the Width and Height boxes.**

Be sure to type the unit of measurement you want to use after the numbers you enter, as shown in Figure 4.12. You can use picas, inches, and other standard units of measurement. Use pixels for Web images, for reasons discussed in Chapter 1.

Use pixels for low-resolution images you plan to print, too. That way, you know that after you crop, the image will still have enough pixels to generate a decent print. Multiply the desired resolution by the desired print size to come up with the pixel values. For example, if you want to output a 4 × 6–inch print at 200 pixels per inch, set the Width and Height values to 800 and 1200 pixels, respectively. Of course, you can't crop to those dimensions unless your original image is at least that large.

5. **Click on your image to display a selection outline.**

6. **Move your cursor inside the outline and then drag the outline over the part of the image you want to keep.**

To fine-tune the outline placement, press the arrow keys. Press once to nudge the outline one pixel in the direction of the arrow. Press SHIFT plus an arrow key to nudge the outline 10 pixels.

7. **Choose Image | Crop.**

Elements crops the image to the boundaries of the selection outline.

In addition to cropping to a specific size, you can use this technique to crop to a particular aspect ratio. Just choose Fixed Aspect Ratio instead of Fixed Size from the Mode pop-up menu in Step 2. This time, drag in the image window to create your selection outline. Elements limits the Rectangular Marquee tool to drawing an outline that matches the proportions you entered in the Width and Height boxes.

Watch Out!

Before printing your cropped image, you need to visit the Image Size dialog box to establish the output resolution and print size, regardless of which crop method you used. For Web images, you may need to adjust the pixel dimensions after cropping.

See Chapter 1 for more information about pixels and output resolution. Chapter 5 provides details about the Rectangular Marquee tool, and Chapter 13 shows you how to prepare photos for printing and the Web.

Trimming with Precision

As covered in Chapter 3, every image in Elements rests on an invisible canvas, which you can resize via the Image | Resize | Canvas Size command. When you reduce the canvas size, Photoshop clips off pixels that fall outside the new canvas area, which means that you can use Canvas Size as a cropping tool.

Time Saver

This option provides the fastest way to clip a specific number of picas, inches, pixels, or whatever from one or more edges of an image. Just match the dimensions of the canvas to the size you want your cropped image to be. Chapter 3 details the process of adjusting the canvas size, so I won't waste space going into everything again here.

Cropping to an Irregular Shape

All digital images are rectangular. But you can create the *illusion* that your image has some other shape by using the Cookie Cutter tool, new to Elements 3. I used this technique to crop the image in Figure 4.13.

In essence, this technique creates a digital matte. If you match the matte color to the paper color or Web page background, it becomes invisible—the eye

Figure 4.13: All digital images are rectangular (top), but a little trickery creates the illusion of an image that has some other shape (bottom).

can't tell where the photo ends and the paper or background begins. (I added a border around the cropped photo in Figure 4.13 so that you can see the actual dimensions of the image.)

The following steps show you how to create the soft vignette effect you see in Figure 4.13. To work along with the steps, open the sample image Butterfly.jpg.

Watch Out!

One word of caution: If your image contains multiple layers, and you want to crop the entire image, flatten the photo before using this technique. Otherwise, you crop only the active layer. (Chapter 6 explains layers.)

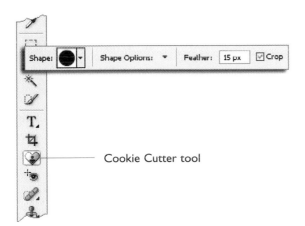

Cookie Cutter tool

Figure 4.14: The Cookie Cutter tool enables you to crop to a variety of shapes.

1. **Select the Cookie Cutter tool, labeled in Figure 4.14.**

2. **Open the Shape Picker by clicking the arrow labeled in Figure 4.15.**

The picker contains icons representing a default collection of shapes. If you open the picker menu, you can load additional shapes. To create the circular matte used in this example, load either the Shapes collection or All Elements Shapes, as shown in the figure.

Click to open Shape Picker

Click to open menu

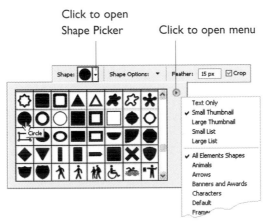

Figure 4.15: To display the entire collection of shapes, choose All Elements Shapes.

3. Click the icon for the shape you want to use.

Many of the shapes aren't suitable to use for this purpose; they're designed for adding simple drawings to pictures, not for cropping. For the sample image, click the Circle icon, as shown in Figure 4.15. (Note that the location of the Circle icon depends on which shape collection you load, the display option you choose from the top of the Shape Picker menu, and whether you enlarge the picker window itself. You can pause your cursor over a shape to see its name.)

4. Display the list of shape options, as shown in Figure 4.16.

These options determine the size and proportions of the initial shape that you draw:

- **Unconstrained** allows you to create a shape with any size or proportions.
- **Defined Proportions** retains the original proportions of the shape.
- **Defined Size** retains the original size of the shape.
- **Fixed Size** allows you to set precise dimensions for the shape by entering values into the Width and Height boxes.
- **From Center** relates to the Unconstrained and Defined Proportions options. For both options, you drag to draw the shape. When From Center is selected, the shape is centered around the start of your drag. Turn the option off, and the shape is centered between the start and end points of your drag.

For the sample project, choose Unconstrained and turn off the From Center box.

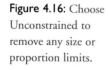

Figure 4.16: Choose Unconstrained to remove any size or proportion limits.

Click to display options

5. Enter a Feather value (optional).

Feathering causes the shape to fade out gradually at the edges. The higher the value, the greater the effect. For the sample image, I set the Feather value to 15. If you want your shape to have crisp, precise edges, set the value to 0.

6. Select the Crop box (optional).

If you select this box, Elements crops the image to the boundaries of the matte after you draw it. Alternatively, you can do the cropping yourself later, using the methods discussed earlier in this chapter. You may as well select the box for the sample project.

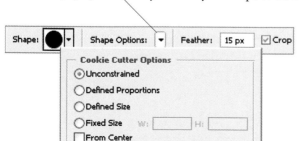

7. **Click or drag in the image window to create the shape outline, as shown in Figure 4.17.**

If you selected the Unconstrained or Defined Proportions option in Step 4, drag to create the shape outline. Otherwise, just click. For the sample image, drag as shown in Figure 4.17. (I added the arrow; it doesn't appear on your screen.)

After you click or release the mouse button, everything outside the outline is replaced by a checkerboard pattern, as shown in Figure 4.18. The checkerboard indicates transparent pixels—or, in this case, pixels that will be transparent after you finish with the Cookie Cutter. You also see a bounding box (outline) with square handles, along with the same controls that appear when you use the Free Transform command, explained earlier in this chapter.

Figure 4.17: In Unconstrained mode, drag to create the initial shape outline.

8. **Adjust the size, shape, and position of the matte as needed.**

You can drag the handles around the bounding box or enter values into the options bar boxes, just as when you use Free Transform. In fact, you can use all the techniques listed in the earlier Speed Keys table to manipulate the matte. Drag inside the bounding box to reposition the matte.

At any time, you can cancel out of the operation by clicking the Cancel button, labeled in Figure 4.18, or by pressing ESC.

Figure 4.18: Drag the
bounding box handles to
adjust your digital matte.

9. **Press ENTER or click the Apply button, labeled in Figure 4.18.**
The bounding box disappears, and everything but the area that was inside the
bounding box officially becomes transparent.

> **Tool Tricks**
> If you set the Cookie Cutter tool to Unconstrained mode, you can still limit the tool
> to retaining the shape's original proportions by pressing SHIFT as you drag.

For single-layer images, you may need to take one additional step. As part of the
Cookie Cutter process, Elements converts the Background layer to a regular layer.
Why? Because the Background layer can't contain transparent pixels, as you'll dis-
cover when you explore Chapter 6.

If you save your image in the PSD or TIFF format with layers enabled, your transparent pixels remain invisible—which means that they take on the paper color
when printed. You can instead fill those areas with color, as I did for Figure 4.19.
For images saved in the JPEG format, you *must* specify a color—JPEG images
can't contain transparent pixels.

Figure 4.19: You can fill the transparent pixels with color.

To add color to the transparent areas, take these steps:

1. Set the background paint color to the color you want to use for the transparent areas.

2. Choose Layer | New | Background from Layer.

This step converts the layer back to a Background layer, but you can always turn it back into a regular layer if needed by choosing Layer | New | Layer from Background.

As an alternative, you can choose Layer | Flatten Image, in which case Elements fills the transparent pixels with white.

Again, don't worry if this whole layer thing is completely baffling at this point—it will make sense after you explore Chapter 6.

Time Saver

The Save for Web utility, explained in Chapter 13, offers a Matte control that enables you to assign a color to transparent pixels and save the file in the JPEG format in one step. This option is helpful when you need a JPEG copy of an image but want to keep a print version that retains the transparent areas.

Selective Editing

5

In a traditional darkroom, photographers sometimes selectively expose the image by covering part of the paper with a light blocking material, or *mask*. The mask prevents the underlying area from being altered by the exposure.

In Elements, you take the opposite approach, specifying the area you *do* want to affect. This process, called *selecting*, is critical: Your selecting technique determines whether the alterations you make are undetectable or scream "this photo's been doctored!" To that end, this chapter provides you with the best (and fastest) ways to expertly select even the most complex subjects.

The Basics of Selecting

To limit the effects of an Elements command to a particular area of your picture, you must select the pixels to be changed before applying the command. If you're familiar with word-processing programs, the concept is the same as highlighting the text you want to modify. For some commands, such as the Free Transform command introduced in Chapter 4, you must take this step even if you want to alter the entire photo.

Selecting isn't a requirement when you work with an editing tool, such as the Brush or Clone tool, but it provides you with a safety net because Elements then limits the tools so that they affect only selected pixels. Suppose that you want to paint a tint over the petals of the water lily in Figure 5.1, for example. If you select the petals, you don't have to worry about accidentally getting paint on the background.

Figure 5.1: The blinking line indicates the boundaries of your selection outline.

Selection outline

To select pixels, you use the tools discussed in this chapter to draw a *selection outline* around the area you want to alter. The outline appears as a blinking, dashed line, as shown in Figure 5.1. The area inside the outline—the region designated as ready for change—is the *selection*.

Because of its appearance, the selection outline is sometimes called a *marquee*—the outline is supposed to resemble a theatre marquee. If that's not creative enough for you, some folks say *marching ants* instead. I'm not keen on that particular bit of selection slang, finding it a little too cutesy, but if Adobe ever puts little heads and feet on the lines, I may convert. I don't use the term *marquee* because I want to avoid confusion when discussing the Marquee tools.

Note that in Figure 5.1, as well as in other figures that show a selection outline, I made the outline thicker and, in some cases, added a tint so that you can see it more clearly. I made these changes in Elements; you can't adjust the actual on-screen appearance of selection outlines. Not to worry—the outlines are perfectly visible on-screen in their natural clothing; they just don't reproduce well in print.

Fading Versus Precise Selection Outlines

Before you create a selection outline, you need to consider whether you want to create a sharp, distinct boundary between the edited and unchanged areas in your photo or have the alteration fade out gradually along that border.

Figure 5.2 illustrates the difference between a hard-edged selection outline and a fading one, which is said to be *feathered*. For both images, I selected and copied part of the water lily image from Figure 5.1 into a new background. To create the example on the left, I selected the flower using an unfeathered selection outline, which gives the copied selection a crisp, well-defined edge.

Remember

Some people use the terms *masking* and *selecting* interchangeably. But technically speaking, *masking* means *preventing* changes to an image area, and *selecting* means marking the pixels that you *do* want to edit. That's how I use the terms in this book.

Figure 5.2: Here you see the results of selecting the water lily from Figure 5.1 using an unfeathered outline (left) and a feathered outline (right).

For the example on the right, I used a feathered outline, setting the feathering effect to spread over 15 pixels. Now pixels along the edge of the copied selection fade gradually into the new background, creating a soft vignette effect.

Whether you should use a hard-edged or feathered selection outline depends on what you're trying to accomplish. If a hard-edged outline creates an unwanted visual break after you apply an edit, undo your changes and try again with a slightly feathered outline. You need to experiment to see how much feathering creates the look you want.

Elements gives you two ways to specify which outline treatment you want:

- Some selection tools can create either type of outline. For these tools, you make the call via the Feather control on the options bar. (The Cookie Cutter tool, explored in Chapter 4, also offers a Feather control.)
- You also can apply feathering after creating a selection outline by choosing Select | Feather, which displays the Feather Selection dialog box, shown in Figure 5.3.

In both cases, a higher value produces a more feathered outline.

Figure 5.3: A higher Feather Radius value produces a more feathered outline.

Anti-aliased Selection Outlines

When you work with some selection tools, the options bar offers an Anti-aliased check box. *Anti-aliasing* is a process that smoothes out the jagged edges that can occur along curved or diagonal lines in a digital image.

To understand the impact of this option, see Figure 5.4. Both examples show a close-up of a portion of the unfeathered, copied selection from Figure 5.2. For the example on the left in Figure 5.4, I created the selection outline with the Anti-aliased option off. Notice the jagged edges? Compare that result with the example on the right. For that version, I created an anti-aliased selection, producing a smoother edge.

Figure 5.4: Without anti-aliasing, curved and diagonal lines appear jagged.

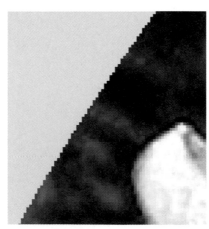

Anti-aliased Off   Anti-aliased On

As with feathering, the decision to anti-alias a selection outline depends on your photo-editing goal. Anti-aliasing can help some edits blend in more naturally. But when you need a precise outline, you may want to turn the feature off because it can cause your outline to stray from the boundaries of the area that you want to alter.

Watch Out!

Be sure to set the Anti-aliased control *before* you create your selection outline. You can't apply this effect after the fact.

Choosing the Right Selection Tool for the Job

The Elements toolbox contains a batch of tools for creating selection outlines, as shown in Figure 5.5. You need to be familiar with all these tools because no single one provides the best solution for all projects. But in general, I recommend tackling selections as follows:

- **Marquee tools**   Grab the Rectangular or Elliptical Marquee to create rectangular or round outlines. (You could no doubt have figured that one out for yourself, but some of your fellow readers may not be as clear-headed.)

- **Lasso tools**   Use the Lassoes to create rough, initial outlines around irregularly shaped objects. The Lasso enables you to create a freeform outline as if you were drawing with a pen. The Magnetic Lasso partially automates the process of selecting an object that's set against a contrasting background. The Polygonal Lasso assists you with creating polygonal outlines—that is, outlines formed by three or more straight lines (think triangle, pentagon, octagon, and so on).

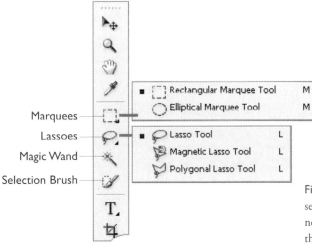

Marquees

Lassoes

Magic Wand

Selection Brush

Figure 5.5: The selection tools live near the top of the toolbox.

- **Magic Wand**   Pick up this tool, which selects pixels based on color, if your subject is different in color from the surrounding area.
- **Selection Brush**   Rely on the Selection Brush to refine a rough outline or to select complex subjects. With this tool, you "paint" a selection outline as if you were working with a paintbrush. Although this tool is a little more complicated to learn than the others, it provides the most flexibility and, in the long run, delivers better results in less time.

Watch Out!

After you create a selection outline, don't click or drag in the image window with the Marquee tools, the Lassoes, or the Magic Wand. When the Selection Mode control on the options bar is set to New Selection, your click or drag eradicates your selection outline and starts a new one. If you accidentally click or drag, just press CTRL-Z (Windows) or ⌘-Z (Mac) to undo your mistake and get your original outline back. See "Adjusting a Selection Outline" later in this chapter for more about the Selection Mode controls.

SPEED KEYS: Selection Tools and Commands

Tool/Command	Windows*	Mac*
Rectangular Marquee	M	M
Elliptical Marquee	M	M
Lasso	L	L
Polygonal Lasso	L	L
Magnetic Lasso	L	L
Magic Wand	W	W
Selection Brush	A	A
Select | All	CTRL-A	⌘-A
Select | Deselect	CTRL-D	⌘-D
Select | Reselect	SHIFT-CTRL-D	SHIFT-⌘-D
Select | Inverse	SHIFT-CTRL-I	SHIFT-⌘-I
Select | Feather	ALT-CTRL-D	OPTION-⌘-D

*Press SHIFT plus the key to toggle through tools that share a shortcut. In OS X, disable conflicting system shortcuts; see Chapter 2.

Selecting Rectangular or Elliptical Areas

When you work with the Rectangular or Elliptical Marquee tool, the options bar offers the controls shown in Figure 5.6. Starting from the left, the controls work as follows:

New Selection

Selection Mode icons

Rectangular Marquee

Figure 5.6: The Marquees create rectangular or elliptical selection outlines.

- **Selection Mode icons**   These icons determine whether the tool creates a new selection outline or adjusts an existing outline. Click the New Selection icon, labeled in Figure 5.6, to begin a new outline; see "Adjusting a Selection Outline" later in this chapter to find out how the neighboring three icons work.

- **Feather and Anti-aliased**   These options work as described earlier in this chapter. The Anti-aliased option is available only for the Elliptical Marquee.

- **Mode**   This option affects the possible proportions and size of the selection outline:
    - **Normal**   In this mode, you can make your outline as tall and wide as you like.
    - **Fixed Aspect Ratio**   This mode limits the tool to creating an outline that adheres to proportions that you establish in the Width and Height boxes. If you want an outline that's twice as tall as it is wide, for example, enter 1 in the Width box and 2 in the Height box.
    - **Fixed Size**   Choose this mode to produce a selection outline with specific dimensions. Enter values in the Width and Height boxes, remembering to type the unit of measurement after the number (inches, pixels, picas, and so on).

In Normal or Fixed Aspect Ratio mode, create your selection outline by dragging from one corner of the area you want to select to the other, as illustrated in Figure 5.7. (I added the arrow; you don't see it on-screen.) In Fixed Size mode, just click in the image.

Figure 5.7: Drag to create a selection outline with the Rectangular or Elliptical Marquee tool.

See "Adjusting a Selection Outline" later in this chapter to find out how to reposition or otherwise refine your initial outline if needed. And for a real-life application of the Rectangular Marquee tool, flip back to the section in Chapter 4 on cropping to a specific size or aspect ratio.

> **Tool Tricks**
> Hold down the SHIFT key while dragging with the Rectangular or Elliptical Marquee to force the tool to draw a square or circular selection outline, respectively.

Selecting with the Lasso Tools

In homage to all the cowpokes in the digital darkroom, Elements provides a selection tool called the Lasso. The Lasso ropes pixels into a selection corral—get it? Anyway, you get three Lasso variations, all accessible from the Lasso flyout menu (refer to Figure 5.5).

Because precision selecting with the Lassoes can be difficult, I use them mostly to draw rough selection outlines before switching to the Selection Brush to finish the job. So that you can take advantage of your Lassoes in the same way, the next three sections walk you through the pixel-ropin' possibilities.

Creating Freeform Outlines with the Lasso

The Lasso, labeled in Figure 5.8, enables you to create a freeform selection outline. Try it using the Hardware.jpg image, part of which appears in Figure 5.8.

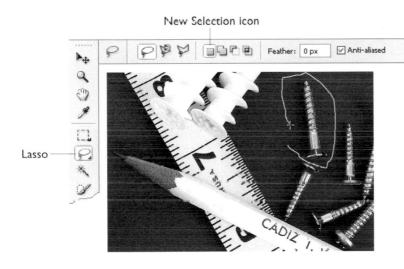

New Selection icon

Lasso

Figure 5.8: Drag around the objects you want to select.

1. Make sure that the New Selection icon on the options bar is pressed in, as shown in Figure 5.8. If not, click it.

2. Set the Anti-aliased and Feather options as desired.

You can read about both options earlier in this chapter.

3. Drag around the area you want to select.

A solid line trails your mouse to show you where the outline will appear, as shown in Figure 5.8. Release the mouse button when you get back to where you started.

Watch Out!

In an attempt to be helpful, Elements automatically closes your selection outline with a straight segment if you release the mouse button before you get back to your starting point. That may or may not be a good thing, depending on the shape of the area you want to select.

Remember

A selection outline sometimes prevents you from getting a clear view of what's happening to your photo. You can hide the outline by pressing CTRL-H (Windows) or ⌘-H (Mac); press again to redisplay the outline.

PART II | PHOTOSHOP ELEMENTS BASICS

Selecting Polygonal Shapes

The Polygonal Lasso simplifies the job of selecting straight-sided polygonal regions. Give it a whirl by selecting the pencil in the Hardware.jpg image, as shown in Figure 5.9.

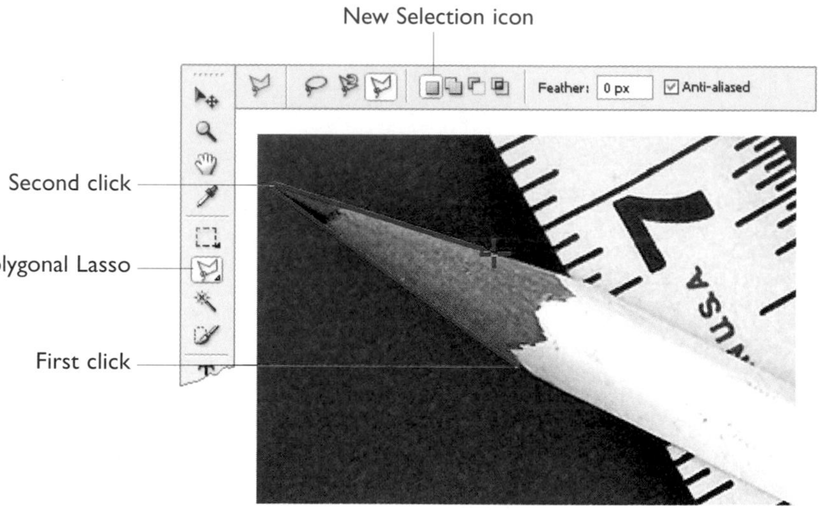

New Selection icon

Figure 5.9: Click to set the endpoints of segments in the outline.

Second click

Polygonal Lasso

First click

1. **Make sure that the New Selection icon is active, as shown in Figure 5.9.**

2. **Set the Anti-aliased and Feather options as desired.**

See the earlier part of this chapter for information on these two options.

3. **Click at the spot where you want the selection outline to begin.**

In the example image, click at the position marked "first click" in Figure 5.9.

4. **Click at the spot where you want to end the first segment in the outline.**

In the example, click the spot marked "second click." Elements creates a straight outline segment between the first and second pixels you clicked.

5. **Keep clicking to create additional segments until you surround the area you want to select with the outline.**

If you mess up, press DELETE to get rid of the last corner you created and then click to redraw the segment. When you reach the start of the outline, Elements displays the tool's icon-style cursor along with a little circle, as illustrated in Figure 5.10. (The icon cursor appears even if you set the cursor preferences option to Precise as suggested in Chapter 2.)

6. **Click to finish the outline.**
You also can double-click to automatically create a final segment between the last pixel you clicked and the starting point.

Selection close cursor

Figure 5.10: When you get back to the selection starting point, a circle appears next to the cursor.

Tool Tricks
Hold down the ALT key (Windows) or OPTION key (Mac) to temporarily shift the Polygonal Lasso into standard Lasso mode, and vice versa. This trick enables you to use either tool to create an outline that contains both curving and straight lines.

Selecting Between Boundaries with the Magnetic Lasso

The Magnetic Lasso is designed to automate the process of selecting an object that's surrounded by contrasting pixels—a light-colored flower set against a dark background, for example. As you move your cursor around the edges of the object, the Magnetic Lasso lays down a selection outline along the boundary between contrasting regions, as if pulled by a magnetic force. (Elements gurus refer to areas where contrasting pixels meet as *edges,* by the way.)

This tool sounds more complex than it really is, but you can't know that until you try it for yourself. So open the sample image WaterLily.jpg and pretend that your creative soul is just dying to select the petals of the flower.

1. **Make sure that the New Selection mode icon is active, as shown in Figure 5.11.**

Ignore all the other tool options except Pen Pressure for now. If you're working with a pressure-sensitive drawing tablet, turn off that option.

2. **Center your cursor over the boundary between the object you want to select and the background.**

Zoom in close on the boundary so you can get a clear view. If you're working with the sample image, place the cursor over the edge of a petal. Your cursor looks like a crosshair within a circle, as shown in Figure 5.11. (See the section in Chapter 2 related to cursor options if your cursor instead looks like the tool icon. Or press the CAPS LOCK key to toggle from the icon cursor to the crosshair cursor.)

New Selection icon

Cursor

Magnetic Lasso

Fastening point

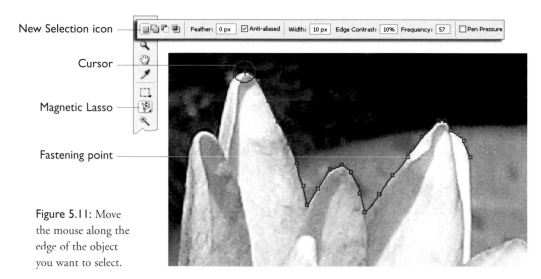

Figure 5.11: Move the mouse along the edge of the object you want to select.

3. **Click to start your selection outline.**

4. **Move your cursor along the perimeter of the object.**

Keep the cursor centered over the edge between the object and the background. As you move the mouse, Elements follows your cursor with a selection outline.

Every so often, the tool shoots out little squares called *fastening points* to tack down the outline. If a segment of the outline doesn't fall where you want it, try these tricks:

- Move your cursor over the last fastening point and press DELETE. The fastening point disappears, and you can re-create that portion of the outline. You can delete as many fastening points as needed.
- Click to add your own selection points. Don't go hog wild; too many points results in a jagged outline.
- Hold down the ALT key (Windows) or OPTION key (Mac) to temporarily switch to the regular Lasso and then drag to create the segment without Elements' help. If you click instead of drag, the tool behaves like the Polygonal Lasso. Release ALT or OPTION to return to the Magnetic Lasso.
- If you really mess up and want to start over, press ESC to get rid of your outline.

5. **When you reach the starting point of the outline, click to complete it.**

To let you know that you've reached the starting point, Elements displays the tool's icon-style cursor with a little circle to the side, similar to the Polygonal Lasso close cursor shown in Figure 5.10. Be careful to single-click and not double-click, or Elements automatically creates a straight segment to join the last fastening point with the starting point.

Like the Lasso and Polygonal Lasso, the Magnetic Lasso offers the Feather and Anti-aliased controls, both explored earlier in this chapter. You also can tweak this tool's behavior by using the following options bar controls, shown in Figure 5.11.

- **Width** This control sets the length of the Magnetic Lasso's leash. If you use a high value, the tool can stray farther from the cursor position to look for an edge. The cursor size reflects the width setting.
- **Edge Contrast** This value controls the tool's sensitivity to contrast. If the contrast between object and background is minimal, use a low value.
- **Frequency** This control enables you to add fastening points at closer or wider intervals. The higher the value, the more points you get.
- **Pen Pressure** This option is designed for users working with a pressure-sensitive tablet. When you select this option, you can adjust the

Width value on the fly by applying more or less pressure with the stylus. I think the Magnetic Lasso is unpredictable enough without throwing in this option, but be your own judge. Note that the value in the Width box doesn't change as you vary pen pressure, but the cursor size does, so that's something.

The Magnetic Lasso does a decent job when a high degree of contrast exists between subject and background. But I can't recommend that you spend hours trying to perfect your Magnetic Lasso technique because you can drive yourself nuts pretty quickly trying to achieve perfection with this tool. So take advantage of the Magnetic Lasso to draw your initial selection outlines if the necessary image contrast exists, but then rely on the Selection Brush, covered later in this chapter, for refining the outline.

Tapping Pixels with the Magic Wand

One of the most valuable selection tools in the Elements arsenal, the Magic Wand tool selects pixels based on color. This option is often the fastest route to a selection outline, especially for selecting subjects shot against a contrasting background.

Using the Magic Wand couldn't be simpler—you just click the color you want to select. But before you click, review the tool options, shown in Figure 5.12. They affect the outcome of your click as follows:

New Selection icon

Figure 5.12: The Magic Wand selects pixels based on color.

Magic Wand

- **Selection Mode icons** Click the New Selection icon, labeled in Figure 5.12, to get rid of any existing selection outline and create a new one. The other three icons shift your tool into modes that enable you to refine an outline, as explained later in this chapter.

- **Tolerance** This setting determines how closely a pixel must match the color of the pixel you click in order to be selected. At a Tolerance value of zero, only exact matches are selected. Raise the value to include more color variations in the selection.

- **Anti-aliased**   Select Anti-aliased to smooth jagged edges along curved or diagonal segments of the outline, as detailed near the start of this chapter.
- **Contiguous**   If you enable this option, Photoshop selects only pixels that are contiguous—directly connected, in plain English—to the pixel that you click. If you turn off the option, the tool can select matching pixels throughout the image.
- **Use All Layers**   This option applies only to multilayered images, which you can learn about in the next chapter. If you turn on the option, Photoshop creates the outline based on the colors of pixels in all layers. This doesn't mean that pixels on all layers are actually selected; a selection outline always affects just the active layer. To base the outline only on colors in the current layer, uncheck the Use All Layers box.

Figures 5.13 through 5.17 illustrate how the Tolerance and Contiguous settings work together to affect the outcome of a Magic Wand selection. After setting the Tolerance value to 35 and selecting the Contiguous check box, I clicked the yellow gumball at the position indicated by the black X in Figure 5.13. The purple areas in Figure 5.14 show the extent of the resulting outline. (I filled the selection with purple to make the illustration clearer; in real life, you see only the dotted selection outline.) Matching pixels in the other yellow gumballs aren't selected because pixels of another color fall between them and the pixel I clicked—those other yellow-gumball pixels are noncontiguous, in Photoshop lingo. Some pixels in the gumball I clicked also miss the cut because they don't meet the Tolerance limit.

Figure 5.13: I clicked at the spot marked by the X to produce the examples in Figures 5.14 through 5.17.

Figure 5.14: With the Contiguous option turned on, matching pixels in other yellow gumballs aren't selected.

Tolerance 35, Contiguous on

Figure 5.15:
Disabling the Contiguous option selected matching pixels in all the yellow gumballs.

Tolerance 35, Contiguous off

For Figure 5.15, I turned off the Contiguous option but left the Tolerance value at 35. This time, the Magic Wand selected matching pixels in all the yellow gumballs.

For Figures 5.16 and 5.17, I raised the Tolerance value to 100. With the Contiguous option enabled, the Magic Wand selected all but a few pixels in the gumball I clicked, as shown in Figure 5.16. When I turned the option off, the tool grabbed nearly all the yellow gumballs regardless of their position in the image. However, if you compare Figure 5.17 with Figure 5.16, you can see that parts

Figure 5.16: Here, I raised the Tolerance value and turned on the Contiguous option.

Tolerance 100, Contiguous on

Tolerance 100, Contiguous off

Figure 5.17: These settings selected nearly all the pixels in the yellow gumballs, but also picked up some areas in the orange gumballs.

Remember

When you work with any selection tool, establish tool settings before you apply the tool. The settings have no impact on a selection outline after the fact.

of the orange gumballs were also selected. At the higher Tolerance value, the Magic Wand includes a broader range of shades in the selection, and the orange gumballs have pixels that fall within that range.

In most cases, a single click of the Magic Wand isn't sufficient to produce a perfect selection outline, no matter what Tolerance/Contiguous combo you use. Not to worry—if the tool didn't grab all the areas you want to select, hold down the SHIFT key and click those areas to add them to the selection outline. If the tool overstepped its bounds, hold down the ALT key (Windows) or OPTION key (Mac) and click the pixels that you want to deselect. You can also use the Selection Mode icons, discussed later in this chapter, to formally set the Magic Wand to Add or Subtract mode, in which case you don't have to press the modifier keys.

Power Selecting: Painting Masks with the Selection Brush

With the Magic Wand, you can create precise selection outlines based on color. But suppose that you wanted to select the scaly subject of the Sleeping Beauty.jpg sample photo, featured in Figure 5.18. The subject and background are too similar in color for the Magic Wand to be of any use. Nor would the Magnetic Lasso be able to pick out the boundary between the two. You could try to draw an outline freeform with the Lasso, but you'd need a mighty steady hand and lots of patience to get the outline just right.

Figure 5.18: To select complex subjects like this, turn to the Selection Brush.

To tackle this kind of selection challenge, turn to the Selection Brush, labeled in Figure 5.19. With this tool, you first paint a mask over the areas you *don't* want to alter, just as if you were brushing on that liquid mask stuff you can buy from the hardware store to protect glass when you're painting your window trim. By default, the mask appears as a translucent red overlay, as shown in the second image in Figure 5.18. (The red overlay is supposed to resemble Rubylith, a masking material used in the traditional darkroom.) After you paint your mask,

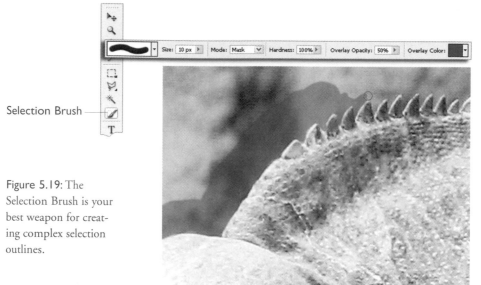

Selection Brush

Figure 5.19: The Selection Brush is your best weapon for creating complex selection outlines.

Elements generates a selection outline that encompasses all the unmasked pixels.

What makes the Selection Brush so powerful is its flexibility. When you paint your mask, you can vary the brush size as needed to get into every nook and cranny, as shown in Figure 5.19. You can work with a hard brush to create a nonfeathered outline or use a softer brush to create a feathered outline. You can even generate an outline that's feathered in one area and nonfeathered in another.

Simply put, the Selection Brush is your best weapon for creating complex selection outlines or refining rough outlines that you draw with the other selection tools. Try it out by selecting our scaly friend from the SleepingBeauty.jpg sample image.

1. Choose the Selection Brush, labeled in Figure 5.19.

Time Saver

To activate the tool quickly, press the A key.

2. Select the Mode control on the options bar to Mask.

3. Zoom the image display to get a close view of the boundary between subject and background, as shown in Figure 5.19.

4. Set the brush shape, size, and hardness.

These options work as detailed in Chapter 2. If you want the selection outline to have an unfeathered edge, set the Hardness value to 100 percent. For a feathered outline, reduce the Hardness value. The lower the value, the more feathering you get. (You can always apply the Feather command after creating your outline if neessary, too.) For the sample image, work with a 10-pixel round brush and set the Hardness value to 100 percent.

5. Paint over the pixels that you want to mask.

That is, paint the areas that you don't want to select. Concentrate first on painting along the boundary between the two areas, adjusting the brush size as needed as you paint. When you've outlined the subject, as shown in Figure 5.20, enlarge the brush and swab over the rest of the area you want to mask. For the sample image, extend the mask over the entire background.

If you accidentally mask pixels that you do want to select, hold down the ALT key (Windows) or OPTION key (Mac) and drag over them. When the ALT or OPTION key is pressed, the Selection Brush removes the mask instead of adding to it. And if you have trouble seeing your image through the default red mask, use the Overlay Opacity and Overlay Color controls to adjust the mask style.

Figure 5.20: Start by outlining the object you want to select.

6. When the mask is complete, set the Mode control to Selection.

The mask overlay disappears, and all unmasked pixels appear inside a selection outline, as shown in Figure 5.21. (Choosing any other editing tool or menu command also displays your selection outline.)

Remember

To quickly adjust brush size, press the bracket keys. Press the left bracket key for a smaller brush; press the right bracket key for a larger brush.

Figure 5.21: Change the Mode control to Selection to convert your mask into a selection outline.

Time Saver

Depending on your photo, you may be able to save some time by drawing a rough selection outline with one of the other selection tools before using the Selection Brush. Try this: Drag with the Lasso around the iguana in the sample photo, including a small margin of background in the selection outline. Then grab the Selection Brush and set the Mode control to Mask. Elements automatically adds the mask to any areas that were outside your initial selection outline. Now you just have to paint around the perimeter of the body to complete the mask.

Adjusting a Selection Outline

However you create a selection outline, don't worry if you don't achieve perfection on the first stab. Remember, you can always pick up the Selection Brush, work in Mask mode to refine the mask, and then regenerate the selection outline. In addition, you can use the techniques outlined in the next several sections to adjust the outline. To practice these tricks, open the sample image Gumballs.jpg, featured in the earlier section on the Magic Wand, and use the Lasso to drag around any gumball that looks particularly gummy.

Moving a Selection Outline

To reposition an outline, first make sure that any selection tool but the Selection Brush is active. Then use either of these techniques:

- **Drag the outline** Put your cursor inside the selection outline. Your cursor changes to look like the one in Figure 5.22. Now drag the outline to move it. You can even drag a selection outline from one image window to another.

Outline move cursor

Figure 5.22: To move a selection outline, move your cursor inside the outline and then drag.

- **Press the arrow keys** Each press of an arrow key moves the outline one pixel in the direction of the arrow. Press SHIFT plus an arrow key to nudge the outline 10 pixels.

Watch Out!

Don't get confused and try to move a selection outline with the Move tool. That tool moves the actual selection—the pixels enclosed in the outline—not just the outline. Again, you can move an outline with the Marquee tools, Lassos, or Magic Wand.

Selecting Additional Pixels

You can use a number of techniques to expand a selection outline:

■ **Add Selection Mode**   When any selection tool but the Selection Brush is active, click the Add icon on the options bar, labeled in Figure 5.23. Then use the tool to select the new pixels you want to add to the selection, as shown in Figure 5.24. You can create as many additional selection outlines as you need.

Figure 5.23: The Selection Mode icons determine whether a selection tool creates a new outline or adjusts an existing outline.

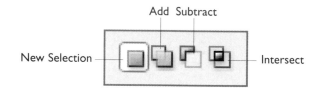

Add Subtract

New Selection

Intersect

Time Saver

You also can simply press and hold the SHIFT key to throw a selection tool into additive mode. This trick works regardless of which Selection Mode icon is active.

■ **Select | Modify | Expand**   To expand an outline by a set number of pixels around the entire perimeter, choose this command. Enter the number of pixels in the resulting dialog box and click OK.

Figure 5.24: In Add mode, you can create multiple selection outlines.

■ **Select | Grow and Select | Similar**   Both commands add pixels to an outline based on color. Grow snatches up adjacent pixels that are similar in color to those at the edges of the selection outline. Similar selects similarly colored pixels no matter where they're located. Both Grow and Similar select pixels based on the current Tolerance setting of the Magic Wand tool, discussed earlier in this chapter. Remember, a low Tolerance value tells Elements to add only pixels that are extremely close in color to the selected ones.

Deselecting Pixels

Round up too many pixels with your initial selection outline? To deselect just some pixels, use these tactics:

- **Subtract Selection Mode**   Pick up any selection tool but the Selection Brush and click the Subtract icon on the options bar, labeled in Figure 5.23. Now your tool works in reverse, deselecting pixels instead of selecting them.

Time Saver

You also can hold down the ALT key (Windows) or OPTION key (Mac) to temporarily throw the tool into deselect mode.

- **Select | Modify | Contract**   Use this command to shrink the outline by a specific number of pixels around the entire perimeter. Enter the number of pixels you want to trim and click OK.

To get rid of a selection outline entirely, walk this way:

- **Select | Deselect**   Press CTRL-D (Windows) or ⌘-D (Mac) to choose the command quickly.
- **Click with a selection tool**   This one works only when the tool is in New Selection mode, and doesn't work at all with the Selection Brush.

Creating Intersecting Outlines

Truth be told, I almost didn't include the Intersect option here, which you access by clicking the Intersect icon (see Figure 5.23) when working with any selection tool but the Selection Brush. In Intersect mode, you can create intersecting selections. Try this: Click the New Selection icon, grab the Rectangular Marquee tool, and draw a small outline. Now click the Intersect icon and create a second outline that overlaps just one corner of your existing outline. Elements then selects just the area of overlap.

PART II

PHOTOSHOP ELEMENTS BASICS

What's my problem with Intersect mode? Nothing; it works fine. I just find it less mentally challenging to create a brand-new outline that selects that overlapping area. But your brain may work differently than mine, so feel free to intersect away!

Reversing a Selection Outline

Tucked away on the Select menu, the Inverse command is incredibly simple—all it does is reverse an existing selection outline, so that pixels that previously were selected become deselected, and vice versa. (Elements experts refer to this process as *inversing the outline*.)

Inverse makes your life easier in two important ways. First, you may sometimes want to apply one correction to a foreground subject and another process to the background. You need only one selection outline to do both jobs. Select the subject, apply the first correction, and then use Inverse to select the background.

Second, you can take a "backward" approach to selecting if the area you *don't* want to alter is easier to select than the region you do want to change. Suppose that you wanted to apply a correction to just the buildings in Figure 5.25. Creating

Figure 5.25: To quickly select the buildings, use the Magic Wand to select the sky and then Inverse the selection outline.

an outline around all the peaks and valleys of those buildings would be a tedious affair. But selecting the sky behind the buildings is a piece of cake with the help of the Magic Wand. With one or two clicks in the sky, you can easily select the entire background and then choose the Inverse command to select the buildings instead.

To try out this backward-selection thing, open the image Indianapolis.jpg and follow these steps:

1. Press w to activate the Magic Wand.
Set the options as shown in Figure 5.25: Tolerance, 25; Anti-aliased and Use All Layers, off; and Contiguous, on.

2. Click anywhere in the sky.

3. Hold down the SHIFT key and keep clicking sky pixels until you've selected the entire sky.

4. Choose Select | Inverse or press SHIFT-CTRL-I (Windows) or SHIFT-⌘-I (Mac).
Now the buildings are selected.

5. Just for kicks, choose Filter | Adjustments | Invert.

Watch Out!

Invert is different from Inverse; Invert is a special-effects feature. It creates a negative image of your selection, as shown in Figure 5.26.

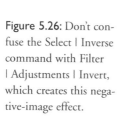

Figure 5.26: Don't confuse the Select | Inverse command with Filter | Adjustments | Invert, which creates this negative-image effect.

Preserving Selection Outlines

"Never do something twice if you can get away with doing it just once"—that's my motto. Some people call that lazy; I call it efficient. If you're of like mind, you'll appreciate the Save Selection and Load Selection commands. These commands enable you to save a selection outline as part of a picture file so that if you later want to alter the same area of your photo, you don't have to create a new outline from scratch.

To store your outline, choose Select | Save Selection to display the Save Selection dialog box, shown in Figure 5.27. Click the Name box, enter a name for the outline, and then click OK.

When you want to reuse the outline, choose Select | Load Selection to display the Load Selection dialog box, which is nearly identical to the Save Selection dialog box. Choose the name of the saved selection from the Selection drop-down list. The Invert option found in this dialog box accomplishes the same thing as Select | Inverse, reversing the outline that the saved selection outline produces.

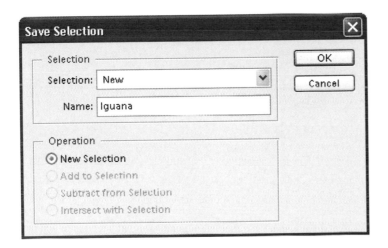

Figure 5.27: Choose Select | Save Selection to preserve a selection outline for future use.

Both dialog boxes also contain a set of four Operation buttons, which enable you to use a current selection outline to modify a saved outline. The buttons work the same as the Add, Subtract, and Intersect options that you get when you work with the standard selection tools. But frankly, I find these options more than my feeble brain can handle—I prefer to load the saved outline, make any adjustments to it in the normal way, and then resave it as an entirely new entity.

Watch Out!

Wherever you find yourself on this last point, note that you must save the image file in the PSD or TIFF file format to preserve a saved selection outline between editing sessions. To delete a saved outline from a file, open the picture and choose Select | Delete Selection. You're then presented with a dialog box in which you specify which saved outline to trash.

Layers: The Photo Editor's Best Weapon

6

When you thumbed through this book looking for a fun place to dive in, you probably weren't drawn immediately to this chapter. First, you may not even know what I mean by *layers*—there's no equivalent in the traditional photographic world. Second, this isn't a topic that lends itself to dramatic illustrations. Heck, I wrote the thing, and even I think it's less visually compelling than, say, the chapters on color and exposure adjustments.

Trust me, though, that what this chapter lacks in eye candy is far overwhelmed by the photo-editing power you'll gain by discovering layers. Like wheels on suitcases, layers are one of those inventions that make you wonder how you ever lived without them after you discover their benefits.

Introducing Layers

Are you old enough to remember overhead projectors? For the young 'uns in the crowd, an overhead projector is the ancestor of today's digital projector. You draw bar charts, company slogans, or whatever on sheets of transparent acetate—transparencies, for short—and the machine projects the transparency contents onto a screen. To present a series of ideas, you can stack one transparency on top of another, with each sheet adding a new element to the projected image.

Elements layers are based on the same idea. Every image begins life with one layer, called the Background layer, which is opaque throughout. On top of the Background layer, you can create additional layers that can be opaque, translucent, or transparent. Wherever a layer is transparent, the underlying layer shows through. Translucent pixels allow underlying pixels to be partially visible.

Figure 6.1: This collage contains three image layers, one each for the background, daisy, and butterfly.

As an example, Figure 6.1 shows a collage that contains three layers. I used a close-up of some tree bark as my Background layer. On top of that, I added a second layer, into which I copied a daisy taken from another photo. Then I created a third layer to hold the butterfly, taken from yet another picture. In Figure 6.2, you see representations of the individual layers; the checkerboard pattern indicates transparent areas.

Figure 6.2: Where a layer is transparent, the underlying layer shows through.

Background layer   Middle layer   Top layer

Each layer exists on its own virtual plane, which gives you several advantages:

- Changes to one layer don't affect other layers. So you could, for example, apply a sharpening filter to the butterfly in the collage without sharpening the flower and wood—and without having to first draw a selection outline around the butterfly. (If you do want to alter several layers at once, you can; see the upcoming sections "Manipulating Multiple Layers" and "Taking Advantage of Adjustment Layers.")
- You can vary the composition of an image by shuffling the vertcal arrangement of the layers—the *stacking order,* in imaging lingo. For example, I swapped the butterfly and flower layers in Figure 6.3. Now the flower petals nearly obscure the butterfly.

Figure 6.3: Swapping the order of the flower and butterfly layers changes the composition.

- You can reposition and rotate layer elements without harming the underlying image. In the image on the left in Figure 6.4, I moved and rotated the butterfly layer, for example. Making the same alteration in a single-layer image creates a hole in your photo, as shown in the image on the right. Elements fills the hole with the background paint color—white, in the figure.

- You can delete an element by simply deleting its layer. In a single-layer image, deleting pixels creates a hole, just as with moving an element.

Figure 6.4: You can reposition objects in a multilayer image (left); moving pixels in a single-layer image creates a colored hole (right).

Upcoming sections show you how to take advantage of these and other layer benefits and provide sample projects that you can use to try layer techniques yourself. But first, explore the next two sections, which cover additional layer fundamentals.

Layer Central: The Layers Palette

The Layer menu contains scores of layer-related commands. But the Layers palette, shown in Figure 6.5, provides quicker access to nearly all those commands.

To display the Layers palette, choose Window | Layers or press F11. If you took my advice in Chapter 2 and dislodged the palette from the Palette Bin, it appears as a free-floating window, as shown in Figure 6.5. Otherwise, the palette hangs out at the bottom of the bin, where it may be collapsed (minimized). To display the entire palette, click the triangle to the left of the palette name.

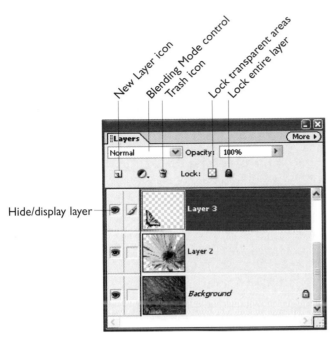

New Layer icon
Blending Mode control
Trash icon
Lock transparent areas
Lock entire layer

Hide/display layer

Figure 6.5: The Layers palette offers quick access to layer-management controls.

At any rate, the palette contains thumbnails representing each image layer, as shown in Figure 6.5. The layers appear according to their stacking order.

Visit the palette to perform these basic layer operations:

- **Make a layer active**   Click a layer name to make that layer the active layer, which is the only one affected by your next edit. The active layer appears highlighted in the palette, and a little brush icon appears to the left of the thumbnail. In Figure 6-5, the butterfly layer is the active layer. (A few commands, such as Crop, Image Size, and Mode, affect all layers; these operations can't be applied on a single-layer basis.)

- **Create a new layer**   Click the New Layer icon, labeled in Figure 6.5. The new layer appears above the layer that was active when you clicked. Elements then makes the new layer the active layer.

- **Delete a layer**   Drag the layer name to the Trash icon, also labeled in the figure. All pixels on the layer go kaput.

- **Hide/display layers**   To hide a layer, click the eyeball icon that appears to the left of the layer name (refer to Figure 6.5). Click the same spot again to redisplay the eyeball icon and the layer.

Remember

Hidden layers do not print. However, when you save the image in a format that supports layers (PSD or TIFF), hidden layers remain part of the file so that you can continue to access them. When you save in other formats, hidden layers get dumped.

Time Saver

You can quickly hide all layers but the one you want to view by ALT-clicking (Windows) or OPTION-clicking (Mac) the eyeball for that layer. ALT- or OPTION-click the eyeball again to redisplay all hidden layers.

■ **Name a layer**   Elements automatically names the bottom layer Background and assigns numbers to new layers—Layer 1, Layer 2, and so on. You can rename any layer but the Background layer by double-clicking the name and typing the new name. Press ENTER to make the change official. Naming layers helps you remember the purpose of each layer.

Watch Out!

Double-clicking the Background layer name produces the New Layer dialog box, which contains a layer-name option. But this action does more than rename your layer. It also converts the Background layer into a regular layer. For more on this subject, see "Freeing the Background Layer," near the end of this chapter.

■ **Prevent changes to a layer**   Use the two Lock icons, labeled in Figure 6.5, to protect layer pixels from accidents. The Lock icon on the left prevents changes to transparent areas, and the one on the right—the padlock—prevents any changes to the entire layer. When you want full editing access to a layer, disable both options. (Clicking the icons toggles the locks on and off.)

Figure 6.6: Changing the blending mode alters how layer pixels mix with underlying pixels.

The Blending Mode and Opacity Controls

You can fine-tune the way that pixels on one layer blend with underlying pixels by fiddling with the Blending Mode and Opacity controls in the Layers palette.

The Blending Mode control, labeled in Figure 6.5, determines how pixels on one layer mix with pixels on the layers below. In Normal mode, the top pixels obscure underlying pixels, assuming that those top pixels are opaque. In other blending modes, Elements uses some properties from the upper layer and some from the underlying layer, which can produce some interesting results. In Figure 6.6, I set the butterfly layer to the Multiply mode and the flower layer to the Pin Light mode. Blend modes aren't just for special effects, however; they also can be useful for retouching, as you'll discover in later chapters.

In the Elements Help system, you can find out exactly how the program manipulates pixels in each blending mode, but frankly, predicting the outcome of a blend mode isn't easy even when you have that information. So when you're not sure which mode to choose, just click your way through all of them and see which one you like best.

The Opacity control, on the other hand, is straightforward. It enables you to reduce the opacity of an entire layer. As you reduce the opacity, the underlying pixels become more visible, as illustrated in Figure 6.7. I reduced the opacity of the flower to 50 percent, producing an area that's half flower, half wood. As an alternative, you can adjust the opacity of just some pixels on a layer by using techniques explored in the upcoming section "Step 2: Erasing Unwanted Layer Pixels."

Figure 6.7: Reducing the opacity of the flower layer to 50 percent allows the underlying wood pixels to become partially visible.

Building a Multilayer Photo Collage

Creating a simple photo collage is a great way to get acquainted with basic layer techniques. The next few sections explain this process; to work along with the steps, you'll need the sample images Wood.jpg, Daisy.jpg, and YellowButterfly.jpg, all shown in Figure 6.8.

Figure 6.8: To create the sample collage, open the Wood, Daisy, and YellowButterfly images.

Step 1: Combining Photos

Your first step in creating a collage is to copy and paste the collage elements into the background image. Click this way:

1. **If the Layers palette isn't visible, open it by choosing Window | Layers or pressing F11.**

2. **Open the image that you want to use as the collage background.**
For the example collage, open Wood.jpg.

3. **Open an image that contains an element you want to add to the collage.**
This time, open Daisy.jpg.

4. **Check the output resolution (ppi) of both images.**

Watch Out!

When you paste one image into another, the pasted image takes on the output resolution (ppi) of its new home. As a result, the relative size of the pasted image may change. To avoid this, match the resolution of each collage element to the background image before you copy and paste.

The sample images already match, so you're good to go. If you're working with your own images, visit Chapter 13 to learn how to use the Image Size command to adjust output resolution.

5. **Draw a loose selection outline around the first collage element, as shown in Figure 6.9.**
For the flower image, use the Lasso tool, explained in Chapter 5, with the Feather value set to 0 and the Anti-aliased option turned off. You don't have to be precise—you'll get rid of unwanted pixels around the flower later.

6. Copy the selected area to the background image.

You can do this in two ways:

- **Copy and Paste commands**   Press CTRL-C (Windows) or ⌘-C (Mac) to quickly apply the Edit | Copy command. Next, click the background-image window and press CTRL-V (Windows) or ⌘-V (Mac), which is the shortcut for the Edit | Paste command.
- **Drag and drop**   Alternatively, arrange the two image windows side by side (choose Window | Images | Cascade and then drag the image windows by their title bars). Press V to select the Move tool, place your cursor inside the selection outline, as shown in Figure 6.9, and drag the selection into the background-image window. See the upcoming section "Step 3: Positioning Layer Elements" for details about the Move tool.

Move tool   Selection move cursor

Figure 6.9: Loosely select the flower and then drag it into the Wood.jpg image.

Your combined image should look something like the one in Figure 6.10. If you check the Layers palette, you see that the copied flower appears on a new layer above the Background (wood) layer.

To continue building the collage, close the daisy image and open the YellowButterfly.jpg image. Following the same process, copy the butterfly

into the background image, creating the third layer in your collage. After you have combined the three elements, save your collage under a new name so you don't accidentally overwrite the original wood file.

Figure 6.10: The wood shows through transparent areas in the flower layer.

Step 2: Erasing Unwanted Layer Pixels

Your next step is to eliminate the unwanted pixels that exist around the perimeter of pasted collage elements—in the sample project, the butterfly and flower. You can do this in two ways:

- **Select and delete**   After creating a selection outline, press the DELETE key. All selected pixels on the active layer become transparent. This option works best for getting rid of large or easy-to-select areas.
- **Rub out with the Eraser**   Touching pixels with the Eraser tool also makes them invisible. Go this route to wipe out small areas or pixels that would be difficult to select with precision. The following steps give you the low-down on the Eraser; try it out using your sample collage.

Watch Out!

Remember, you can't make Background-layer pixels transparent; these techniques apply just to other layers. On the Background layer, Elements paints pixels with the current background color when you delete or erase.

Figure 6.11: On any layer but the Background layer, the Eraser makes pixels transparent or translucent.

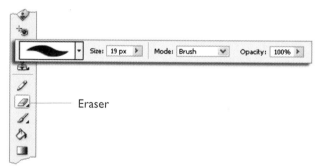

Eraser

1. **In the Layers palette, click the layer containing the pixels you want to erase.**

For the sample collage, click the Daisy layer.

2. **Make sure that the Lock icons in the palette are inactive.**

3. **Select the Eraser tool, labeled in Figure 6.11.**

4. **Choose a tool mode (Pencil, Brush, or Block) from the Mode control.**

In Brush or Pencil mode, the Eraser works just like the Brush or Pencil tool, respectively, except that it "paints" transparency onto pixels instead of applying the foreground color. You can adjust the brush size and, when working in Brush mode, work with either a hard or soft brush. In Block mode, you get a hard, square brush that can't be adjusted.

For the example project, set the tool mode to Brush and choose the hard, round, 19-pixel brush from the Brushes palette. With a hard brush, your Eraser strokes produce a nice, clean edge.

Tool Tricks

Although the Eraser doesn't offer a custom Hardness control like the Brush and Pencil tools, you can adjust hardness by pressing these keyboard shortcuts: Press SHIFT-[(left bracket) to reduce the Hardness value by 25 percent. Press SHIFT-] (right bracket) to increase the Hardness value by 25 percent.

5. Set the tool Opacity (Brush and Pencil mode only).

At any setting less than 100, pixels aren't completely erased but instead become translucent. Each swipe of the Eraser makes the pixels more translucent. For the sample project, use 100 percent.

6. Hide all other layers (optional).

Just ALT-click (Windows) or OPTION-click (Mac) the eyeball icon for the active layer. If you're working on the sample project, you now see just the flower image, as shown in Figure 6.12. Remember, the checkerboard pattern indicates transparent areas.

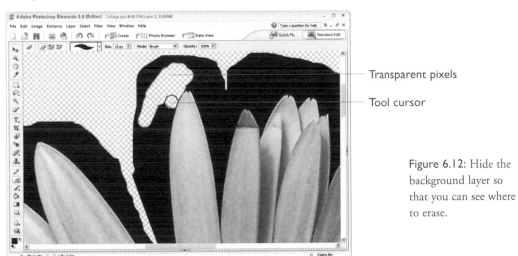

Transparent pixels

Tool cursor

Figure 6.12: Hide the background layer so that you can see where to erase.

7. Drag over or click on the pixels you want to erase.

Assuming that you hid other layers in Step 6, the pixels you erase are replaced by the checkerboard pattern, as shown in Figure 6.12. You may need to adjust the brush size as you work.

That's all there is to it. Just keep dragging or clicking with the Eraser until you get rid of all the extraneous pixels on your layer. Then ALT-click (Windows) or OPTION-click (Mac) the layer's eyeball icon to redisplay other layers, if you hid them.

To continue building the sample collage, repeat the preceding steps, this time working on the Butterfly layer. Then press CTRL-S (Windows) or ⌘-S (Mac) to save the collage file again.

> **Time Saver**
>
> Keep in mind, though, that you can combine the select-and-delete erasing technique with the Eraser tool. With the daisy layer, for example, you could use the Magic Wand to select most of the darkest areas of the background, press DELETE, and then clean up the remaining areas with the Eraser. (Sorry that I didn't offer this time-saving option before you worked through the steps, but I wanted you to have lots of background available for your Eraser practice.)

Of course, you can eliminate the need to do *any* erasing by precisely selecting your collage elements before copying and pasting them. But even when you're careful, you can easily miss a few of the element pixels when you draw your selection outline. For that reason, I prefer to include a small boundary of unwanted pixels in the original selection—I find erasing excess pixels easier than returning to the original image and grabbing pixels that I missed on the first try.

Step 3: Positioning Layer Elements

After pasting elements into your collage, you can easily reposition them as necessary to devise a composition you like—as long as they remain on their individual layers, that is. The next four sections show you how.

Manipulating Multiple Layers

You can reposition two or more layers at the same time by *linking* them. In the Layers palette, click the name of one of the layers that you want to move. For the other layers, click the column between the layer name and the eyeball to display a link icon, as shown in Figure 6.13. Now when you move the layers, they'll travel together as a unit. To unlink the layers, just click that link icon to make it disappear.

If you want to include the Background layer in the link group, you must first convert it to a regular layer, as explained in the upcoming section "Freeing the Background Layer."

Moving Layer Elements

The Move tool, labeled in Figure 6.13, is key to moving objects on layers. To select the Move tool, click its toolbox icon or press V.

> ### Tool Tricks
> When you're working with any tool other than the Hand, Shape, Red Eye Removal, or Cookie Cutter tools, you can temporarily access the Move tool by holding down the CTRL key (Windows) or ⌘ key (Mac). Release CTRL or ⌘ to return to the previously active tool.

When the Move tool is selected, the options bar offers these controls:

- **Auto Select Layer**   If you enable this option, Elements automatically activates the layer that contains the pixel you click with the Move tool, saving you a trip to the Layers palette. This feature works great unless your layers hold very small or translucent elements, In which case clicking just the right pixel to grab the layer you want can be a challenge. I normally leave the option turned off for that reason.

- **Show Bounding Box**   This option, when selected, displays a dotted outline around the contents of the selected layer. The outline enables you to see clearly the boundaries of the layer contents, but it's also dangerous for new users. If you drag an edge of the outline, you shift into layer-transformation mode, as if you had selected the Free Transform command, introduced in Chapter 4 and revisited in the next section.

To sum up, I recommend that you turn off both Move tool options. Then use the tool as follows to position your collage elements:

1. **In the Layers palette, click the layer that contains the object you want to move.**

2. **To move only some pixels on the layer, select them using the techniques outlined in Chapter 5.**

3. **Drag with the Move tool or press the arrow keys to move the element.**

Figure 6.13: Use the Move tool to reposition a selection or entire layer.

Move tool

Link icon

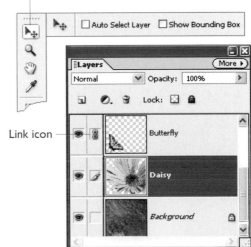

Just drag with the Move tool, releasing the mouse button at the spot where you want to position the moved pixels. You also can press an arrow key to nudge the selection or layer one pixel in the direction of the arrow. Press SHIFT plus an arrow key to nudge the selection ten pixels in the direction of the arrow. Use this technique to fine-tune the position of moved pixels.

Tool Tricks

SHIFT-drag with the Move tool to restrict it to moving a selection in 45-degree increments. ALT-drag (Windows) or OPTION-drag (Mac) to copy a selection instead of moving it. (You can't drag to copy linked layers, however.)

Rotating a Layer

If you've been working through the steps of building the sample collage, you probably noticed right away that in the original flower and butterfly images, shown in Figure 6.8, both elements appear at different orientations than they do in the final collage, shown in Figure 6.1. Again, as long as pasted elements remain on separate layers, you can rotate them freely, as I did for my collage.

Follow these steps to rotate the contents of any layer but the Background layer:

Figure 6.14: Drag near a corner handle to rotate the layer contents.

1. Select the layer by clicking its name in the Layers palette.

To rotate multiple layers, link them as described in the preceding section.

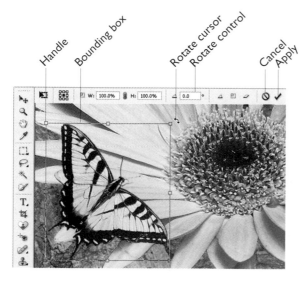

2. Select any tool except the Cookie Cutter or Shape tool.

When either tool is active, you lose access to the command you'll use next.

3. Choose Image | Transform | Free Transform or press CTRL-T (Windows) or ⌘-T (Mac).

A rectangular outline, known as a *bounding box,* appears around the nontransparent layer pixels, as shown in Figure 6.14. Tiny squares called *handles* appear around the perimeter of the box, and several transformation controls appear on the options bar.

4. **Position your cursor outside the box, near one of the corner handles.**

The cursor turns into a curved, two-headed arrow, as shown in Figure 6.14.

5. **Drag to rotate the contents of the layer.**

You also can enter a specific rotation angle in the box labeled in Figure 6.14. Enter a value up to 180 to spin the layer clockwise. Enter a minus sign before the value to rotate counterclockwise.

6. **Press ENTER or click the Apply check mark, labeled in Figure 6.14, to apply the rotation.**

You must press ENTER twice if you typed a specific rotation value. (Should you instead decide not to go through with the rotation, click the Cancel button, labeled in Figure 6.14, or press ESC.)

Time Saver

As an alternative, you can use the commands on the Image | Rotate submenu to quickly rotate a layer 90 or 180 degrees or to flip the layer horizontally or vertically. But be sure to choose the command from the second set of submenu commands—the ones that include *Layer* in the command name. Otherwise, you rotate the entire image.

However you go about it, try not to apply more than one rotation to a layer. Every time you rotate, Elements has to shuffle the pixels to rebuild the rotated element, a process that can lead to a loss of picture quality.

For information about the other changes you can make with Free Transform, see the section related to correcting convergence in Chapter 4.

Changing the Layer Stacking Order

By changing the layer stacking order, you can alter its composition, as illustrated by Figures 6.1 and 6.3.

To change the stacking order of a layer, just drag the layer name up or down the list of layers in the Layers palette. As you drag, your cursor changes to a little clenched fist to let you know you've got a layer by the tail, as shown in Figure 6.15.

Figure 6.15: Drag a layer up or down to change its position in the layer stack.

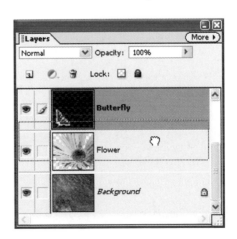

If you want to reposition the Background layer, see "Freeing the Background Layer," later in this chapter.

Step 4: Adding Shadows with Layer Styles

A final bit of business completes the sample collage: adding a soft shadow underneath both the flower and butterfly to create some separation between them and the wood. You can do this easily with a feature known as *layer styles*.

Watch Out!

When you're building your own collages, you may see shadows in the original photos and be tempted to simply copy and paste the shadows along with the objects. Be careful; the colors of the original shadow, which may exhibit some hues from surrounding objects, may look unnatural against the new background. Usually, you're better off leaving the shadow behind and then reintroducing it by using layer styles.

Follow these steps to cast a shadow:

Figure 6.16: Open the Styles and Effects palette to access drop-shadow effects.

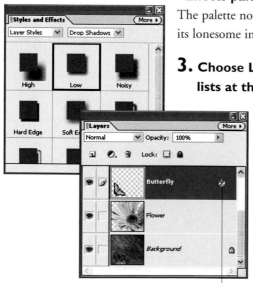

Layer Style icon

1. In the Layers palette, click the layer to which you want to add the shadow.

2. Choose Window | Styles and Effects to display the Styles and Effects palette, shown in Figure 6.16.

The palette normally appears docked in the Palette Bin; I elected to show it by its lonesome in the figure. See Chapter 2 for more about working with palettes.

3. Choose Layer Styles and Drop Shadows from the drop-down lists at the top of the palette, as shown in Figure 6.16.

The palette then displays icons representing a variety of shadow styles.

4. Click the icon that most resembles the style of shadow you want to create.

For the sample collage, choose Low. The shadow appears in the image, and a little *f*—for *effects*—appears next to the layer name in the Layers palette, as shown in Figure 6.16. I labeled this the Layer Style icon in the figure.

5. **To modify the shadow effect, double-click the Layer Style icon.**
Or choose Layer | Layer Style | Style Settings. You then see the Styles Settings dialog box, shown in Figure 6.17. Play with the available controls until you get the shadow just so, turning on the Preview box so that you can monitor the changes in the image window. Click OK to close the dialog box and apply the changes.

To remove the shadow or any other layer style, choose Layer | Layer Style | Clear Layer Style.

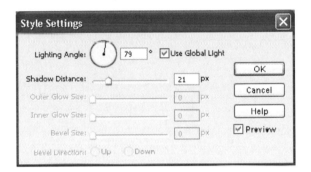

Figure 6.17: Double-click the Layer Style icon in the Layers palette to open this dialog box and adjust the shadow effect.

Layers in the Retouching Room

Layers give you an extra safety net when you're retouching photos—or making any alterations to an image, for that matter. Instead of working directly on your photo, you can make the alterations on a separate layer, thereby protecting the image from irreparable harm. If you mess up, you just delete the edited layer.
You also can fine-tune how edited and original pixels mix by using the layer Blending Mode and Opacity controls, which often leads to more natural results.

Some retouching work calls for a new, empty layer, but other projects involve copying existing pixels to a new layer. I specify which route to take when providing instructions elsewhere in the book; for now, familiarize yourself with these techniques for creating your editing layers:

■ **Create a new, empty layer** Click the New Layer icon in the Layers palette, labeled in Figure 6.18. Or choose Layer | New | Layer to display the New Layer dialog box and then click OK. (Leave the dialog box options at their default settings; you can change all those options later if needed.)

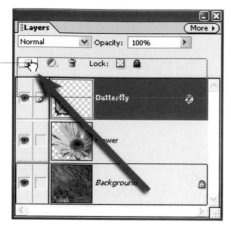

New Layer icon

Figure 6.18:
Duplicate
a layer by
dragging it
to the New
Layer icon.

- **Copy a selection to a new layer** After creating a selection outline (as explained in Chapter 5), press CTRL-J (Windows) or ⌘-J (Mac). Or choose Layer | New | Layer via Copy.
- **Duplicate an entire layer** Drag the layer name to the New Layer icon, as illustrated in Figure 6.18. If no selection outline is active, you also can use CTRL-J (Windows), ⌘-J (Mac), or the Layer via Copy command.
- **Move a selection to a new layer** Press SHIFT-CTRL-J (Windows) or SHIFT-⌘-J (Mac) or choose Layer | New | Layer via Cut.

In all cases, the new layer appears above the one that was previously active.

Taking Advantage of Adjustment Layers

Adjustment layers are a special breed of layer that offer a convenient way to apply the most frequently used exposure and color filters as an independent layer.

Filters that you apply via an adjustment layer affect not just the active layer, but all layers below, which saves you the trouble of correcting each layer individually. And because an adjustment layer is at heart a layer, it offers all the other layer features, including the option to adjust layer opacity, blending mode, and so on. Adjustment layers even come with a built-in *layer mask,* a feature that enables you to change which areas are affected by the filter by simply painting on your image.

The following steps show you the basic workings of adjustment layers. (Later chapters explain the specific filters that you can apply.) To work along with the steps, open the butterfly collage you created earlier in this chapter.

Remember

You can select all nontranspaent pixels on a layer quickly by CTRL-clicking (Windows) or ⌘-clicking (Mac) the layer name in the Layers palette. To quickly select all transparent pixels, first select nontransparent areas and then choose Select | Inverse.

1. In the Layers palette, click the top layer that you want to receive the filter.

Remember, an adjustment layer affects all layers beneath it. For the sample project, click the flower layer so that your filter will affect the flower and the wood but not the butterfly.

2. Select the area that you want to alter (optional).

Normally, a selection outline affects just the active layer, but in this case, the selected area will change on *all* layers underneath the adjustment layer.

You don't have to create a selection outline if you want to edit all pixels on the affected layers, as is the case for the sample image.

3. Click the Adjustment Layer icon, labeled in Figure 6.19, to display a pop-up menu of filter choices.

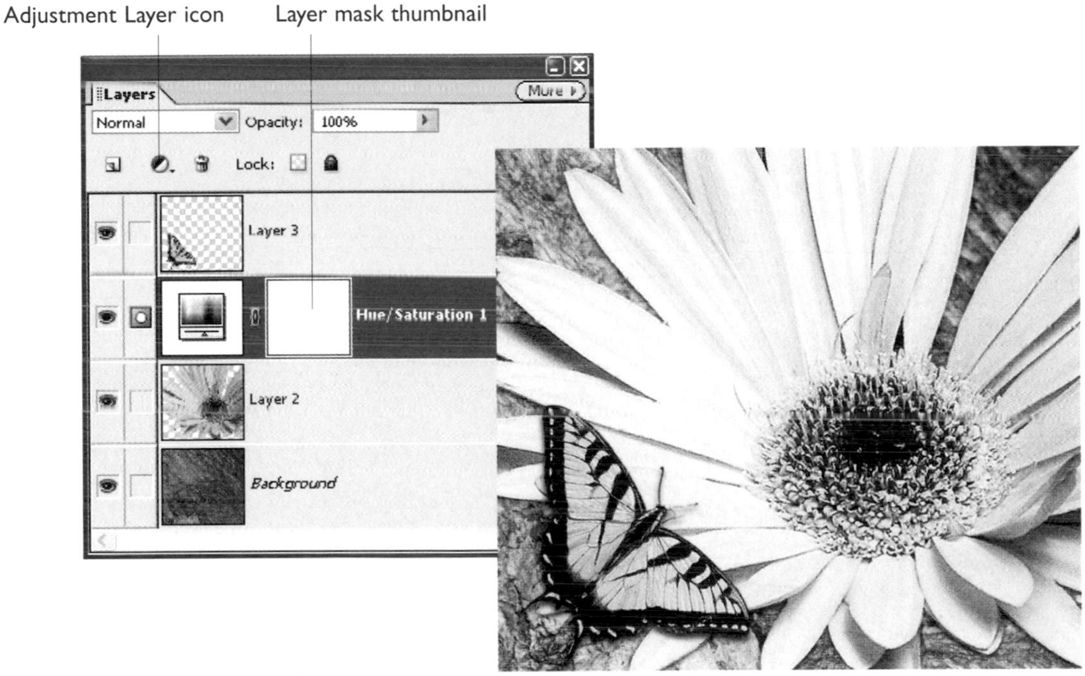

Adjustment Layer icon   Layer mask thumbnail

4. Click the name of the filter you want to apply.

For this example, choose Hue/Saturation. Elements adds an adjustment layer item to the Layers palette, as shown in the figure, and opens a dialog box containing options for the filter you selected.

5. In the dialog box, establish the filter settings you want to use.

For the example collage, do something drastic, like cranking the Saturation value all the way down, so that you can clearly see the effects of the adjustment layer. The photo in Figure 6.19 shows the result of completely desaturating the affected layers.

Figure 6.19: I applied a Hue/Saturation filter to the flower and background layer via an adjustment layer.

6. **Click OK to close the dialog box.**

In your sample collage, the flower and wood are turned to gray, as shown in Figure 6.19. If you drew a selection outline before creating the adjustment layer, only selected pixels in the underlying layers are affected.

7. **Adjust the layer mask if needed.**

In the Layers palette, you see two thumbnails for the adjustment layer. In the layer mask thumbnail, labeled in Figure 6.19, white areas represent pixels affected by the filter and black areas represent unchanged areas. In the sample image, no pixels were selected when you added the adjustment layer, so the entire mask thumbnail is white.

After clicking the mask thumbnail, you can paint in the image window with black to hide the filter or paint with white to extend the filter effect over new areas. For example, try painting with black over the interior of the flower in the sample image to restore color to that area, as shown in Figure 6.20. You can use any painting tool to make this adjustment—Brush, Pencil, whatever. You don't see black or white paint on the image itself; instead, the black or white paint appears in the mask thumbnail, and the image updates to show you the result of adding or removing the filter effect.

As long as you retain the adjustment layer, you can modify the filter effect at any time by using these techniques:

■ **Change the filter settings** To redisplay the filter dialog box, double-click the thumbnail labeled *dialog box thumbnail* in Figure 6.20.

■ **Refine the layer mask** Click the mask thumbnail and paint on your image with black to hide the filter effect; paint with white to reveal it.

To partially restore or reveal

Dialog box thumbnail

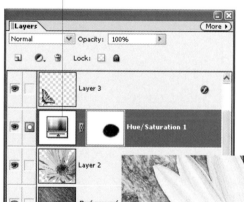

Figure 6.20: After clicking the layer mask thumbnail, paint with black to remove the filter effect from the pixels you touch with your paint tool.

the filter effect, just lower the opacity of your paint tool. For example, if you set the paint tool to 50 percent opacity and painted over the petals with black, they would come back to only 50 percent of their original saturation.

- **Change the adjustment layer's opacity and blend mode**   To lessen the effect of the filter without changing the filter settings, reduce the layer opacity, as explained earlier in this chapter. You also can vary the blend mode to create different effects.

- **Apply the adjustment to different layers**   By changing the stacking order of the adjustment layer, you change what layers are affected by the filter. If you were to move the adjustment layer in the example image to the top of the layer stack, for example, all three layers would become desaturated.

- **Delete the adjustment layer**   Drag the layer to the Trash icon in the Layers palette.

Time Saver

You can copy an adjustment layer from one image to another, which gives you a quick way to apply the same correction to multiple photos. Just drag the adjustment layer from the Layers palette into the image window of the other photo you want to correct.

Freeing the Background Layer

To transform the Background layer into a normal layer, double-click the layer name in the Layers palette or click the layer name and then choose Layer | New | Layer from Background. The New Layer dialog box opens, as shown in Figure 6.21. Give the layer a new name or stick with the default name, *Layer 0*. Keep the Mode and Opacity values at their default settings (Normal and 100) and just click OK to close the dialog box.

Although you can now create transparent areas on the Background layer, the empty areas of that layer—or whatever layer you put at the bottom of the layer stack—are filled with a solid color if you save the image in any format but TIFF or PSD. You also must enable the Layers check box in the Save As dialog box.

Figure 6.21: To turn the background layer into a regular layer, choose Layer | New | Layer from Background and then click OK in this dialog box.

Merging Layers

Every layer taxes your computer's resources. So when possible, combine finished layers, using these techniques:

- **Combine a layer with the one immediately below**   Click the top layer in the pair and choose Layer | Merge Down or press CTRL-E (Windows) or ⌘-E (Mac).

- **Combine multiple, nonconsecutive layers**   First, hide all the layers that you don't want to merge (by clicking their eyeball icons in the Layers palette). Choose Layer | Merge Visible or press SHIFT-CTRL-E (Windows) or SHIFT-⌘-E (Mac). Then redisplay the hidden layers.

- **Combine all layers**   To merge all layers, known as *flattening* the image, choose Layer | Flatten Image. If any layers are hidden, Elements displays a warning box asking for your permission to discard the hidden layers. To instead preserve the layer content, click Cancel, redisplay the layers, and choose the Flatten command again.

Watch Out!

After you flatten the image, you can no longer manipulate image elements, adjust transparency, or do any of those other things that make layers so useful. Your image exists solely on the Background layer. So before flattening, always make a backup copy in a format that preserves layers. See the next section for more information.

SPEED KEYS: Layer Shortcuts

Action	Windows	Mac
Copy selection to a new layer	CTRL-J	⌘-J
Move selection to a new layer	SHIFT-CTRL-J	SHIFT-⌘-J
Merge layer with underlying layer	CTRL-E	⌘-E
Merge visible layers	SHIFT-CTRL-E	SHIFT-⌘-E

Preserving Layers

When you save your image file, you must select either the Elements (PSD) or TIFF file format if you want your image layers to retain their independence. Select any other format, and Elements flattens the image upon saving. Also be sure to select the Layers check box in the Save As dialog box, which you can explore in Chapter 3.

For works-in-progress, choose PSD over TIFF. This format enables Elements to process your edits more quickly. The layered TIFF option is provided for users who need to share TIFF files with others or import the files into a publishing program. Not all programs can work with layered TIFFs, however. Chapter 13 talks more about saving in the TIFF format.

Too Light?
Too Dark?
No Problem!

Photography books and magazines are loaded with information designed to help you expose your pictures properly. But even if you manage to digest all that advice, the occasional exposure problem is inevitable. Sometimes the film isn't as sensitive as the manufacturer claims. Sometimes the camera's autoexposure sensor or your light meter falters. And sometimes, the universe just wants to mess with you and blows a cloud over the sun just as you press the shutter button.

Whether your exposure problems stem from inexperience, mechanical failures, or bad karma—I recommend excuse number two, by the way—this chapter shows you how to fix pictures that are too light, too dark, or a bit of both.

Making Quick Changes with Screen and Multiply

One of the fastest routes to a darker or lighter image involves layer blending modes, introduced in Chapter 6. After copying the under- or overexposed areas to a new layer, you set the blending mode of that layer to Multiply to darken the image or Screen to lighten the image. Try the Multiply version of this technique using the too-light sample image Seaside.jpg, shown in Figure 7.1.

Figure 7.1: An overexposed image may be a candidate for the Multiply blend mode.

1. Select the problem areas and copy them to a new layer.

Use the selection techniques discussed in Chapter 5 to select the improperly exposed areas and then choose Layer | New | Layer via Copy or press CTRL-J (Windows) or ⌘-J (Mac).

If you're working with a single-layer image and the entire photo needs fixing—as is the case with the example photo—just duplicate the Background layer by dragging it to the New Layer icon, labeled in Figure 7.2.

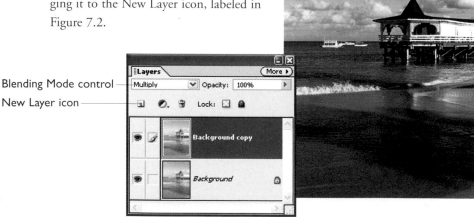

Blending Mode control

New Layer icon

Figure 7.2: After duplicating the Background layer, set the blending mode to Multiply to darken the image.

2. Set the blending mode of the new layer to Multiply or Screen.

Choose Multiply to darken the image; choose Screen to lighten it.

3. If the picture became too dark or too light, reduce the layer's Opacity value.

For example, the multiplied sample image, shown in Figure 7.2, got too intense for my taste. To produce the more subtle change shown in Figure 7.3, I lowered the opacity of the multiplied layer to 70 percent. You also can use the Eraser, introduced in Chapter 6, to erase pixels that became too light or dark.

4. Merge the screened or multiplied layers with the original.

Now that you've got the hang of this trick, try a variation, this time using the Screen blending mode to lighten just the buildings in the sample image Monument.jpg, shown in Figure 7.4. Use the Magic Wand to select the sky and then choose Select | Inverse to swap the selection outline so that the buildings and monument are selected instead. (See Chapter 5 for details about selecting.) Then choose Layer | New | Layer via Copy or press CTRL-J (Windows) or ⌘-J (Mac) to copy the selection to a new layer. Finally, set the layer blending mode to Screen. Your photo should look similar to the one in Figure 7.5.

Figure 7.3: Adjust the layer's Opacity value to lessen the Screen or Multiply effect.

Figure 7.4: In this image, strong backlighting led to an underexposed foreground.

Figure 7.5: You can screen or multiply just the problem areas by copying only those pixels to a new layer.

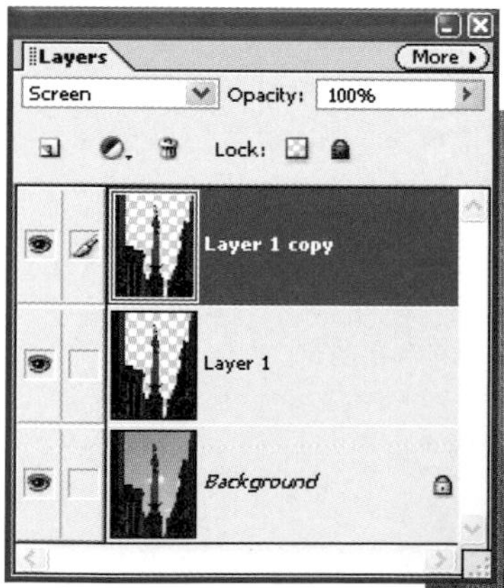

Figure 7.6: To produce a more pronounced effect, duplicate the screened or multiplied layer.

With the sample image, one screened layer doesn't bring the buildings completely out of the shadows. So duplicate that screened layer by dragging it to the New Layer icon. The foreground becomes even brighter, as shown in Figure 7.6.

You can duplicate the screened or multiplied layer as many times as needed. If the effect becomes too strong, just lower the Opacity value of the topmost screened or multiplied layer or use the Eraser to erase pixels that became too dark or light.

There is one important drawback to this quick-and-easy exposure fix: it doesn't affect white or black pixels. So if you're trying to fix blown highlights—areas that are so over-exposed that they're completely white—Multiply won't help. Nor will Screen rescue shadow details that have gone to absolute black. In fact, you're not likely to get the results you want from any of the exposure tools; try using the touch-up techniques covered in Chapter 10 instead.

Brightening Shadows and Darkening Highlights

The Shadows/Highlights filter enables you to lighten shadows and tone down highlights. The sample image Windowsill.jpg, shown in Figure 7.7, offers a good example for putting the filter through its paces. I was attracted to this scene by the way the strong afternoon sun came through the window to strike just a few areas

of the pots and windowsill, and wanted to capture that contrast. But the shadows are too dark, obscuring the leftmost pot as well as the textures in the wall and window frame. I fixed the problem by taking the following steps:

1. Select and copy the problem area to a new layer.

Remember, you can copy a selection to a new layer by choosing Layer | New | Layer via Copy or simply pressing CTRL-J (Windows) or ⌘-J (Mac). If you want to correct the entire image in a single-layer photo like the sample image, just duplicate the Background layer by dragging it to the New Layer icon in the Layers palette.

Figure 7.7: Too-dark shadows obscure the interesting wooden textures and one of the pots.

2. **Choose Enhance | Adjust Lighting | Shadows/Highlights to display the dialog box shown in Figure 7.8.**

3. **Adjust the sliders as needed.**

Raise the Lighten Shadows value to brighten the shadows; raise the Darken Highlights value to darken the brightest pixels. Raise the Midtone Contrast value to increase contrast in the image midtones. Doing so tends to deepen shadows and brighten highlights as well, however. A negative Midtone Contrast value reduces contrast.

Figure 7.8: An application of the Shadows/Highlights filter reveals details formerly hidden in the shadows.

For the sample image, using the values shown in Figure 7.8 brings the darkest areas of the pots out of the shadows and makes the rough texture in the wood more apparent. I chose not to darken the highlights too much because I wanted to retain the window glare caused by the strong sun.

4. **Click OK to apply the filter.**

Because your adjustment exists on its own layer, you can modify the effect by lowering the layer's Opacity value or using the Eraser to rub away pixels in areas that became too dark or too light. When you're happy with the finished project, merge the adjusted layer with the underlying image, using the techniques covered in Chapter 6.

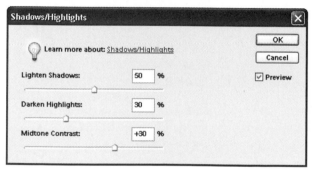

Although the Shadows/Highlights filter can work really well in the right circumstances, be aware that you can make dramatic exposure shifts easily with this filter. As you play with the filter sliders, keep an eye out for *posterization*—large areas of flat color where you should have a smooth gradation of many different tones. (Turn on the Preview option in the dialog box so that you can see the filter effects in the image window.) Also, never apply the filter directly to your image; always copy the problem area to a new layer first, as instructed in Step 1.

Adjusting Exposure and Contrast with the Levels Filter

With the Levels filter, you can darken shadows and brighten highlights—the exact opposite of the changes you can make with the Shadows/Highlights filter. You also can manipulate the brightness of midtones with Levels.

The next section explains *histograms,* a key component of the Levels filter. After that, you'll find general steps for applying the filter.

Analyzing Exposure and Contrast

To get acquainted with the Levels filter, open the sample image Peppers.jpg, shown in Figure 7.9. Can you say "bland?" In addition to lacking contrast, the image is underexposed.

Stay away from the Brightness/ Contrast filter and the automatic exposure/contrast filters, including Auto Levels and Auto Contrast. These quick-fix exposure filters are easy to use but often destroy shadow and high- light detail.

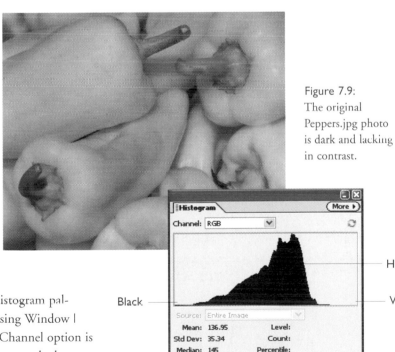

Figure 7.9: The original Peppers.jpg photo is dark and lacking in contrast.

Black — Histogram — White

Below the photo, you see the Histogram pal- ette, which you display by choosing Window | Histogram. Make sure that the Channel option is set to RGB, ignore all the numbers at the bottom of the palette, and concentrate on the graph in the middle. Called a *histogram,* this graph plots image brightness values, with the darkest pixels on the left and the brightest pixels on the right.

PART III EXPOSURE AND COLOR TECHNIQUES

Possible brightness values range from 0 (black) to 255 (white). The vertical axis of the histogram shows you how many pixels fall at a particular brightness value. For example, the histogram in Figure 7.9 shows that nearly all the pepper pixels are clustered near the midpoint of the brightness spectrum.

Some photographers really get into reading histograms and base all their exposure moves on what they read in that little black graph. Personally, I think the histogram gives you a good idea of what changes need to be made but should never take a front seat to what your eyes tell you when you look at the picture itself. (Be careful, however, that your monitor is properly calibrated so that you get a reasonably accurate view of things. See Chapter 12 for help.)

At any rate, the Levels dialog box contains its own histogram, so you can close the palette for now. But any time you're not using that filter and want to know where your image measures in the brightness department, remember that the Histogram palette is available.

Remember

If colors appear faded after an exposure correction, use the Hue/Saturation filter, explained in Chapter 8, to strengthen them.

Applying the Levels Filter

You can access Levels from the Enhance | Adjust Lighting submenu, but doing so applies the correction directly to your image. Instead, always apply Levels via an adjustment layer, a feature introduced in Chapter 6. That way, if you decide down the road that you aren't happy with the correction, you can modify the filter settings or simply trash the adjustment layer and start over. You also can tweak the correction by lowering the adjustment layer's opacity or changing the blending mode.

Follow these steps to apply the filter, working along with the sample image Peppers.jpg if you're in the mood.

1. In the Layers palette, click the topmost layer that you want to correct.

Remember, an adjustment layer affects all layers underneath it. For single-layer photos like the sample image, you can skip this step.

2. Select the area that you want to adjust (optional).

If you want the adjustment to affect all pixels on underlying layers, you don't need a selection outline. For the example, don't select anything.

3. **Click the Adjustment Layer icon at the top of the Layers dialog box, labeled in Figure 7.10.**

Clicking the icon displays a pop-up menu of the filters you can apply via adjustment layers (not shown in the figure).

4. **Choose Levels from the pop-up menu to display the Levels dialog box, shown in Figure 7.11.**

You can also create your adjustment layer by choosing Layer | New Adjustment Layer | Levels and then clicking OK in the resulting dialog box. Either way, select the Preview check box in the Levels dialog box so you can preview your corrections in the image window.

Adjustment Layer icon

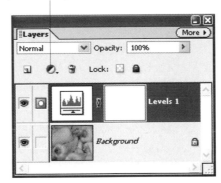

Figure 7.10: Apply exposure and color corrections via an adjustment layer.

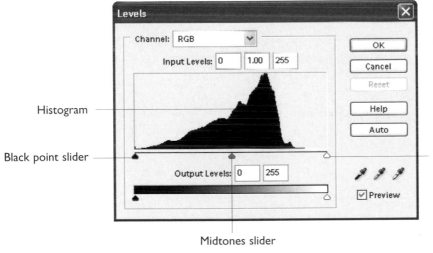

Histogram

Black point slider

Midtones slider

White point slider

Figure 7.11: Drag the sliders to tweak shadows, midtones, or highlights.

5. **Select RGB from the Channel menu.**

6. **Drag the sliders underneath the histogram to adjust exposure and contrast.**

You get three sliders, labeled in Figure 7.11. Use the sliders as follows:

- **Deepen shadows**   Drag the black point slider to the right to make the darkest pixels darker. Elements finds all the pixels whose original brightness value corresponds to the new slider position and makes them black. Then it reassigns other pixels along the rest of the brightness spectrum.
- **Brighten highlights**   Drag the white point slider to the left to make the brightest pixels brighter. This time, Elements makes pixels located at the new slider position white, again reassigning other pixels accordingly.
- **Adjust midtones**   Drag the midtones slider, also called the *gamma* control or *midpoint* control, to the left to brighten midtones. Drag to the right to darken them.

Figure 7.12: To brighten highlights, drag the highlight slider to the left.

To maximize contrast, drag the black point and white point sliders to the positions where the histogram indicates at least a handful of pixels. For the sample image, for example, drag the sliders to the positions shown in Figure 7.12 to produce the results you see in the accompanying photo.

As you move the shadow or highlight slider, the midtones slider moves as well. You can adjust the midtones slider after setting the new black or white point if needed.

7. **Click OK to close the dialog box.**

Because you applied the correction on an adjustment layer, you can refine the results using all the techniques outlined in Chapter 6. A quick recap:

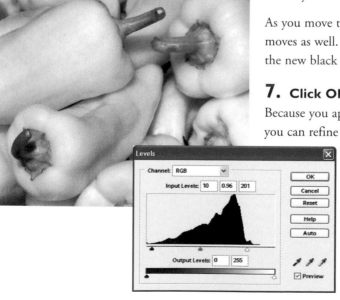

- Double-click the dialog box thumbnail, labeled in Figure 7.13, to open the Levels dialog box and change the slider settings.
- Click the mask thumbnail, also labeled in the figure, and then use the Brush tool to paint with black over areas where you want to hide the correction. (Set the tool's opacity to 100 percent to hide the filter effect fully.) Remember, although you do your painting in the image window, the black paint appears only in the mask thumbnail. The image itself reflects the result of removing

the adjustment layer effect. (If you created a selection outline before creating the adjustment layer, the nonselected areas already appear black in the mask.) Paint with white to restore the effect. For fun, try painting with black to remove the Levels adjustment from the pepper stems, as shown in Figure 7.13.

■ Lower the opacity of the adjustment layer to lessen the impact of the filter without changing the filter settings.

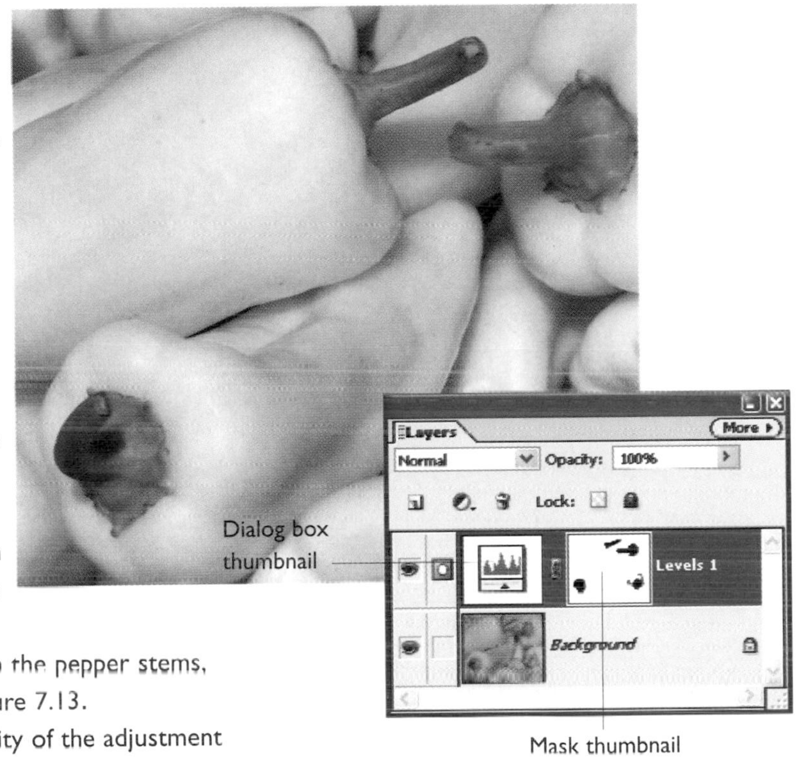

Dialog box thumbnail

Mask thumbnail

As for the other Levels dialog box controls, most aren't terribly useful, allow you to harm your image, or are designed for making color changes, not exposure changes. See Chapter 8 for information on using Levels in color-correction projects.

Watch Out!

Remember that if you merge the adjustment layer with the underlying image, you lose the opportunity to easily modify the effect. Again, Chapter 6 spells out adjustment layers in more detail.

Applying a Fading Exposure Correction

Consider the photo in Figure 7.14. Exposure is good on the right half of the image, but is too dark in the left half. You can just barely make out the waterfall that has the leftmost penguin so interested.

Figure 7.13: To remove the filter effect from portions of the image, click the mask thumbnail and paint over those areas with black.

Figure 7.14: This image needs a gradual exposure correction that grows stronger toward the left of the scene.

To fix images like this, you must apply a gradual exposure change, fading the correction to full strength where the image needs the most help. The secret is to add a *gradient*—fading—mask to your adjustment layer.

The following steps show you how to apply the Levels filter with this technique, but you can translate the steps to any filter that is available as an adjustment layer. Try it out using the sample image Penguins.jpg.

1. Select the area that you want to adjust (optional).

For the sample image, don't select anything.

2. In the Layers palette, click the topmost layer that you want to alter.

You can skip this step if you're working with a single-layer image like the penguins photo.

3. Create a Levels adjustment layer.

You can do this in two ways: Click Layer | New Adjustment Layer | Levels and then click OK in the resulting dialog box. Or click the Adjustment Layer icon in the Layers palette and choose Levels from the pop-up menu.

4. Adjust the Levels sliders as needed to correct the problem areas.

For the example image, drag the midtones slider left to brighten the image but leave the highlights and shadows sliders alone. Concentrate on improving exposure in the left half of the photo, and don't worry if the right half gets too bright.

5. Click OK to close the Levels dialog box.

6. Set the foreground paint color to black and the background paint color to white, as shown in Figure 7.15.

7. Select the Gradient tool and establish the gradient options shown in Figure 7.15.

Choose the first gradient in the gradient picker, which will produce a black-to-white gradient, and select the Linear style icon, labeled in the figure.

Figure 7.15: Use the Gradient tool to produce a fading mask for an adjustment layer.

8. Drag to create a gradient mask.

Drag from the edge of the image that's properly exposed to the point where you want the exposure change to occur at full strength. In the example, drag from the right side of the image to a little ways past the leftmost penguin, as shown in Figure 7.15.

After you release the mouse button, notice the adjustment layer's mask thumbnail, labeled in Figure 7.16. You see a mask that fades gradually from black to white. And in the image itself, your Levels adjustment now fades from full strength

Figure 7.16: By using a gradient mask, you can create a fading exposure adjustment.

to zero. (Remember, where the mask is black, the Levels adjustment is not applied; where the mask is white, the effect is applied at full strength.)

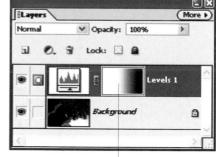

Mask thumbnail

If needed, you can use the tricks discussed in Chapter 6 to refine the adjustment layer's mask. Or, if you want to redraw the gradient entirely, click the mask thumbnail, grab the Gradient tool, and have at it. (Just remember to click that mask thumbnail first so that you create the gradient on the mask, not on the image itself.)

Dodging and Burning

Occupying the very bottom slot in the Elements toolbox, the Dodge and Burn tools take their names from traditional darkroom exposure techniques. Dodging lightens an image; burning darkens it. However, these two tools don't really supply the same results as you get in the darkroom.

Dodge and Burn do lighten and darken pixels, but they also desaturate colors. If you drag over medium blue pixels with the Burn tool, for example, you don't get navy pixels but a darker, grayish blue. Similarly, Dodge would give you a brighter, but also grayish, shade of blue, not the pure, light blue you may expect.

That's not to say that these tools are useless, however. First, if you're working on a grayscale image, all the pixels are already desaturated, so the tools produce good results. Just dab at your image with the Dodge tool to make pixels lighter and swab with the Burn tool to make them darker. (See the next section for advice regarding tool options.) In the color world, Dodge makes an excellent teeth-whitener when you're retouching portraits, and Burn can emphasize eyes. The next sections show you these techniques.

Remember

To preserve independent layers between editing sessions, save the image in the PSD or TIFF format, with the Layers option enabled.

Watch Out!

Unlike Levels, you can't apply Dodge and Burn corrections as an adjustment layer. So before you pick up either tool, copy the problem area to a new layer and then do your editing on that layer. See Chapter 6 for the full story on layers.

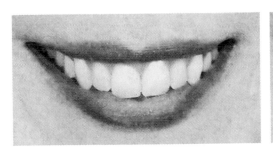 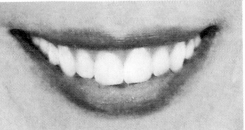

Whitening Teeth with the Dodge Tool

Although the Dodge tool isn't terribly useful for general exposure corrections, it comes in handy for portrait retouching work. You can use it to whiten teeth, as outlined in the following steps. If you don't have a photo of your own choppers, work along with the sample image Teeth.jpg. Figure 7.17 shows before and after views to give you an idea of the results you can achieve. Well, actually, you can go even whiter, but only if you want the teeth to look fake. Remember, teeth are supposed to be "pearly white," not bleach white.

Figure 7.17: Use the Dodge tool to brighten and whiten teeth.

1. Select the teeth.

2. Copy the selection to a new layer by pressing CTRL-J (Windows) or ⌘-J (Mac).

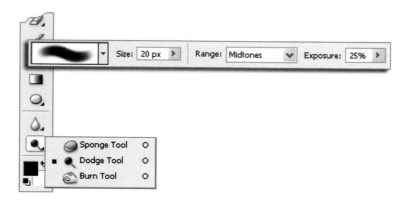

Figure 7.18: The Dodge and Burn tools share a flyout menu in the toolbox.

3. Select the Dodge tool, shown in Figure 7.18.

4. Choose a small, slightly soft, round brush.

If you need help with this step, see Chapter 2. Note that although the Dodge and Burn tools don't offer a Hardness control, you can adjust hardness by using these keyboard shortcuts: Press SHIFT-] to increase hardness by 25 percent; press SHIFT-[to decrease hardness.

5. Set the Range control to Midtones.

The Range control determines whether the Dodge and Burn tools affect shadows, highlights, or midtones. Normally, Midtones is the best lead-off hitter.

6. Limit the tool impact by lowering the Exposure value.

The Exposure value determines how much change you get from a single click or drag with the tool. The default value, 50 percent, is too high in most cases; try 25 percent or even lower to start. You can apply the tools repeatedly to the same area to make the pixels progressively lighter or darker.

7. Drag over dark areas in the teeth to lighten and whiten them.

If any very dark areas remain, try using the tool with the Range option set to Shadows. Don't use the Highlights setting; you'll blow out subtle details in the teeth.

8. Merge the lightened layer with the underlying layer, as covered in Chapter 6.

Emphasizing Eyes with the Burn Tool

With the Burn tool, you can add a little extra "pop" to eyes by darkening eyebrows, eyelashes, and pupils, as illustrated in Figure 7.19. To produce the lower image, I just dragged over the brows and lashes and then clicked a few times on the pupil. The results are subtle but make a big impact in calling attention to the eyes.

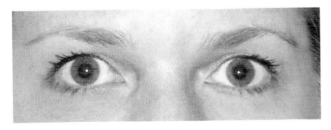

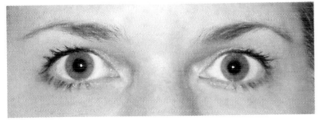

Figure 7.19: Draw attention to the eyes by using the Burn tool to darken lashes, brows, and pupils.

To achieve this effect, follow the same steps outlined in the preceding section, selecting the Burn tool instead of the Dodge tool in Step 3. Again, start with the Range control set to Midtones, and then follow up with the tool set to Shadows if necessary. For the lashes, drag outward from the eye to the tip of a lash, just as if you were applying mascara. When darkening the pupil, take care not to alter the catch light (that little white highlight caused by reflecting light). For further eye emphasis, you may want to follow up this enhancement by using the Dodge tool to brighten the whites of the eyes.

When Good Colors Go Bad

8

Compared with exposure corrections, tweaking colors in Photoshop Elements is child's play. Well, young adult's play, at the least. With the tools discussed in this chapter, you can remove color casts, play with color balance, adjust saturation, and repair red-eye with surprising ease.

Before doing any color work, however, calibrate your monitor so that you can evaluate your pictures on a neutral canvas. Chapter 12 walks you through the process and explains a few color-management options that also affect on-screen colors.

Removing Red-Eye

The top image in Figure 8.1 suffers from an all-too-common problem: red-eye. Fortunately, removing red-eye in Elements is easier than ever, thanks to a new, improved red-eye removal tool. To try it out, open the image RedEye.jpg and work through these steps:

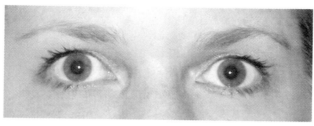

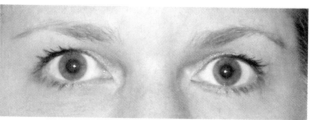

Figure 8.1: Red-eye removal takes only seconds.

Figure 8.2: One click on the eye with the Red Eye Removal tool may solve the problem.

1. Select and copy the eyes to a new layer.

You don't have to be precise—just use the Lasso or one of the Marquee tools to draw a rough selection outline. Then press CTRL-J (Windows) or ⌘-J (Mac) or choose Layer | New | Layer via Copy.

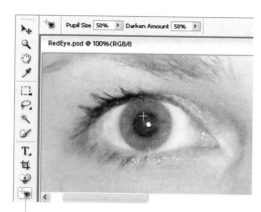

Red Eye Removal tool

2. Select the Red Eye Removal tool, labeled in Figure 8.2.

Start with the default tool options, shown in the figure.

3. Click on a red pixel in one of the eyes.

After a few seconds, the red-eye pixels are replaced, hopefully with a color that seems natural. If not, choose Edit | Undo, adjust the Pupil Size and Darken Amount values on the options bar, and try again. Also try this alternative method of working with the tool: Instead of clicking, drag to enclose the entire eyeball in a small selection outline and then wait for the replacement to occur.

4. **Repeat the process to correct the other eye.**

5. **Merge the corrected eye layer with the underlying image by using the commands discussed in Chapter 6.**

Now, a word of commentary: The Elements 3 Red Eye Removal tool is a great improvement over similar tools of the past, which almost never produced natural results. But if you can't solve your red-eye issues after a few clicks or drags with the tool, don't waste any more time; the image may be such that the tool simply isn't up to the job. Instead, use this "old-fashioned" method of red-eye removal:

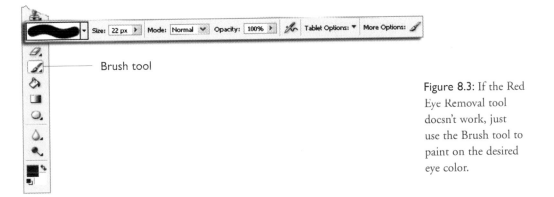

Brush tool

Figure 8.3: If the Red Eye Removal tool doesn't work, just use the Brush tool to paint on the desired eye color.

1. **Select the Brush tool, labeled in Figure 8.3.**
Choose a small, round, slightly soft brush—about 90 percent Hardness works well. Set the other options as shown in Figure 8.3 and turn off brush dynamics in the Tablet Options palette. (See Chapter 2 for a review of these brush settings.)

2. **Set the Foreground color to match the desired pupil color.**

Time Saver

To get a good match quickly, ALT-click (Windows) or OPTION-click (Mac) on a pupil pixel that isn't red or a dark pixel somewhere else in the eye.

3. **Create a new, layer and set the layer blend mode to Color.**

Choose Window | Layers or press F11 to open the Layers palette and then click the New Layer icon, labeled in Figure 8.4. Set the blending mode to Color as shown in the figure. Create the new layer directly above the layer that contains the red-eye pixels.

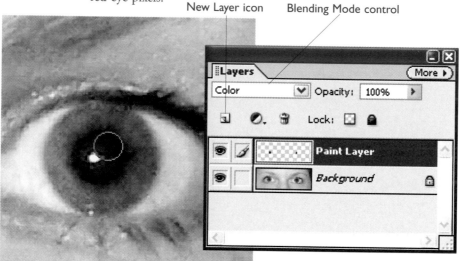

Figure 8.4: For natural results, paint on a new layer set to the Color blending mode.

4. **Paint over the red pixels, working on the new layer.**

Elements uses the color information from the Color layer—your paint layer—but takes shadow and highlight information from the underlying layer, which contains the original eyes. This setup retains the tonal details in the eyes. You may need to dab on a few different colors to get natural results, depending on how much of the eye appears red. Remember, too, that you can adjust the darkness of the resulting eye color by using the Levels filter, explained in Chapter 7. So that the filter affects only the paint pixels, apply it directly to the paint layer by choosing Enhance | Adjust Lighting | Levels instead of creating an adjustment layer.

5. **Merge the paint layer with the underlying layer by choosing Layer | Merge Down.**

For animal pictures, you may need to vary this technique. If the eyes are white (or very light) instead of red, the Color blending mode doesn't work. Instead, use the Normal blending mode and lower the paint layer's opacity as needed.

Neutralizing Color Casts
with the Levels Filter

If you shoot with a digital camera, you're probably familiar with *white balancing*.
This feature enables the camera to compensate for the fact that every light source
infuses a scene with its own color cast. By manipulating the white balance control,
you ensure that colors are rendered accurately regardless of the light source.

Problem is, if you forget to adjust the white-balance setting when you change light
sources, you can wind up with odd color casts like the one in Figure 8.5. (I should
fess up and add that you usually encounter this error only if you think you're
smarter than the camera's automatic white-balancing option and switch to manual
control, as I did for shots taken before this one.) Color casts can also occur when
you shoot with old film, use the wrong lens filter, scan an old print, or do business
with a particularly inept photo lab.

Figure 8.5: An incorrect white-balance setting on my digital camera caused a reddish color cast.

Whatever the cause of the problem, Elements offers two tools designed to help you solve it. Let's address the most obvious option first: Enhance | Adjust Color | Remove Color Cast. This command brings up a simple dialog box that instructs you to click any image pixel that should be gray, white, or black. After you click, the program analyzes the pixel you clicked and tries to neutralize the color cast. Although the filter works okay on some photos, it can be overzealous, not only removing color casts but monkeying with contrast and saturation. Sometimes, it even adds a tint to formerly white pixels, creating a new problem in the process of fixing another.

Feel free to investigate Remove Color Cast as you see fit; apply the filter to a duplicate of your original image layer for added safety. I think, though, that you'll get better results from a color-correction tool found inside the Levels dialog box, introduced in Chapter 7. You can apply this filter as an adjustment layer, and you can make exposure and contrast adjustments at the same time you remove the color cast. Try this technique with the sample image CityPark.jpg.

1. **Choose Window | Layers or press F11 to open the Layers palette.**

2. **If your image contains multiple layers, click the topmost layer that you want to correct.**

Remember that an adjustment layer affects all underlying layers. If you want the filter to affect only certain areas of those layers, create a selection outline as explained in Chapter 5. (For the sample image, you can skip this step entirely.)

3. **Create a Levels adjustment layer.**

Just click the Adjustment Layer icon in the Layers palette, shown in Figure 8.6, and select Levels from the pop-up menu that appears. The Levels dialog box opens.

Figure 8.6: Start your correction by creating a Levels adjustment layer.

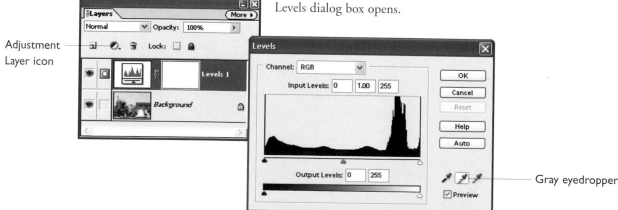

Adjustment Layer icon

Gray eyedropper

4. In the Levels dialog box, click the gray eyedropper, labeled in Figure 8.6.

5. In the image window, click a pixel that should be medium gray.

For the sample image, click at the spot marked with a white X in Figure 8.7. Elements finds all the pixels that match the one you click and recolors them medium gray, and then adjusts the rest of the image using the same formula. This step should eliminate most, if not all, of your color cast.

> **Watch Out!**
>
> If you don't get good results, click the Reset button in the dialog box and try again. Don't simply keep clicking with the eyedropper—repeated manipulation of the color values isn't a good thing.

> **Remember**
>
> Adjustment layers affect all underlying layers. To correct one layer without changing underlying layers, duplicate that layer and then apply the filter directly from the Enhance menu.

6. **Tweak exposure and contrast if necessary.**

Chapter 7 explains how to make these adjustments using the three sliders under the histogram (that chart-like thingy in the middle of the dialog box). For the sample image, drag the middle slider left to brighten the image; aim for results that look similar to Figure 8.8.

7. **Click OK to close the Levels dialog box.**

Figure 8.7: Click with the gray eyedropper on a pixel that should be medium gray.

You can adjust the correction at any time by editing the adjustment layer as explained in Chapter 6. But don't spend *too* much time trying to achieve perfection with this technique; just eliminate as much of the color cast as possible. You can use other color and exposure filters to fine-tune the image.

PART III | EXPOSURE AND COLOR TECHNIQUES

Figure 8.8: I removed the color cast and brightened the image with a single Levels adjustment layer.

Shifting Color Balance

Although the gray eyedropper in the Levels dialog boxes is a great tool, it's effective only for neutralizing a color cast. To manipulate color with more flexibility—for example, to tone down reds and play up blues—use the Color Variations filter.

Figure 8.9: The Color Variations filter is based on the color wheel.

This filter is based on the *color wheel,* a graph used to plot out the color spectrum. Chapter 1 introduces the wheel; Figure 8.9 shows it again. With Color Variations, you reduce the amount of one color by introducing more of the color that's directly opposite on the wheel, as indicated by the arrows in Figure 8.9. This process is called *color balancing.*

The following steps show you how to apply the Color Variations filter. As a sample image, work with StillLife.jpg, shown in its original state in Figure 8.10. This image leans too much to the cool (bluish) side of the spectrum for my taste. Increasing red and yellow, which decreases cyan and blue, produces the warmer version shown in Figure 8.11.

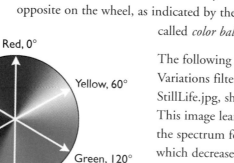

Figure 8.10: This still
life is heavy on blues
and cyans, giving it a
cool tone.

1. **Copy the area you want to alter to a new layer.**

For the sample photo, the entire image needs help, so duplicate the Background layer by dragging it to the New Layer icon in the Layers palette. (Refer to Figure 8.4.) Or just make sure that no selection outline is active and choose Layer | New | Layer via Copy. If you're starting with a multilayer image, make sure to put your duplicate layer above the problem layer. (See Chapter 6 for a refresher

Figure 8.11: I created a warmer image by bumping up the reds and yellows, which in turn reduces blues and cyans.

course in layers.) Of course, you can create a selection outline before making the copy if you want to limit the changes to specific areas of a layer.

2. **Choose Enhance | Adjust Color | Color Variations to display the Color Variations dialog box, shown in Figure 8.12.**

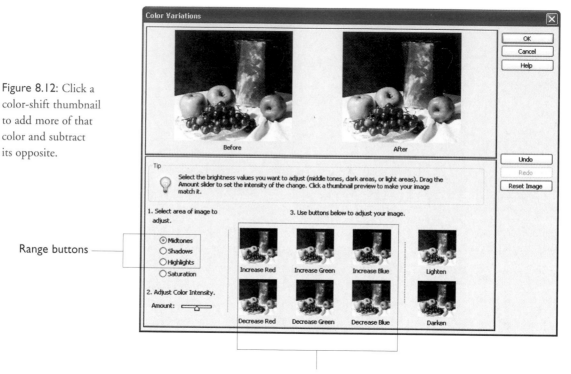

Figure 8.12: Click a color-shift thumbnail to add more of that color and subtract its opposite.

Range buttons

Color-shift thumbnails

3. **Select a range button (Shadows, Midtones, Highlights).**
With this filter, you adjust shadows, midtones, and highlights separately. Specify the range you want to alter by clicking one of the three Range buttons, labeled in Figure 8.12. For the sample image, start with the Midtones button.

4. **Click the color-shift thumbnails, labeled in Figure 8.12, to adjust the image.**
You get three pairs of thumbnails, one each to adjust reds, greens, and blues. Click a thumbnail to increase or decrease the amount of that color. To change

the impact of each click, drag the Amount slider. Drag the slider to the right to produce bigger shifts in color; drag left to make more subtle changes. The After thumbnail at the top of the box shows you the results of your changes.

What about the cyan, yellow, and magenta components of the color wheel, you ask? Well, remember that when you increase one color, you decrease the color that lies opposite on the wheel. So although the thumbnail labels don't mention cyan, magenta, or yellow, you can adjust those hues as follows:

- To increase cyan, click Decrease Red; to decrease cyan, click Increase Red.

- To increase magenta, click Decrease Green; to decrease magenta, click Increase Green.

- To increase yellow, click Decrease Blue; to decrease yellow, click Increase Blue.

For the sample image, set the Amount slider in the middle of the bar. Then click once on the Increase Red and the Decrease Blue thumbnails.

5. Adjust the remaining two brightness ranges as needed.

Again, click the Shadows, Midtones, or Highlights button, depending on which range you want to adjust. Then click the color-shift thumbnails as before. For the sample image, apply the same changes as you did in Step 4 to the shadows and highlights.

At any time, you can restore the image to its original appearance by clicking the Before thumbnail or the Reset Image button. The dialog box also offers Undo and Redo buttons for times when you want to undo or redo just some of your color changes.

6. Click OK to close the dialog box.

7. When you're satisfied with the image colors, choose Layer | Merge Down to merge the corrected layer with the original.

Figure 8.13: Colors in
this autumn scene are a
little lackluster.

Adjusting Saturation

Saturation refers to color purity or intensity.
A fully saturated pixel is pure, undiluted
color, containing not a hint of white, gray, or
black. A completely desaturated pixel can be
only white, black, or gray.

Figure 8.14: A
quick trip to the
Hue/Saturation
dialog box gives
colors some
oomph.

Increasing satura-
tion can sometimes
improve the impact
of a photo, as
illustrated by the
examples in Figures
8.13 (original) and
8.14 (adjusted). The
original image didn't
reflect the vibrancy
of the colors that I

saw when I snapped this shot. A slight boost to saturation restored the intense palette that drew me to the scene.

That's not to say that boosting saturation is always the way to go, however. Some images may call for a more subtle color palette, and thus a slight decrease in saturation. Reducing color strength also sometimes allows subtle tonal details to emerge. Either way, Elements gives you two tools for adjusting saturation: the Hue/Saturation filter, which you can apply via an adjustment layer, and the Sponge tool, which enables you to "brush on" saturation changes as if you were working with a magical paint brush.

Applying the Hue/Saturation Filter

Adjusting saturation via the Hue/Saturation filter is one of the easiest things you'll ever do in Elements. To prove it to yourself, open the sample image AutumnReflections.jpg, shown in Figure 8.13, and play along:

1. Select the area that you want to adjust (optional).

If you want to affect an entire, single-layer image—as is the case with the sample image—bypass this step. In a multilayer image, open the Layers palette and click the topmost of the layers you want to change. You also can draw a selection outline to limit the filter to just some pixels on affected layers; see Chapter 5 for help.

2. Create a Hue/ Saturation adjustment layer.

The quickest route: Click the Adjustment Layer icon in the Layers palette (see Figure 8.15) and select Hue/ Saturation from the pop-up list. You see the Hue/ Saturation dialog box, also shown in Figure 8.15.

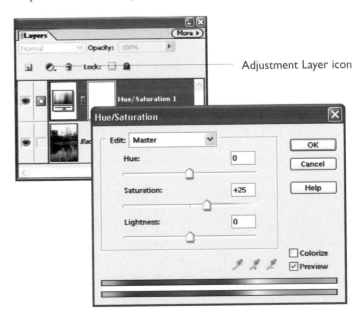

Adjustment Layer icon

Figure 8.15: Select Master from the Edit drop-down list to adjust saturation for all colors.

3. **Select the Preview check box.**

4. **Deselect the Colorize check box.**

This option enables you to desaturate your entire image and then add a color tint. Chapter 9 discusses this and other color effects.

5. **Select the range of colors you want to adjust from the Edit drop-down list.**

For the sample image, choose Master. When Master is selected, as in Figure 8.15, all colors receive the saturation adjustment. But you also can adjust the reds, yellows, greens, cyans, blues, and magentas individually. Just select the color range that you want to manipulate from the Edit drop-down list. Note, however, that Elements does not limit the saturation change to the pure form of the selected color, but also adjusts closely related colors.

6. **Drag the Saturation slider to adjust saturation.**

Drag right to increase saturation; drag left to decrease saturation. You also can enter a specific value in the box above the slider. Acceptable values range from −100, which completely desaturates the image, to 100, which is well beyond the limits of polite society and the capabilities of most printers. For the sample image, raise the value to 25.

7. **Click OK to close the dialog box.**

If you later want to tweak saturation further, see Chapter 6 to find out how to edit your Hue/Saturation adjustment layer.

Watch Out!

One additional point: The options that appear at the bottom of the dialog box when you select a color range from the Edit drop-down list enable you to modify the range of colors that will be affected. I don't recommend that novices fool with these options, because you can introduce banding—noticeable color breaks where you should have smooth, subtle color transitions. If you want to know more, however, the program's Help system details the options.

Applying Saturation Changes with a Sponge

When you want to tweak saturation in a small area or in an object that would be difficult to select, consider using the Sponge tool. With this tool, you simply click on or drag over pixels to adjust saturation.

To try it out, open the sample image Rope.jpg, shown on the left in Figure 8.16. Adding saturation to the rope creates some needed contrast between it and the fence, as shown in the right image. If you wanted to make this change via the Hue/Saturation filter, you would need to select the rope or add a mask to the adjustment layer after applying the filter—both time-consuming operations. Assuming that you have a fairly steady hand, you can probably get the job done much faster by simply dragging along the coils of rope with the Sponge tool.

Follow these steps to use the tool:

Figure 8.16: Increasing the saturation of the rope helps set it apart from the fence.

1. Copy the area that you want to adjust to a new layer.

If the region you want to tweak occupies most of the image, as is the case with the sample photo, duplicate the entire image by dragging the Background layer to the New Layer icon in the Layers palette (see Figure 8.18 later in the chapter). Otherwise, use the Lasso or one of the other selection tools to draw a rough outline around the area that you want to edit. Then choose Layer | New | Layer via Copy or press CTRL-J (Windows) or ⌘-J (Mac) to copy the selection to a new layer.

Watch Out!

Never apply this or any of the editing tools directly to your original image—you lose flexibility and risk permanently damaging your photo. Always work on a duplicate layer.

2. **Select the Sponge tool, labeled in Figure 8.17.**

Found near the bottom of the toolbox, the Sponge tool shares a flyout menu with the Dodge and Burn tools. (If this is your first trip to the flyout menu, the Dodge tool will be the selected tool in the toolbox.)

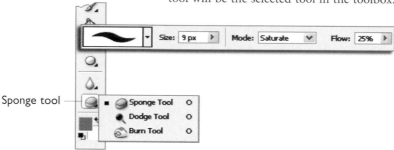

Sponge tool

Figure 8.17: Use the Sponge tool to "paint on" saturation changes.

3. **Set the brush size, shape, and other options.**

The Sponge tool is a brush-based tool, which means that you can customize the brush size and shape, as explained in Chapter 2. For the sample image, work with a brush that's about the diameter of the rope, as shown in Figure 8.18. (The right size will depend on how much you zoom in on the image.) Note that although you don't get a Hardness control as you do with some other brush-based tools, you can adjust hardness in 25 percent increments by pressing the bracket keys. Press SHIFT plus the left-bracket key ([ ) to lower the value; press SHIFT plus the right-bracket key ( ]) to raise it.

4. **Select a Mode option (Saturate or Desaturate).**

Select Saturate to boost saturation; select Desaturate to suck out color. Sorry, didn't mean to insult your intelligence.

5. **Set the Flow value to adjust the tool impact.**

For the Sponge tool, the Flow value determines how much impact you make with each click or drag. Set this one according to your personal taste, keeping in mind that your clicks and drags are cumulative. I usually start with a relatively low setting—say, 25 percent—and then just keep swabbing those pixels until I reach the saturation I want.

6. **Click on or drag over the areas you want to tweak, as shown in Figure 8.18.**

For the sample project, try to swipe each part of the rope the same number of times so you don't get an uneven result.

That's all there is to it. When you're happy with your image, merge the corrected layer with the underlying image by choosing Layer | Merge Down or using one of the other techniques outlined in Chapter 6.

New Layer icon

Figure 8.18: Always apply the Sponge and other editing tools on a duplicate layer

Tool Tricks

When using the Sponge tool, press the number keys to raise or lower the Flow value, which controls the tool's impact. Press 0 for 100 percent, 9 for 90 percent, 85 for 85 percent, and so on.

More Color Tricks

When you're taking pictures, you may use filters or special films to emphasize a part of the color spectrum. Most portrait photographers put a warming filter on the lens to give skin a golden glow, for example, while landscape photographers often work with films that render highly saturated blues and greens.

For times when you forget to load your camera bag—or just don't want to lug all those bits and pieces around—this chapter shows you how to create a variety of color effects in the digital darkroom. You'll also find out how to convert color pictures to black-and-white images and produce the look of a hand-tinted photo.

Replacing the Color of an Object

Chapter 8 introduces you to filters that enable you to make subtle color adjustments—slightly reducing red tones or boosting blues, for example. To completely replace the color of an object, use the techniques described in the next two sections. (If you're not sure what color you want the object to be, try the first method; to apply a specific color, opt for technique number two.)

Recoloring Pixels with the Hue/Saturation Filter

Figure 9.1: Drag the Hue slider to shift selected pixels around the color wheel, represented in linear form at the bottom of the dialog box.

The easiest way to change the color of an object is to use the Hue control provided with the Hue/Saturation filter. This control is based on the *color wheel*. As discussed in Chapter 8, a color wheel is a circular graph that plots out the color spectrum. Red sits at 0 degrees; yellow, 60 degrees; green, 120 degrees; cyan, 180 degrees; blue, 240 degrees; and magenta, 300 degrees. The top color bar in the Hue/Saturation dialog box, shown in Figure 9.1, is a linear representation of the wheel, with 0 degrees set at the midpoint of the bar.

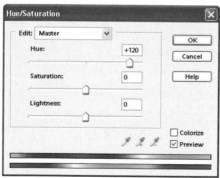

Changing the Hue value in the dialog box spins pixels around the color wheel. For example, if you enter +120 as the Hue value, red pixels move from 0 degrees to 120 degrees and become green. Green pixels become blue, and blue pixels become red. In Figure 9.2, setting the Hue value to +120 changed the gumballs image on the left to the version on the right.

Figure 9.2: I created the variation on the right by applying the Hue setting shown in Figure 9.1.

Original

Hue, +120

To try the Hue color-spinning technique, take the following steps, working along with the sample image Gumballs.jpg. The steps apply the Hue/Saturation filter as an adjustment layer, a concept you can explore in Chapter 6.

1. **In a multilayered image, open the Layers palette and click the topmost layer that you want to recolor.**

The sample image contains just one layer, so you're good to go.

2. **Select the area that you want to recolor (optional).**

If you don't select anything, all pixels on the active layer and any underlying layers will be changed. For the sample image, skip this step.

3. **Create a Hue/Saturation adjustment layer.**

Choose Layer | New Adjustment Layer | Hue/Saturation and then click OK in the resulting dialog box. Or just click the Adjustment Layer icon at the top of the Layers palette and choose Hue/Saturation from the pop-up menu. Either way, you see the Hue/Saturation dialog box, shown in Figure 9.1.

4. **Turn off the Colorize option and select the Preview box.**

5. **Select a color range from the Edit drop-down list.**

To affect all colors, as I did for the image in Figure 9.2, choose Master. Alternatively, you can manipulate a specific color range by selecting it from the list. Note, however, that the filter adjusts a range of hues, not just that single, pure color. For example, if you spin the Reds range in the gumballs image, you alter not just the red gumballs, but also many pixels in the pink, yellow, and orange gumballs.

6. **Drag the Hue slider to adjust the colors.**

Drag right to move pixels clockwise around the color wheel; drag left to move pixels counterclockwise. You also can enter a specific value into the box at the right end of the slider bar. (You don't have to enter the plus sign for positive values, but you need a minus sign for negative values.)

7. **Use the Saturation and Lightness controls to fine-tune the colors if needed.**

Both controls affect the range selected from the Edit drop-down list.

8. **Click OK to close the dialog box.**

After closing the dialog box, use the adjustment layer techniques explained in Chapter 6 to alter the filter effect if needed.

The Hue technique does have two shortcomings: First, it doesn't work on grays, whites, or blacks. Notice that the white gumball in the sample image changed only minimally, for example—it has a slight pinkish cast in the original, reflecting the colors of the neighboring gumballs. In the altered image, the cast shifts to a lighter, less obvious green-blue.

Second, because Hue/Saturation shifts all shades within a particular color range by the same degree, you can't easily convert multiple hues to a single color. The solution to both problems lies in the technique outlined next.

Painting on New Colors

To produce a color shift you can't achieve via Hue/Saturation, you can pick up any paint tool and simply brush on the desired color. However, there's a secret to getting natural results instead of a flat, unnatural blob of paint like what you see on the top lip in Figure 9.3. Try it out with the sample image Teeth.jpg, shown in the figure.

Figure 9.3: To create natural color shifts, set the blending mode of the paint layer to something other than Normal.

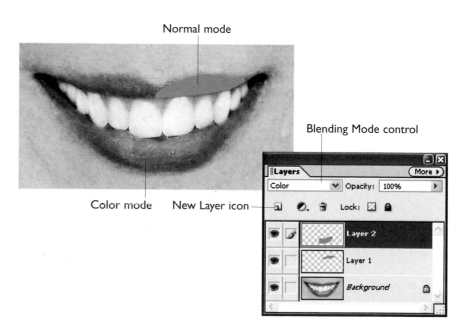

Normal mode

Blending Mode control

Color mode   New Layer icon

1. Create a new layer above the pixels that you want to recolor.

Just click the New Layer icon in the Layers palette, labeled in Figure 9.3.

2. Set the layer blending mode to Color, as shown in Figure 9.3.

3. Add the paint to the new layer.

For small areas like the lips in the sample image, use the Brush tool or, if you need precise, sharp lines, the Pencil. See Chapter 2 to find out how to choose a brush tip and paint color.

For larger areas, create a selection outline as explained in Chapter 5. Set the foreground color to the desired paint color and then choose Edit | Fill Selection to open the Fill Layer dialog box, shown in Figure 9.4. Select Foreground Color from the Use drop-down list, set the Mode to Normal, set the Opacity to 100 percent, turn off the Preserve Transparency check box, and click OK.

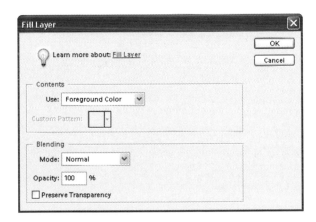

Figure 9.4: To fill a selection with the foreground paint color, choose Edit | Fill Selection and use the options shown here.

4. Experiment with other layer blending modes.

Each blending mode produces different results, and the best mode depends on your ultimate color goal. I used the Color mode for the bottom lip in Figure 9.3. In Figure 9.5, I set the mode to Multiply for the top lip and Overlay for the bottom lip.

Figure 9.5: Changing the layer blending mode produces different results.

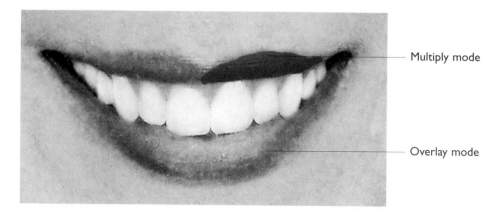

— Multiply mode

— Overlay mode

Try these tricks if you can't achieve the color mix you want by simply changing the blending mode in the Layers palette:

- Vary the paint layer's opacity, using the control in the Layers palette.
- To recolor white and black pixels, change the blending mode of the paint layer to Normal but reduce the layer's Opacity value.
- Use the Hue control in the Hue/Saturation dialog box to nudge the colors on the paint layer around the color wheel, as described in the preceding section. But this time, don't create an adjustment layer. Instead, apply the filter directly to the paint layer by choosing Enhance | Adjust Color | Adjust Hue/Saturation.
- Use the Levels filter to lighten or darken the paint layer color. Again, apply the filter directly to the paint layer, choosing the Levels command from the Enhance | Adjust Lighting submenu. See Chapter 7 to find out how to use the Levels filter.

Applying Virtual Warming and Cooling Filters

Using the Color Variations filter, discussed in Chapter 8, you can warm or cool shadows, highlights, and midtones independently. For a faster way to apply an overall warming or cooling effect, however, take advantage of the Photo Filter command, which produces effects similar to what you can achieve with traditional lens filters.

These steps explain how to apply the filter as an adjustment layer. Try it out with the Cabin.jpg sample image, shown on the left in Figure 9.6. I used the Photo Filter to produce the subtle warming effect you see in the right image.

1. Select the area that you want to alter (optional).

For a multilayer image, open the Layers palette and click the top layer that you want the filter to affect. You can limit the filter to specific pixels on the affected layers by creating a selection outline, explained in Chapter 5.

In a single-layer image, skip this step if you want to apply the filter to the entire image, as is the case with the sample photo.

2. Create a Photo Filter adjustment layer.

You can choose Layer | New Adjustment Layer | Photo Filter and click OK in the resulting dialog box. Or click the Adjustment Layer icon in the Layers palette and choose Photo Filter from the pop-up menu. You see the Photo Filter dialog box, shown in Figure 9.7.

3. Select the Preview check box.

Figure 9.6: Add a virtual warming filter by creating a Photo Filter adjustment layer.

Figure 9.7: Drag the Density slider to adjust the strength of the filter.

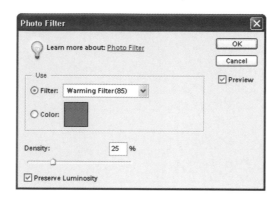

4. **Select a filter from the Filter drop-down list.**

The list offers four filters that mimic traditional warming and cooling filters: 81 and 85 warming filters along with 80 and 82 cooling filters. (With traditional filters, higher numbers indicate a more intense effect.) For the sample image, choose Warming Filter (85). In addition, the list offers a choice of specific colors. You also can click the Color swatch and choose a custom color from the Color Picker, explained in Chapter 2.

5. **Adjust the Density and Preserve Luminosity options as needed.**
Raise the Density value to produce a stronger effect. Turn off the Preserve Luminosity option to give Photoshop permission to adjust image brightness as it adjusts colors. Experiment with both options; the correct settings depend on the look you want.

6. **Click OK to close the dialog box.**
The standard tips and reminders about editing adjustment layers apply; see Chapter 6 for the full story.

Replacing a Backdrop

When circumstances prevent you from catching your subject against a flattering background, you can create a new, more appropriate backdrop in Photoshop.

Figure 9.8 offers an example of the dramatic impact you can make by swapping out the background. The stark white backdrop does nothing to complement the pitcher, and the harsh shadow caused by too-strong lighting is distracting. I solved both problems by filling the background area with a textured blue pattern and then adding a new, softer shadow behind the pitcher.

Remember

Play with the Opacity and Blending Mode controls in the Layers palette to vary the impact of an adjustment layer.

Figure 9.8: A boring white background and harsh shadow do nothing to flatter the pitcher; replacing the background and creating a new, softer shadow improve the image.

The following steps walk you through the process of creating the textured backdrop shown in Figure 9.8. To work along with the steps, open the sample image Pitcher.jpg.

1. Select the area that you want to replace.

For the sample image, use the Selection Brush in Mask mode to mask the pitcher and the table, as instructed in Chapter 5. Set the Hardness value for the Selection Brush to 100 percent. When your mask is complete, change the tool mode to Selection, which produces a selection outline around the background. As an alternative, you can also use the Magic Wand in Contiguous mode to select the background. Turn off the Anti-aliased option and turn on the Contiguous option.

2. Create a new empty layer by clicking the New Layer icon, labeled in Figure 9.9.

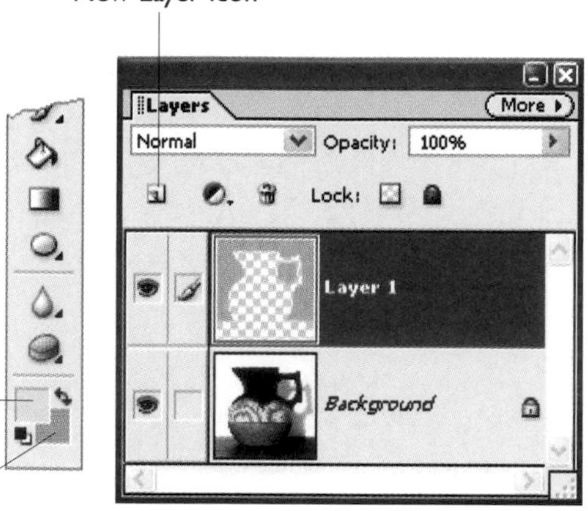

New Layer icon

Figure 9.9: On a new layer, fill the background area with a solid color or texture.

Foreground color

Background color

This layer initially will hold your new backdrop. Position the layer on top of the layer that contains the background area you want to replace, as shown in the figure.

3. **Establish the backdrop colors by setting the foreground and background colors.**

For the sample image, set the foreground paint color to pale blue and the background to a slightly darker shade of the same hue, as shown in Figure 9.9. (If you need help with this step, see Chapter 2.)

4. **Fill the selected backdrop area with the foreground paint color by pressing ALT-DELETE (Windows) or OPTION-DELETE (Mac).**

5. **Get rid of the selection outline by pressing CTRL-D (Windows) or ⌘-D (Mac).**

6. **Check your work.**

Zoom in so that you can get a good view of the boundary between the subject and the new backdrop. Does the backdrop cover any subject pixels? If so, use the Eraser to wipe away the stray background pixels, revealing the hidden subject pixels. Or, if the new backdrop doesn't completely extend over the old backdrop, use the Brush tool to cover the missing areas with the foreground paint color. It's important to get the boundary exact before you go any further. (Chapter 6 explains the Eraser; Chapter 2 offers help with the Brush tool.)

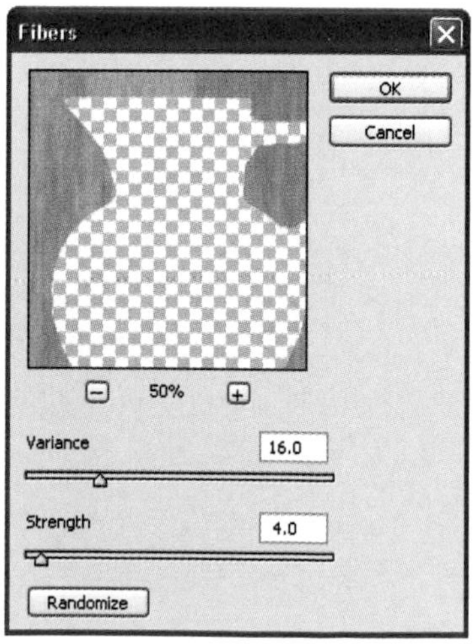

Figure 9.10: You can use the Fibers filter to produce a great textured backdrop.

7. **Choose Filter | Render | Fibers to display the Fibers dialog box, shown in Figure 9.10.**

This filter creates the fiber-like texture that you see in Figure 9.8, basing the effect on the current foreground and background colors.

8. **Play with the filter settings to produce a textured effect you like and then click OK.**

If the preview area in the dialog box reveals only the transparent areas of the layer—indicated by the checkerboard pattern—drag inside the preview to display a portion of the layer that you filled with color. You can also click the plus and minus signs under the preview to zoom the display. I used the settings shown in Figure 9.10 for the sample image. Click OK to apply the effect and close the dialog box.

9. **Add a shadow behind the subject (optional).**

This step creates additional separation between subject and background, often producing a more realistic image. Move on to the next step to add the shadow. If you *don't* want to add a shadow, skip to Step 14.

10. **Select the subject to which you want to add the shadow.**

For the sample image, you need to select the pitcher but not the table.

Time Saver

You can get a head start on your selection outline by CTRL-clicking (Windows) or ⌘-clicking (Mac) the new backdrop layer in the Layers palette. This step selects all nontransparent pixels—in this case, your backdrop. Choose Select | Inverse to reverse the outline so that the pitcher and table are selected instead. Next, switch to the Selection Brush and set the Mode control on the options bar to Mask. Voilà—everything but the pitcher and table appear under the mask. Now just paint with the Selection Brush to extend the mask over the table. When you finish, set the tool mode back to Selection to generate the selection outline around the pitcher.

11. **Copy the subject that will get the shadow to a new layer.**

For the sample image, first click the pitcher layer (the original Background layer) in the Layers palette. Then choose Layer | New | Layer via Copy or press CTRL-J (Windows) or ⌘-J (Mac).

12. **Drag the duplicated subject layer above the new backdrop layer, as shown in Figure 9.11.**

Figure 9.11: After copying just the pitcher to a new layer, move it above the new backdrop and add a shadow via the Styles and Effects palette.

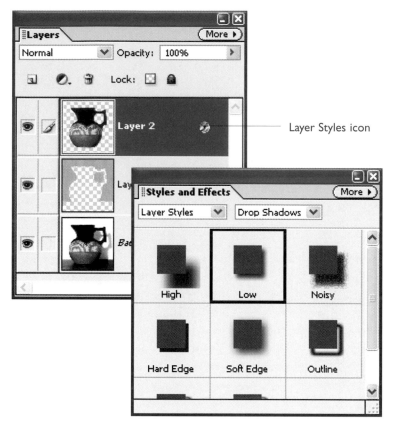

Layer Styles icon

13. Add a shadow to the pitcher layer via the Styles and Effects palette, shown in Figure 9.11.

To display the palette, choose Window | Styles and Effects. (As with other palettes, I've dragged this one free of the Palette Bin in Figure 9.11; see Chapter 2 if you want to do the same or need help using palettes that you leave in the bin.) Set the two controls at the top of the palette to Layer Styles and Drop Shadows, as shown in the figure. Then click a shadow type icon to apply it to the layer. You can tweak the shadow by double-clicking the Layer Styles icon in the Layers palette, labeled in Figure 9.11, and adjusting the settings in the resulting dialog box.

14. When you're happy with the image, merge all the layers by choosing Layer | Flatten.

If your image contains other layers that you don't want to merge, hide them first (by clicking their eyeball icons in the Layers palette) and then choose Layer |

Merge Visible instead of using the Flatten command. See Chapter 6 for more help with layers.

You can create unlimited variations on this backdrop theme by applying different special-effects filters in Step 7. Two of my favorites are Filter | Texture | Texturizer and Filter | Render | Clouds. The latter produces a random cloud pattern that resembles the backdrops that many studio photographers use when doing portrait work. (You may need to vary the foreground and background paint colors from those used in the example to produce suitable results with other filters.)

Converting Color Photos to Grayscale Beauties

In the photography world, most people use the term *black-and-white* to refer to non-color images. But in digital imaging circles, a black-and-white picture is one that contains just those two colors. Photos that also contain shades of gray are known as *grayscale* images. I go with *grayscale,* mostly because I find traditional photography enthusiasts more easy-going about such things than digital imaging wonks, who spend too much time with uncooperative computers and so are usually a bit on the edge.

To complicate the issue, Elements enables you to convert an image to the official Grayscale color mode. A color model, as explained in Chapter 1, is a formula for defining a spectrum of colors. In the Grayscale mode, an image can contain just 256 colors: white, black, and shades of gray. (You do not have to make this conversion to produce a non-color image, however.)

To avoid confusion, I use the term *Grayscale* with a capital *G* only when referring to an image that has been converted to the official Grayscale color mode. I use a lower-case *grayscale* when I use the term in a general descriptive sense.

With that bit of administrative business covered, the following sections explain two techniques for converting your color images to grayscale.

Converting to the Grayscale Mode

The fastest way to produce a grayscale image is to convert it to the 256-color Grayscale color mode. To try this technique, open the sample image Iris.jpg, shown on the left in Figure 9.12, and take the following steps.

Original RGB

Image | Mode | Grayscale

Figure 9.12: I used the Image | Mode | Grayscale command for this conversion.

1. Save a copy of your color original.

Watch Out!

Don't skip this step! After you apply the command and save the image, you can't get your original colors back.

2. Choose Image | Mode | Grayscale.

What happens next depends on your image. If your image contains just one layer, you see an alert box asking for permission to discard the original color information; click OK to move forward. If your image contains multiple layers, you instead see an alert box that gives you the option of flattening (merging) the layers or keeping them independent.

If the image contains some types of adjustment layers, the program warns you that if you keep the layers independent, the adjustment layer will be discarded. Click OK to eliminate the adjustment layer and retain the individual layers; click Flatten to merge all layers, including the adjustment layer. In any case, Photoshop converts your image to the 256-color Grayscale mode.

3. Save your image under a new name.

Watch Out!

Be sure to use a new name, otherwise, you overwrite your color original.
See Chapter 3 for help on saving files.

For casual work, Image | Mode | Grayscale produces acceptable results and is quick and easy. The image on the right in Figure 9.12 shows the Iris image converted with this command.

With some images, however, you can lose tonal details because of the formula Elements uses to convert the original color values to gray values. It's a one-size-fits-all approach that sometimes doesn't work as well as the next technique, which gives you more control over the conversion.

Creating Custom Grayscale Blends

By taking advantage of two filters, Gradient Map and Hue/Saturation, you can manipulate the tones in your grayscale conversion. Even better, you can apply both filters as adjustment layers, which enables you to retain the original color values and the grayscale values *in the same image file*, assuming that you save the file in the PSD or TIFF format with the Layers feature enabled. So if you do the conversion one day and decide the next to emphasize different details in the grayscale version, all you have to do is edit the adjustment layers. You don't have to start over from scratch.

Try these steps, again using the Iris.jpg image as your crash-test dummy. (If you completed the steps in the preceding section and your iris image is currently in the Grayscale mode, choose Edit | Undo to get back to the full-color original before you try this technique. Or, if you already saved the grayscale version, reopen the Iris.jpg original.)

1. Make sure that no selection outline is active.
To quickly get rid of an active selection outline, press CTRL-D (Windows) or ⌘-D (Mac).

PART III | EXPOSURE AND COLOR TECHNIQUES

2. **In a multilayer image, open the Layers palette and click the topmost layer name.**

Again, this step ensures that you want your entire image to receive the grayscale effect. If your image contains just a single layer (the Background layer), you can skip this step.

3. **Set the foreground and background paint colors to black and white, respectively.**

Just press D to make it so.

4. **Create a Gradient Map adjustment layer.**

You can click the Adjustment Layer icon in the Layers palette (see Figure 9.14) and choose Gradient Map from the pop-up menu. (Be sure to choose Gradient Map, not plain old Gradient.) Or choose Layer | New Adjustment Layer | Gradient Map and click OK when the New Layer dialog box appears. You then see the Gradient Map dialog box, shown in Figure 9.13.

The Gradient Map filter reassigns—*maps*—the colors in your image to different colors based on the gradient style you choose in the dialog box. *Gradient* is simply a fancy name for a gradual blend between two or more colors. Click the arrow labeled in Figure 9.13 to open the gradient palette and click the first gradient style icon, as shown in the figure, to select a gradient based on the current foreground and background paint colors (black and white, in this case). Deselect the Dither and Reverse check boxes and click OK.

Click to open palette

Elements then adjusts your image so that pixels fill the black-to-white spectrum, creating the image shown in Figure 9.13. If you notice any banding—choppy transitions between similar tones—choose Edit | Undo and try again, this time with the Dither option selected. (This option adds random noise in an effort to reduce banding.)

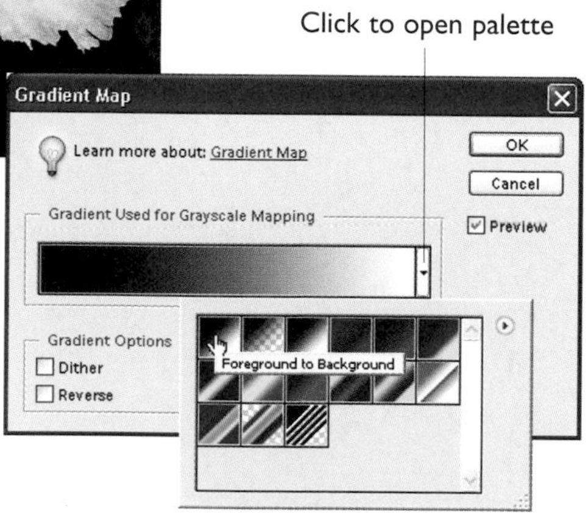

Figure 9.13: You can apply a Gradient Map adjustment layer to reassign pixels so that they fall across the entire black-to-white spectrum.

Gradient Map

Learn more about: Gradient Map

OK
Cancel
☑ Preview

Gradient Used for Grayscale Mapping

Gradient Options
☐ Dither
☐ Reverse

Foreground to Background

5. Add a Hue/Saturation adjustment layer to manipulate the grayscale tones (optional).

If you want to play with the tonal values in your mapped image, create a Hue/Saturation adjustment layer *underneath* the Gradient Map adjustment layer, as shown in Figure 9.14. To properly position the Hue/Saturation adjustment layer, click the layer directly under the Gradient Map layer in the layers palette before adding the adjustment layer. (For the sample image, click the Background layer).

In the Hue/Saturation dialog box, turn off the Colorize option and select a color range other than Master from the Edit drop down-list. Then just play with the Hue, Saturation, and Lightness sliders. As you do, you alter the colors of the pixels in that color range, which affects the outcome of the Gradient Map adjustment layer. For example, I tweaked the Blues and Reds ranges to produce Figure 9.15.

As you can see, the variations that you can achieve via the Hue/Saturation dialog box can be subtle—in the example photo, look closely at the center of the iris and the edges of the flower. How much control you have depends on the original colors of your photo. If you do a lot of grayscale conversions, you may want to invest in a third-party color effects plug-in, such as nik multimedia's Color Efex Pro (www.nikmultimedia.com), which offer more sophisticated tools for this task.

Adjustment Layer icon

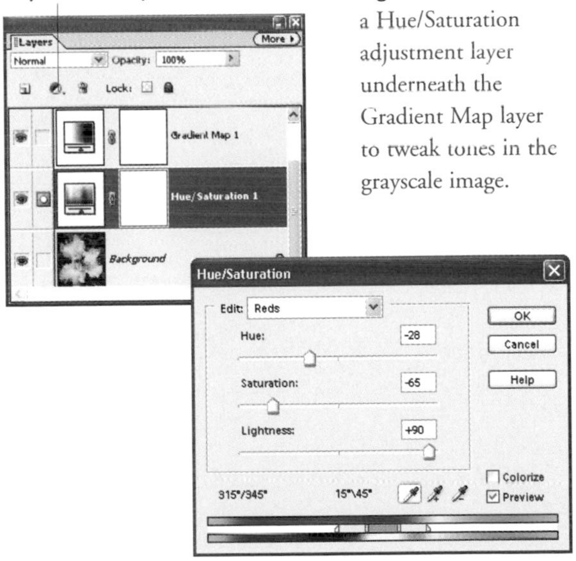

Figure 9.14: Add a Hue/Saturation adjustment layer underneath the Gradient Map layer to tweak tones in the grayscale image.

Figure 9.15: To produce this variation, I adjusted the Reds and Blues ranges in the Hue/Saturation dialog box.

Also keep these other tips in mind:

- Remember that your grayscale effect exists as an adjustment layer, so you can use all the tips outlined in Chapter 6 to refine the effect if necessary.
- If you don't want tones in your photo to span the entire black-to-white spectrum, just set the foreground and background colors to whatever shades of gray you want to use in Step 3. The Gradient Map filter will then use those two colors as the start and end of the color spectrum in your grayscale conversion. (You can also create some interesting color effects by using two different hues—say, red and blue—as the foreground and background colors or by clicking one of the other gradient icons in Step 4.)
- You can tweak your grayscale image using the Levels filter, the Shadows/ Highlights filter, and the Dodge and Burn tools, all covered in Chapter 7, too.
- If you want to create a version of the image in the official Grayscale color mode, first flatten the image by choosing Layer | Flatten. Then choose Image | Mode | Grayscale. Photoshop retains the grayscale values you assigned with the Gradient Map and Hue/Saturation filters when doing the mode conversion.

Creating Antiqued and Hand-Tinted Effects

Want to give your photo that antiqued, sepia tone without waiting a hundred years for the process to occur naturally? You can add the sepia tint—or any other tint color—in a flash. If you care to go even further, you can create the effect of a hand-painted photo.

Watch Out!

For both effects, your image must be in the RGB color mode. If you want to tint or "hand-paint" an image that has been converted to the Grayscale mode, first choose Image | Mode | RGB Color to convert it to RGB.

The following steps show you the easiest way to tint your image. If you want to try the technique with the Iris.jpg sample image and you used that photo for the grayscale project outlined in the preceding section, choose Edit | Revert to Saved to return to the original, full-color version of the image. (If you already saved the grayscale image, just reopen the Iris.jpg color original.)

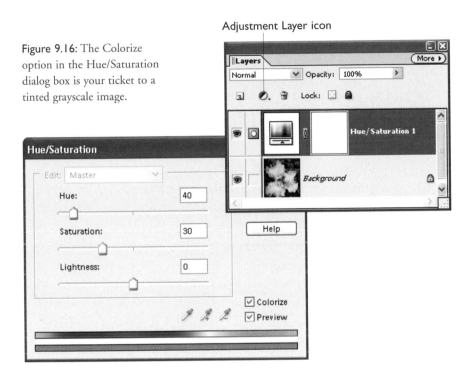

Adjustment Layer icon

Figure 9.16: The Colorize option in the Hue/Saturation dialog box is your ticket to a tinted grayscale image.

1. Create a Hue/Saturation adjustment layer.

Just click the Adjustment Layer icon in the Layers palette (see Figure 9.16), and choose Hue/Saturation from the pop-up menu.

2. In the Hue/Saturation dialog box, select the Colorize and Preview boxes.

3. Drag the Hue, Saturation, and Lightness sliders to specify the tint color and intensity.

When the Colorize option is turned on, the Hue slider works a little differently than previously described. Instead of spinning pixels from one position on the 360-degree wheel to another, you're selecting a particular tint color from the wheel. Possible Hue values range from 0 (red) to 360 (also red). Saturation values in Colorize mode range from 0 (no color) to 100 (full-intensity color). By default, Elements starts you out at a Saturation value of 25.

Don't spend too much time mulling over all this: Just play with the sliders until you get the tint color and intensity you want. The bottom color bar in the dialog box reflects the tint color at the current values.

I used this technique to produce the sepia version of the flower shown in Figure 9.17. If you're playing along with the home version of our game, featuring the Iris.jpg sample image, use the Hue/Saturation values shown in Figure 9.16.

You can produce hand-painted effects like the one you see on the right in Figure 9.17 in two ways. Starting with your full-color image, try these techniques:

Figure 9.17: I used the Colorize option to create the sepia tint (left) and produced the hand-painted effect by simply decreasing saturation (right).

- **Lower the image saturation**   Create a Hue/Saturation adjustment layer and reduce the image saturation. Starting with the original, full-color iris image, I produced the picture on the left in Figure 9.16 by lowering the Saturation value to −50. After making this change, you can further manipulate colors by adjusting the Hue and Lightness values for the individual color ranges inside the dialog boxes. (Choose the range you want to alter from the Edit drop-down list.)

- **Desaturate and then paint on a Color layer**   Alternatively, create your Hue/Sat layer and completely desaturate the image by lowering the Saturation value to −100 percent. Then create a new, empty layer above the Hue/Sat layer and set the layer blending mode of the new layer to Color. Now you can paint on the image using the Brush tool or any other paint tools. The section "Painting on New Colors," earlier in this chapter, offers more specifics.

Spot Removal and Other Touch-up Work

10

Every photographer knows the disappointment of those "almost perfect" pictures—the would-be stunners spoiled by small imperfections. Lens flare pierces a brilliant blue sky. Blown highlights mar a poignant portrait. A stray candy wrapper distracts the eye from a skateboarder caught flying down the street.

With techniques presented in this chapter, you can eradicate these and other picture-wrecking problems. You'll find out how to remove unwanted objects, dab digital cover-up cream on small blemishes, and more.

In This Chapter:

☐ Power retouching with the Clone tool

☐ Quick cover-ups with the Healing Brush

☐ Dust removal with the Spot Healing Brush

☐ How to create custom patches

☐ Repairs for blown highlights

Covering Up Problem Areas

Cropping can eliminate flaws around the perimeter of an image. But what do you do when the problem occurs in an area you don't want to crop away? Depending on the photo, you may be able to duplicate untainted pixels from another part of the image and use the copies to cover the bad spots—sort of like performing a photographic skin graft.

The upcoming sections introduce you to tools for doing this kind of repair work: the Clone tool, Healing Brush, and Spot Healing Brush. Investigate the Clone tool first—it's the most difficult to master but will be your workhorse retouching weapon. The Healing Brush and Spot Healing Brush are variations of the Clone tool, so getting acquainted with cloning will help you better understand those tools.

Cloning Over Defects

Figure 10.1: I cloned over the tattoos with pixels from the surrounding skin.

One of the most useful Elements tools, the Clone tool "paints" with existing image pixels, enabling you to easily copy and paste good areas over bad. In Figure 10.1, for example, I covered the temporary tattoos that decorated the girls' arms with pixels cloned from the surrounding skin.

Because the Clone tool has no real-life equivalent, it can be perplexing at first. So instead of diving right into specifics, the next section explains the general concept and one important tool option.

Getting Familiar with Cloning

My astute technical editor, Kathy Eyster, offers a great analogy for the cloning process: It's just like working with an ink pad and rubber stamp. First, you press the stamp into the ink pad to transfer ink onto the stamp. Then you stamp that ink over the area of the paper you want to cover. Using the Clone tool—officially called the Clone Stamp tool—involves the same two-step approach.

1. **First, establish the initial clone source.**

The *clone source* refers to the pixels that you want to copy and paste over the problem pixels. To set the initial clone source point, you hold down the ALT key (Windows) or OPTION key (Mac) to display a target cursor, as shown in the left image in Figure 10.2. Then you click the initial pixels you want to copy. (The cursor looks more like a bull's-eye target if you didn't set the Other Cursors option in the Preferences dialog box to Precise as suggested in Chapter 2.)

Set Source cursor   Source cursor   Tool cursor

2. **Click or drag to paint copies of the source pixels over the problem pixels.**

If you click, you lay down one cursor's worth of copied source pixels. If you drag, Elements lifts a swath of source pixels as wide and long as your brushstroke. A crosshair cursor appears to show you the position of the pixels currently being cloned. The crosshair cursor moves in tandem with your tool cursor, so as you move the tool cursor, you clone a different part of the photo.

Figure 10.2: ALT-click (Windows) or OPTION-click (Mac) to set the initial clone source (left); then drag over the problem pixels (right).

For example, in Figure 10.2, I set the initial clone source at the position indicated in the left image. Then I dragged down over the tattoo, as indicated by the white arrow in the right image. (The circle is the Clone tool cursor; again, the cursor appearance depends on the options you choose in the Preferences dialog box.) As I dragged down, the crosshair cursor moved the same distance and direction, following the path indicated by the black arrow, cloning a continuous strip of good skin pixels onto the tattoo.

What happens with your second click or drag depends on the Aligned control on the options bar:

- **Aligned on**   Elements continues cloning from the current position of the clone source cursor. This option prevents you from cloning the same area each time you click or drag with the Clone tool.
- **Aligned off**   When you release the mouse button after each click or drag, the clone source cursor returns to the initial clone-source position you set when you ALT- or OPTION-clicked. This option allows you to clone the same pixels repeatedly.

Figure 10.3 illustrates this difference. Suppose you decide that instead of erasing the tattoo, you want to duplicate it, so you set your initial clone source at the position shown in the left image. If you drag four times across your image with the Aligned option on, you get the result shown in the example on the top right. Each time you release the mouse button and begin a new drag, Elements simply continues cloning from the point where you left off so you get an exact duplicate of the heart. If you turn the Aligned option off, the source cursor resets to the initial position after each drag, and you duplicate the same strip of pixels four times, as shown in the example on the lower right.

Figure 10.3: Turn off the Aligned option to clone the same source pixels repeatedly.

Initial clone source

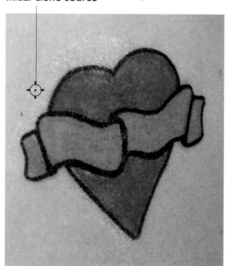

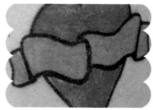

Aligned on

Aligned off

There's no right or wrong setting. Sometimes you need to clone the same area repeatedly, and sometimes you don't. Either way, you can reset the clone source at any time by ALT- or OPTION-clicking again.

Now that you have a better idea of how cloning works, the next section gives you specifics on using the Clone tool.

Applying the Clone Tool

In a practiced hand, the Clone tool can remove almost any unwanted object from a photo. Practice, however, is the operative word. You can't get good cloning results without it. So open the sample image Tattoo.jpg, featured in Figure 10.3, and work along with the steps.

1. Create a new layer to hold your cloned pixels.

Just click the New Layer icon in the Layers palette, shown in Figure 10.4. Place the new layer above the layer that contains the problem pixels.

2. Select the Clone tool, labeled in Figure 10.5.

The official tool name is Clone Stamp, but nearly everyone in the Elements world drops the "Stamp." Whatever you call it, the tool shares a flyout menu with the Pattern Stamp tool. (The Pattern Stamp has little practical use in everyday photographic projects, so I don't cover it.)

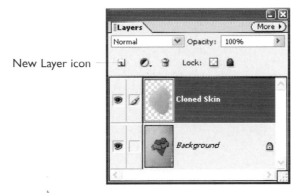

New Layer icon

Figure 10.4: Always do your cloning on a separate layer.

3. Set the brush options.

Select a brush from the brush palette, detailed in Chapter 2. For normal cloning, use the Mode and Opacity settings shown in Figure 10.5 (Normal and 100 percent).

Clone tool

Figure 10.5: The Clone tool is one of your best retouching weapons.

If the area you're fixing is in soft focus, a soft brush helps your cloning strokes blend with the surrounding area. In areas that feature sharp focus, work with a harder brush. Unfortunately, you don't get a real hardness control with the Clone tool, but you can adjust brush hardness in 25 percent increments by pressing these shortcuts: SHIFT-[(left bracket) to reduce hardness; SHIFT-] (right bracket) to increase hardness. For the sample image, start with the 45-pixel soft brush. Then press SHIFT-] twice to raise the hardness to 50 percent.

4. Set the Aligned option.

As explained in the preceding section, this option affects what happens on your *second* click or drag during a cloning session. A quick recap:

- **On** With each new click or drag, you continue cloning from the point where you left off, picking up new source pixels as you move your tool cursor.
- **Off** Each time you release the mouse button, the clone cursor returns to its original starting position. So you clone from the same source pixels each time you click or drag.

For the sample image, turn the option off. You'll need to clone the same skin pixels more than once to cover the entire tattoo.

5. Turn on the Use All Layers check box.

This option allows the Clone tool to see through the new, empty cloning layer and grab the pixels from all underlying layers. If you don't want to clone pixels from a particular layer, hide the layer by clicking its eyeball icon in the Layers palette.

6. ALT-click (Windows) or OPTION-click (Mac) to set the initial clone source.

Remember your click tells Elements what pixels you want to clone. Again, think of this step as pressing a rubber stamp into an ink pad—but in this case, the ink pad is filled with pixels. For the sample repair job, use the surrounding skin pixels as the clone source.

7. Click or drag over the area you want to hide.

The cloned pixels appear underneath your tool cursor. If necessary, you can clone from another area of the image by simply resetting the clone source. Change the brush size and hardness as needed as you go.

Tool Tricks

Press the bracket keys to change the brush size without bothering with the options bar controls. Press the left bracket key to reduce brush size; press the right bracket key to increase brush size.

8. **When you're satisfied with the repair, merge the cloning layer and underlying layer as explained in Chapter 6.**

Now, I want to stress that unless you're some sort of cloning savant, you may have trouble getting to Step 8 with the sample image. I purposely chose this example because cloning skin is one of the toughest repairs you'll ever do, and if you have success with this image, you're well on your way to becoming a master cloner.

What makes this image especially difficult is that the tattoo is bordered by darker skin on the right and lighter hues on the left. Your cloned skin has to create a natural fade between those two tones, but there's little good skin from which to build that bridge. You have to clone the same areas repeatedly, and all those strokes with a semi-soft brush can lead to blurring. (A hard brush would create more problems because the edges of your strokes become noticeable.) As a result, your initial tattoo-removal job may look something like what you see in the image on the left in Figure 10.6—blotchy and uneven, with areas that are noticeably softer than the surrounding skin.

Figure 10.6: I blended the uneven skin patch (left) by cloning again at reduced opacity (middle) and then rebuilding texture using the Grain filter (right).

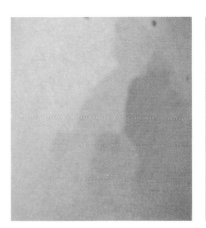

Whether you're working with skin or some other tricky subject, here are some secrets you can use to turn a noticeable cloning job into a more invisible repair:

■ To soften abrupt color shifts, set the clone source on either the light or dark side of the color boundary, set the Opacity control on the options bar to 50 percent, and then drag over the border. This produces a strip of cloned pixels that's an even mix of the two colors. You may need to repeat this process several times, lowering the tool opacity between each stroke as you move outward from the color boundary. (The proper tool opacity will depend on the area you're fixing, so you'll need to experiment.) I used this technique to produce the smoother blend of colors you see in the middle image in Figure 10.6.

■ To rebuild texture that's been softened by repeated cloning, try applying the Grain filter or the Add Noise Filter to the cloned layer. See the section "Painting Over Blown Highlights," later in this chapter, for help with applying both filters. An application of the Unsharp Mask filter, explained in Chapter 11, can also do the trick. I took both steps to produce the textured version of the skin patch on the right in Figure 10.6. If, on the other hand, you've introduced hard edges that you want to eliminate, drag over them with the Blur tool, also described in Chapter 11.

■ For some repairs, allowing the original pixels to remain partially visible produces a smoother result, so experiment with adjusting the opacity of the cloned pixels. To change the opacity of the entire cloning layer, use the Opacity control in the Layers palette. To set the opacity for your next cloning stroke, adjust the Opacity value on the options bar.

■ Adjusting the brightness or color of the cloned pixels is sometimes necessary. See Chapters 7 and 8 for help.

■ You can use the Eraser tool to rub out cloned pixels that don't look right, as explained in Chapter 6. Or just trash the cloning layer and try again.

■ If you can't find any good pixels to clone in the current image, check your archives; you can clone from one photo to another. Open both photos, arrange the image windows side by side, and set the clone source in the window that contains the usable pixels.

Patching Small Defects with the Healing Brush

Like the Clone tool, the Healing Brush copies pixels from one area of the image and paints them on the pixels under your tool cursor. But the Healing Brush adjusts the texture, opacity, and brightness of the cloned pixels to match the surrounding pixels. This adjustment can be good or bad, depending on what you're trying to do. If you want the copied pixels to retain their original appearance, the Healing Brush isn't your tool; use the Clone tool instead.

To get a feel for this tool, try using it to repair the sample image Sunset.jpg, shown in Figure 10.7. You can't shoot a sunset without pointing your lens toward the sun, and if you're too mesmerized by the scene to notice, those last rays of the day can cause lens flare, as happened here. Follow these steps to quickly patch over the flare with some surrounding water.

Figure 10.7: Lens flare ruins a sunset image (left); a single swipe with the Healing Brush fixes the problem (right).

1. Create a new layer to hold the Healing Brush strokes.
Just click the New Layer icon in the Layers palette (refer to Figure 10.4).

2. **Select the Healing Brush tool, shown in Figure 10.8.**
The tool shares a flyout with the Spot Healing Brush, explained next.

Click to display brush options

3. **Set the brush options.**

Click the arrow labeled in Figure 10.8 to display a mini-palette containing a Diameter (brush size) control and a Hardness control. As always, the correct size and hardness depends on the area you're fixing. For the sample image, set the Diameter value to 20 pixels. The area surrounding the lens flare is in soft focus, so set the Hardness value to 0. Leave the Angle, Roundness, and Spacing options alone. If

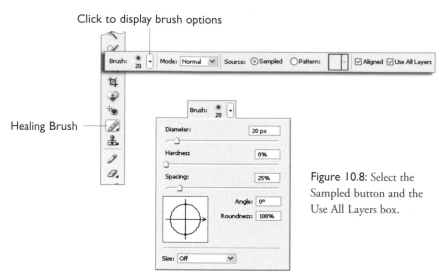

Healing Brush

Figure 10.8: Select the Sampled button and the Use All Layers box.

you're using a pressure-sensitive tablet, set the Pen Pressure option to Off until you get familiar with the Healing Brush. (This option enables you to adjust the brush size by changing stylus pressure or moving the stylus thumbwheel.)

4. **Set the Mode control to Normal and select the Sampled button.**
5. **Set the Aligned option.**
This check box has the same impact as for the Clone tool; see the earlier section "Getting Familiar with Cloning." For the sample repair, turn the option on.

6. **Select the Use All Layers check box.**
7. **ALT-click (Windows) or OPTION-click (Mac) the pixels that you want to use to "heal" the blemish.**
Your click does the same thing as when you use the Clone tool: It tells Elements what pixels to use as the *source pixels*—the pixels to copy and paste over the problem pixels. As with the Clone tool, you see the target cursor when you hold down ALT or OPTION. For the sample portrait, ALT- or OPTION-click at the location shown in the top image in Figure 10.9.

8. **Place your cursor over the blemish and then click or drag to heal it.**

Elements paints the source pixels over the pixels underneath your cursor. In addition to your tool cursor, you see a crosshair cursor, as shown in Figure 10.9. The crosshair indicates what pixels are currently being used as the source pixels. If you drag with the Healing Brush, the crosshair cursor moves in tandem with your tool cursor. In the figure, the white X indicates the spot where I began dragging with the Healing Brush. When you release the mouse button, Elements adjusts the color and brightness of the copied pixels to match their surroundings.

9. **When the repair is done, merge the healed layer with the under lying layer as discussed in Chapter 6.**

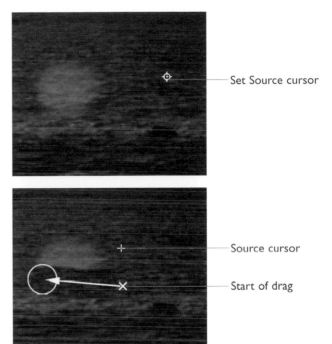

Set Source cursor

Source cursor

Start of drag

Figure 10.9: After setting the Healing Source (top), drag over the defect to repair it (bottom).

After repairing the lens flare, give the Healing Brush another whirl, this time trying to eradicate the telephone wires in the Turtle.jpg image shown in Figure 10.10. Here's a case where the Healing Brush doesn't work. Because Elements adjusts the color, texture, and intensity of the copied area to match the neighboring area, the patch areas nearest the sculpture are too dark. Try as you might, you won't be able to fix the sky with this tool.

So remember: Pick up the Healing Brush only if you want Elements to blend the edges of the copied pixels with the surrounding pixels. Otherwise, use the Clone tool or the custom patching method described at the end of this chapter. If the Clone tool does seem to be blending the cloned pixels with the surrounding pixels, reduce the brush hardness; a too-soft brush can cause this problem.

Figure 10.10: The Healing Brush adjusts the cloned pixels to match the surrounding pixels, making the sky patch too dark in areas nearest the sculpture.

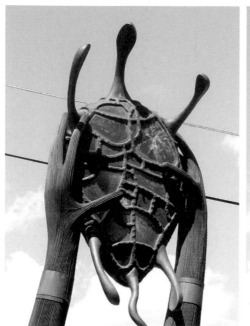

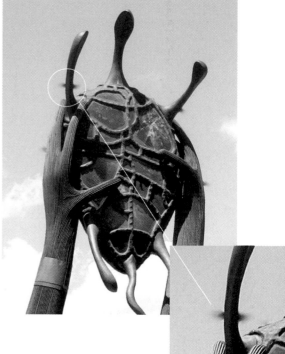

Zapping Dust and Other Specks

A variation of the Healing Brush, the Spot Healing Brush is designed to get rid of very small blemishes such as dust specks that sometimes turn up in scanned images. If you don't have your own grimy scan, open the sample image Pagoda.jpg, shown in Figure 10.11. The inset gives you a close-up look at the crud in a portion of the sky. Zoom in on a bit of dust and follow these steps to produce the spot-free image shown in Figure 10.12.

1. Copy the problem area to a new layer.

You can copy a selection by pressing CTRL-J (Windows) or ⌘-J (Mac). To duplicate an entire layer, use those same shortcuts or drag the layer to the New Layer icon in the Layers palette. For the sample image, duplicate the entire Background layer.

2. Select the Spot Healing Brush, shown in Figure 10.13.

Figure 10.11: Tiny dust specks often plague scanned images.

Figure 10.12: You can wipe away dust easily with the Spot Healing Brush.

Figure 10.13: When working with the Spot Healing Brush, use a brush that's slightly larger than the blemish.

3. Choose a brush size that's slightly larger than the blemish, as shown in Figure 10.13.

Generally, you get the best results with a hard brush. With a soft brush, the edges of the repair are feathered and the repair pixels sometimes don't fully cover the problem pixels.

4. Set the Type control.

For normal spot removal, choose Proximity Match. The Create Texture option adds noise, an effect that gives an area a speckled look.

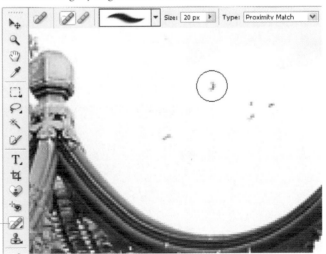

Spot Healing Brush

5. **Click the blemish.**

After surrounding the blemish with a selection outline, Elements scratches its head for a few seconds and then tries to replace the blemish with pixels that match the surrounding area. (You also can drag with the tool over the blemish, but clicking typically works best.)

If you don't get good results, choose Edit | Undo, raise the brush size, adjust the brush hardness—or both—and try again. Still no good? Don't waste any more time; your flaw isn't compatible with the Spot Healing Brush, so try one of the other methods presented in this chapter instead.

When you do repair the blemish, merge the correction layer with the underlying layer as discussed in Chapter 6.

Saving Time with Patchwork

Figure 10.14: Just as I snapped this photo, the black butterfly landed and tried to steal the scene.

When you need to hide a large defect, you may be able to save time by creating a patch instead of using the Clone tool or Healing Brush. Simply select an area to use as a patch, copy it to a new layer, and drag the copied pixels over the problem area.

Try using this technique to cover up the left butterfly in the BlueBeauty.jpg sample image, shown in Figure 10.14. Just as I pressed the shutter button to capture

the blue butterfly, a winged pal intruded into the shot. And of course, that caused the blue butterfly to take off, eliminating my chance to take the picture again. So I covered the interloper with a patch created out of empty areas of the rock. To improve the composition of the patched photo, I then cropped away the excess background to produce Figure 10.15.

1. Select the area that you want to use as a patch.

For the example project, select the Lasso tool, set the Feather value to 10, and turn on the Anti-aliased option. Then drag around the area shown in Figure 10.16.

As explained in Chapter 5, feathering creates a selection outline that fades gradually at the edges. For the sample image, slight feathering will help the patch blend in with the surrounding rock. For your own photos, you'll need to experiment to see whether a feathered or unfeathered patch works best. Ditto for anti-aliasing.

If you draw your selection outline with a tool that doesn't offer a Feather control on the options bar, you can feather the outline via the Select | Feather command.

Figure 10.15: I hid the intruder with a custom patch and then cropped the image to further improve composition.

Figure 10.16: Select an area to use as a patch.

2. Copy the selection to a new layer by pressing CTRL-J (Windows) or ⌘-J (Mac).

Or choose Layer | New | Layer via Copy. The copied selection will serve as your patch. Make sure that the new layer is above the layer that contains the problem pixels, as shown in Figure 10.17. If not, drag it up the layer stack in the Layers palette, as explained in Chapter 6. (Unless you rename your patch layer, as I did for Figure 10.17, the layer name will be Layer 1.)

Move tool

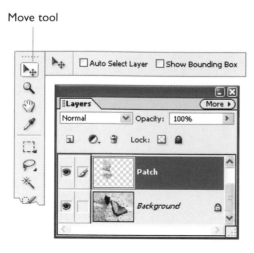

Figure 10.17: After copying the patch pixels to a new layer, use the Move tool to drag them over the defect.

3. **Press v to select the Move tool, labeled in Figure 10.17.**

Turn off the Auto Select Layer and Show Bounding Box options.

4. **Drag the copied selection over the problem pixels.**

You also can nudge the patch into place by pressing the arrow keys. Press an arrow key to move the patch one pixel in the direction of the arrow. Press SHIFT plus an arrow key to move the patch 10 pixels in that direction.

5. **Refine the patch as needed.**

Your patch probably won't be perfect at first. Use these techniques to adjust it so that it blends invisibly into the surrounding pixels:

- If the patch doesn't cover the entire area, create a second patch and drag it over the remaining problem pixels. You can simply duplicate the patch layer (drag it to the New Layer icon in the Layers palette) or create an entirely new patch.
- Use the Eraser, covered in Chapter 6, to rub away any excess patch pixels.
- You can rotate, scale, and otherwise manipulate the patch via the Free Transform command, explained in Chapter 4.
- Experiment with different layer blending modes and opacity settings.
- Adjust the color and exposure of the patch by using the techniques discussed in Chapters 7 and 8. Apply the correction directly to the layer, via the commands on the Enhance menu rather than using an adjustment layer. That way, your changes affect only the patch pixels.
- If you still can distinguish the edges of the patch, erase a few pixels all the way around its perimeter with the Eraser tool opacity set to 50 percent. This will give you a border that's a blend of the original and patch pixels.

6. **When the patch looks good, merge the patch layer with the underlying layer, as explained in Chapter 6.**

Watch Out!

Be careful not to introduce noticeable patterns into areas that should be random, as I did in the area to the left of the butterfly in Figure 10.18. You can avoid this by using several areas as your patch material. Or, after dropping the patch in place, use the Clone tool to randomly copy pixels from one part of the patch to another, so that you interrupt the pattern.

Figure 10.18: Unnatural patterns in the area to the left of the butterfly are a dead giveaway that the image has been altered.

SPEED KEYS: Retouching Tool Shortcuts

Tool	Shortcut
Brush tool*	B
Clone Stamp tool*	S
Eraser*	E
Eyedropper	I
Healing Brush or Spot Healing Brush*	J
Move tool	V

*Shares shortcut with other tools; press SHIFT plus the shortcut key to cycle through the tools.

Painting Over Blown Highlights

Chapter 7 shows you how to fix a photo that is slightly overexposed. But no exposure tool can repair *blown highlights*—areas so overexposed that they're completely white, devoid of any detail. In the photo of the old train car in Figure 10.19, for example, the top of the yellow wheel and some areas in the ladder suffer from this problem.

Figure 10.19: Areas of the wheel and ladder were so overexposed that they

Blown high-

You can take two approaches to repairing blown highlights:

- Use the Clone tool to copy properly exposed pixels over the problem pixels. The first section in this chapter shows you how.
- Use the Brush tool to paint in the missing color.

I prefer the second approach for fixing areas such as the wheel and ladder rungs in the sample photo. Staying within the bounds of such a narrow area with the Clone tool can be tricky. In most cases, painting enables you to produce good results in less time. Painting is also the way to go when you can't find any good pixels to clone.

The following steps show you how it's done. Experiment on the sample image Train.jpg, shown in its repaired state in Figure 10.20. (Figures 10.22 and 10.23 show close-ups of the before and after images.)

Figure 10.20: I repaired the blown highlights by painting over them and then adding some texture.

1. **Select the Brush tool and set the tool options as shown in Figure 10.21.**

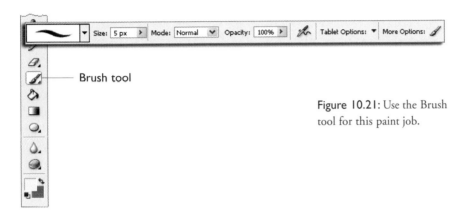

Brush tool

Figure 10.21: Use the Brush tool for this paint job.

For the sample project, work with a small, round brush, and set the Hardness value to 90 percent. Other repair jobs may call for a different brush size or Hardness value. (For the Brush tool, you access the Hardness control by clicking the More Options button.) While you're first learning this technique, also turn off brush dynamics, controlled in the Tablet Options palette at the right end of the options bar. After you understand how the technique works, however, you may want to enable dynamics so that you can vary paint opacity on the fly if you use a pressure-sensitive tablet. (Chapter 2 details all these options.)

2. **Set the foreground color to the color you want the object to be.**

Time Saver

If the color exists elsewhere in the image, press ALT (Windows) or OPTION (Mac) to temporarily access the Eyedropper and then click the color. For the sample image, click a yellow pixel near the blown highlights you need to repair.

To select a color that's not in the image, use the Color Picker as described in Chapter 2.

3. **Create a new layer above the layer that holds the blown highlights.**

Just click the New Layer icon in the Layers palette (refer to Figure 10.22). (I named the new layer Paint Layer in the figure to make the illustration clearer; your new layer will be labeled Layer 1. You can rename a layer by double-clicking the layer name, typing the new name, and then pressing ENTER.)

4. **Paint over the blown highlights, as shown in Figure 10.22.**

As you paint near the edges of the blown highlights, lower the tool's Opacity value (on the options bar) to better blend the paint with the surrounding area. If you spill paint on surrounding pixels, use the Eraser to remove it. (Chapter 6 shows you how.)

Figure 10.22: Paint over the highlights on a new, empty layer.

New Layer icon

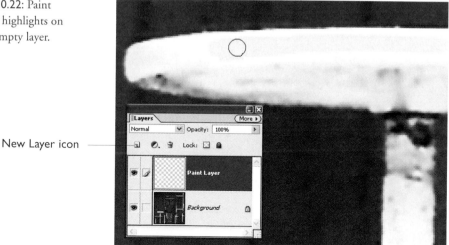

Tool Tricks

Press a number key to adjust the opacity of the next stroke you paint with the Brush tool or Clone tool. Press 0 for full opacity, 9 for 90 percent opacity, 8 for 80 percent opacity, and so on. To adjust opacity in increments smaller than ten, type the specific value: 85, 23, or whatever.

5. Study the painted area to see whether a texture fix is needed.

When you finish, your painted highlights may look something like what you see on the left in Figure 10.23. The color is correct, but something's missing: texture. Compare the top of the wheel, which I painted, with the underlying area. The unpainted regions contain subtle variations of color, while the repaired area is a flat strip of solid color—definitely not natural.

If the repaired area is small, this problem may not be noticeable, in which case you can skip to Step 7. Otherwise, move on to Step 6.

6. Apply the Grain filter to add texture to the painted area (optional).

Choose Filter | Texture | Grain to access the Grain filter, which adds random speckles of color to a selected area. You see the Filter Gallery, shown in Figure 10.24 (the title bar of the gallery window reflects the selected filter). Experiment with the filter settings to find the right texture match for the image, zooming the image if necessary by clicking the plus and minus buttons underneath the preview. For the Grain Type setting, Enlarged usually works well; use this option for the sample

Figure 10.23: The painted area looks flat compared to the rest of the wheel (left); an application of the Grain filter adds texture (right).

image. The other two options control the strength and contrast of the grain effect. For the sample image, set the Intensity control to 15 and the Contrast value to 10. Click OK to apply the effect and close the dialog box.

Figure 10.24: Experiment with the Grain Type option to see which setting produces the best texture match.

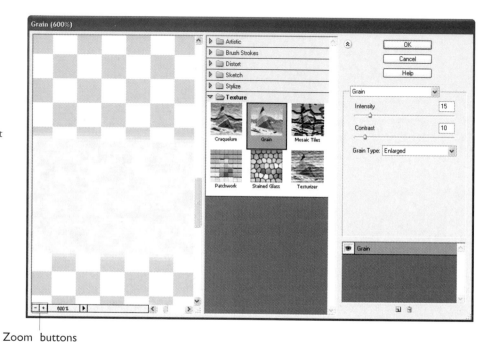

Zoom buttons

After closing the filter dialog box, you can adjust the opacity of the paint layer if needed by using the Opacity control in the Layers palette.

7. **Merge the paint layer with the underlying image as described in Chapter 6.**

For paint jobs that require small-grain texture, also try the Add Noise filter in Step 6. This filter simulates a defect called noise, discussed in the next chapter. Choose Filter | Noise | Add Noise to display the dialog box shown in Figure 10.25. The Amount value controls the strength of the effect. Experiment with the Distribution options; Uniform produces a more subtle effect than Gaussian. Select the Monochromatic box to create noise based solely on tones of the paint color, without introducing any other colors.

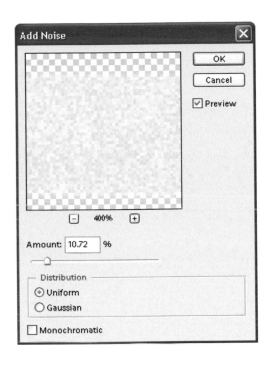

Figure 10.25: To add small-grain texture, try the Add Noise filter.

One final note: If you've explored Chapter 9, which shows you how to replace the color of an object by using the paint tools in combination with certain layer blending modes—Color, Multiply, and so on—you may be wondering why you can't use that same technique here. Unfortunately, that technique doesn't work on pixels that are absolutely white. So you must use the approach covered here if you want to add color to blown highlights.

Focus Tricks

11

In This Chapter:

- What sharpening can—and can't—do

- Professional sharpening with Unsharp Mask

- How to blur focus with Gaussian Blur

- Recipes for manipulating depth of field

- Techniques for using the Sharpen and Blur tools

When you consider that everything that occurs in Elements is the result of a mathematical calculation, some of its features become even more amazing. The filters and tools described in this chapter are a case in point. With the techniques presented here, you can manipulate focus, either to make soft images sharper or to create the illusion of a shortened depth of field. Imagine how many formulas and pieces of computer code must be involved in that bit of digital manipulation!

On second thought, don't—it will only boggle your mind, and we're boggled enough already. Instead, just take advantage of these focus-related features and join me in a 21-click salute to the Adobe wizards who make them possible.

Sharpening Focus

No photo-editing program, even one as capable as Elements, can pull an extremely blurry image into sharp focus—no matter what you've seen people do in Hollywood spy thrillers. But when an image is only slightly soft, such as the flower in Figure 11.1, you can improve it through a process called *sharpening*. Figure 11.2 illustrates the results you can achieve.

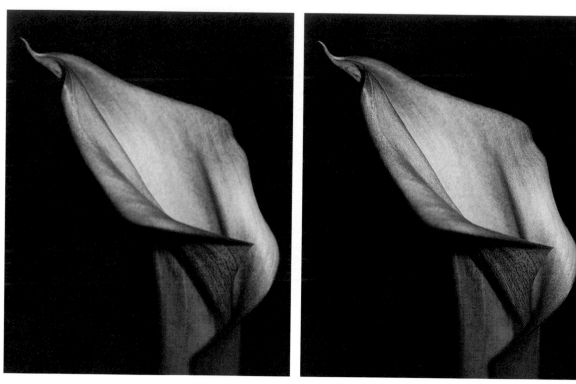

Figure 11.1: Camera shake caused a slight case of the blurs.   Figure 11.2: Sharpening creates the illusion of better focus.

You can approach sharpening in two ways:

- To sharpen an entire photo or a large region, rely on the Unsharp Mask filter.
- To sharpen very small areas, try the Sharpen tool.

The next two sections walk you through both techniques. But before you try either, it's important to understand that a sharpening filter doesn't really adjust focus. Instead, it increases contrast along the border where one color meets another, which tricks the eye into thinking that the picture is in sharper focus.

Figure 11.3, which features a magnified view of the flower, gives you a close-up look at the effect. The left version is untouched; the right one was sharpened. Notice the light and dark halos that appear along the fold in the petal, running diagonally through the frame? That's sharpening. Pixels on the light side of a color boundary get lighter; pixels on the dark side get darker.

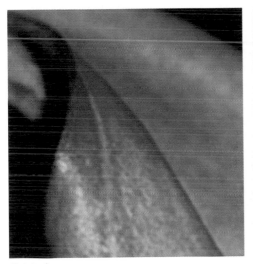

Original

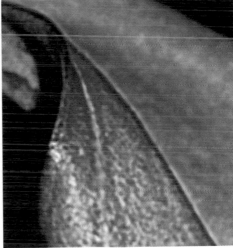

Sharpened

Figure 11.3: Sharpening tricks the eye by increasing contrast in areas where one color meets another.

Watch Out!

When you sharpen, be careful not to go too far. Oversharpened photos have a rough, grainy look with noticeable sharpening halos, as shown in Figure 11.4. In addition, never sharpen until you establish the final pixel dimensions and output resolution, as dicussed in Chapter 13. The appropriate amount of sharpening depends on these two values.

Figure 11.4: Oversharpened photos have a sandpaper-like texture, with visible sharpening halos.

Applying the Unsharp Mask Filter

Clicking Filter | Sharpen opens a submenu containing four sharpening filters: Sharpen, Sharpen Edges, Sharpen More, and Unsharp Mask. But only Unsharp Mask gives you control over how the effect is applied, so ignore the others.

The following steps explain the technique that I use for applying the Unsharp Mask filter. To try it out, open the sample image Lily.jpg, which is the blurry original from Figure 11.1.

1. Copy the area that needs sharpening to a new layer.

If your image contains just one layer and you want to sharpen the entire photo, drag the Background layer to the New Layer icon in the Layers palette, labeled in Figure 11.5. Go this route for the sample image. (I named the new layer Sharpened for the illustration; you don't need to do the same.) Otherwise, select the area you want to sharpen and then choose Layer | New | Layer via Copy or press CTRL-J (Windows) or ⌘-J (Mac).

2. Choose Filter | Sharpen | Unsharp Mask.

You see the Unsharp Mask dialog box, shown in Figure 11.6.

Remember

If your photo remains slightly soft after a reasonable amount of sharpening, try increasing contrast with the Levels filter, covered in Chapter 7. Sometimes, an overall contrast boost can further bolster the illusion of sharper focus.

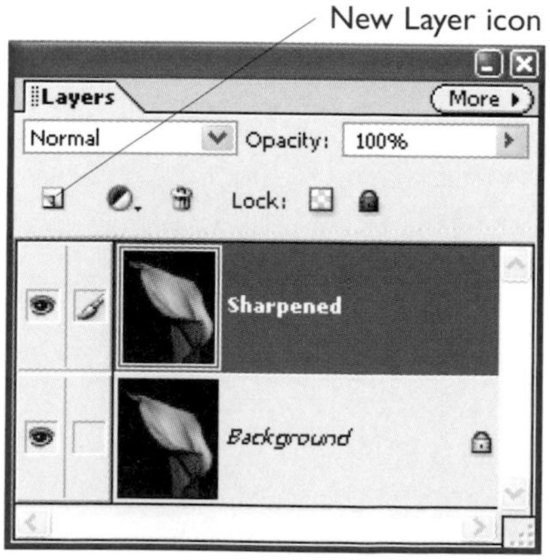

New Layer icon

Layers
Normal | Opacity: 100%
Lock:

Sharpened

Background

Figure 11.5: Always apply sharpening on a duplicate layer.

3. Select the Preview check box so that you can preview the effect in the image window.

You can preview the effect both in the image window and in the small preview inside the dialog box. Zoom the dialog box preview by clicking the plus and minus buttons underneath the preview; drag inside the preview to view a different part of the image.

If you set the dialog box preview to a magnified view, as shown in Figure 11.6, keep the view in the image window zoomed out. This enables you to keep an eye on both the overall image and the close-up details while you're sharpening.

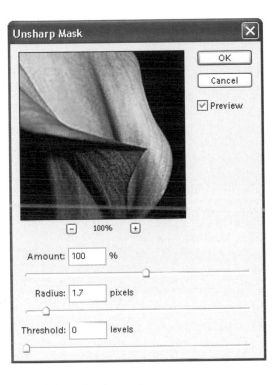

Figure 11.6: Click the plus and minus buttons to zoom the dialog box preview.

4. Use the Amount, Radius, and Threshold controls to adjust the sharpening effect.

These controls work as follows:

- **Amount** The higher the value, the stronger the effect.
- **Radius** This value determines the thickness of the sharpening halos discussed in the preceding section. For print photos, values under 2.0 usually do the trick. On-screen images generally need narrower halos; anything more than 1.0 is typically too much.

Remember

Magnify the view in the image window by pressing CTRL-+(Windows) or ⌘-+ (Mac). Zoom out by pressing the minus key instead of the plus key.

- **Threshold**   If you leave this set to 0, the sharpening is applied anywhere a color change occurs. Raise the value to limit the effect to areas of high contrast—*edges*, in imaging lingo. In portraits, try a value in the 3 to 5 range to sharpen without adding unwanted texture to skin. Also bump up the Threshold value if sharpening starts to bring out noise, grain, or compression artifacts in areas of flat color. (See the end of this chapter for more information about these defects.)

Don't worry if you have to slightly oversharpen some areas in order to get others into decent focus; you can tone down the oversharpened regions later. For the sample image, use the settings shown in Figure 11.6.

5. **Click OK to close the dialog box and apply the effect.**

6. **Evaluate the image.**

First, view the image at its intended output size. For a photo destined for the Web or other on-screen use, choose View | Actual Pixels. For a print image, choose View | Print Size. (Note that the latter view is just an approximation of the print size.) Then zoom in to inspect details. Look for areas that are oversharpened, exhibiting noticeable texture or obvious sharpening halos. For print images, you may want to make a test print to see how the image translates to paper. If everything looks fine, you're done.

7. **If necessary, use the Eraser to rub out oversharpened areas.**

Select the Eraser, labeled in Figure 11.7, and erase areas that became too sharp. Set the tool Opacity value (on the options bar) to 100 percent to completely eliminate the sharpening effect; reduce the tool opacity if you just want to soften the effect. For example, erasing at 50 percent opacity reduces the sharpening effect by half. In the sample image, erase at full opacity to eliminate the too-strong sharpening halos along the fold line that runs diagonally through the image. Then set the tool opacity to 50 percent and drag over the green underside of the flower and the stem.

In the Layers palette, the sharpening layer's thumbnail displays a checkerboard pattern in areas you erase, as shown in Figure 11.8. (Again, your layer will be named Layer 1 unless you renamed

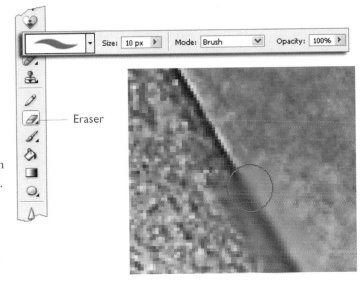

Eraser

Figure 11.7: To soften oversharpened areas, drag over them with the Eraser.

it.) In the image window, your original, unsharpened image shows through areas that you make fully transparent. Where you make pixels translucent—by erasing at less than 100 percent opacity—you get a blend of the original and sharpened layers. The checkerboard pattern in the Layers palette is only partially visible in translucent areas.

The beauty of this technique is that you can concentrate on the softest areas when applying the filter, knowing that you can always lessen the sharpening in other areas by erasing them later. And as long as you retain the sharpening layer, you also can lessen the sharpening effect throughout the entire image by simply reducing the layer opacity, using the control in the Layers palette.

When you're satisfied with the sharpening effect, merge the sharpened layer with the underlying image using the techniques discussed in Chapter 6.

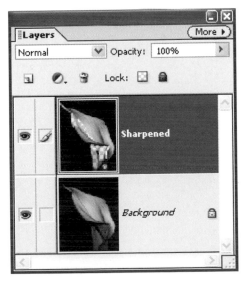

Figure 11.8: The checkerboard pattern in the sharpened layer indicates areas that you've erased, allowing the original image to become visible.

Remember

If you want a
sharpening or
blur effect to
fade in gradually,
use a feathered
or gradient
selection outline,
as explained later
in the upcoming
section "Creating
aGradual Blurring
Effect."

Heightening Focus with the Sharpen Tool

With the Sharpen tool, you can sharpen by dragging over or clicking on the area you want to alter. I'm not terribly fond of this tool; I find its impact too unpredictable, which means a lot of trial and error to get the right amount of sharpening. The tool also doesn't offer the same range of control you get with Unsharp Mask—you can adjust the sharpening amount, but you don't get a Radius or Threshold option. As a result, you can easily end up with an area that looks unnaturally grainy instead of sharper.

That said, when you want to sharpen small or hard-to-select areas, you may be able to save time by using the Sharpen tool instead of the Unsharp Mask technique. Experiment with this option by dragging over the ironwork in the sample image Iron.jpg, which is the first image in Figure 11.9. I used the Sharpen tool to emphasize the rough texture and rusty areas in the iron—a perfect use of the tool, given its tendency to "rough up" pixels.

Figure 11.9: Dragging
over the ironwork
with the Sharpen tool
emphasized its texture.

1. Create a new layer above the layer you want to sharpen.
Just click the New Layer icon in the Layers palette (refer to Figure 11.10).

2. Select the Sharpen tool, labeled in Figure 11.10.
Located near the bottom of the tool palette, the Sharpen tool shares a flyout menu with the Blur tool and Smudge tool.

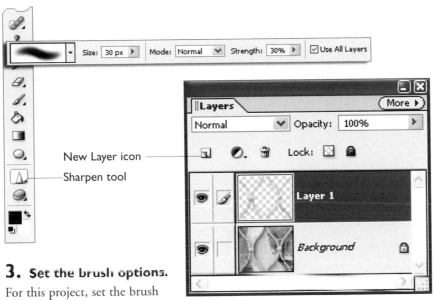

New Layer icon

Sharpen tool

Figure 11.10: With the Sharpen tool, you can click or drag to sharpen the area under your cursor.

3. Set the brush options.

For this project, set the brush size slightly larger than the iron bars, as shown in Figure 11.11, and work with a soft, round brush. Set the Mode control to Normal and lower the Strength value to 30 percent. The Strength value determines how much impact you make with each click or drag of the tool; the default setting of 50 percent typically produces too much change.

4. Select the Use All Layers option.

This step is critical; when the option is turned off, the Sharpen tool can't reach pixels outside the new layer. If you don't want to sharpen a layer, hide it by clicking its eyeball icon in the Layers palette.

5. Click or drag on the area you want to sharpen.

If the sharpening effect isn't strong enough, click or drag again. Notice the thumbnail for the sharpening layer in the Layers palette: Elements puts your sharpened pixels on that layer. You can lessen the impact of your changes by lowering the Opacity value for the layer. You also can use the Eraser tool to wipe out any mistakes. (Of course, Edit | Undo is always at your disposal, too; see Chapter 3 for details.)

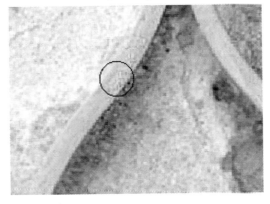

Figure 11.11: Center the Sharpen brush over the ironwork and drag.

Remember

You can increase the hardness of the selected brush in 25 percent increments by pressing SHIFT-] (right bracket). Press SHIFT-[(left bracket) to decrease hardness.

6. **Merge the sharpened layer with the underlying image as explained in Chapter 6.**

> ## Tool Tricks
> To sharpen or blur in a horizontal or vertical line, SHIFT-drag with the tool. To sharpen or blur in a straight line at any other angle, click once at the start of the line and then SHIFT-click again at the end. These tricks work for any brush-based tool.

Blurring Focus

Whereas sharpening increases contrast along color boundaries, blurring reduces contrast to create the illusion of softer focus. By blurring a picture background, you can produce the effect of a reduced depth of field. Blurring also works wonders for softening laugh lines and diminishing digital camera noise, film grain, and compression artifacts.

Blurring Large Areas with Gaussian Blur

When you want to blur a large area, apply the Gaussian Blur filter as outlined in

Figure 11.12: I used the Gaussian Blur filter to soften the background, creating a shortened depth of field.

the following steps. I used this technique to produce the illusion of a shortened depth of field in the ChinaGarden.jpg sample image, featured in Figure 11.12.

1. **Select the area that you want to blur, using the techniques outlined in Chapter 5.**

For the sample image, use the Selection Brush in Mask mode to paint a mask over the garden figure. Then switch the tool to Selection mode to generate a selection outline around the background.

2. **Copy the selection to a new layer, as shown in Figure 11.13.**

Just press CTRL-J (Windows) or ⌘-J (Mac). Or choose Layer | New | Layer via Copy. As I did elsewhere, I changed the name of the new layer to Blur Layer for purposes of illustration; your new layer will be called Layer 1.

3. **Choose Filter | Blur | Gaussian Blur.**

You see the Gaussian Blur dialog box, shown in Figure 11.13.

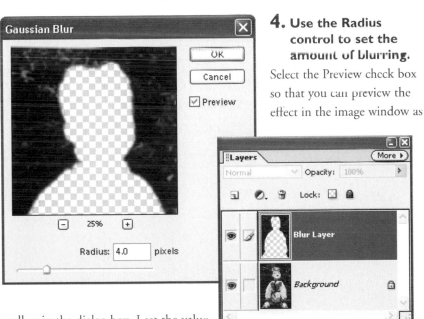

4. **Use the Radius control to set the amount of blurring.**

Select the Preview check box so that you can preview the effect in the image window as

Figure 11.13: Apply the Gaussian Blur filter on a duplicate layer.

well as in the dialog box. I set the value to 4.0 for the sample image.

5. **Click OK to close the dialog box and apply the blur.**

6. Evaluate and refine.

The one hang-up with this and most blurring filters is that the effect often spills a little beyond the boundaries of your selection outline. To remedy the problem, use the Eraser tool on the blur layer, dragging over areas that shouldn't be blurred. For the garden image, for example, you may need to drag along the border between the background and the figure's jacket to bring the sharpness back to the fringes of the flowers. Use a very small, soft brush for this bit of clean-up work. If the blur effect instead missed some pixels that you want to be soft, pick up the Blur tool, discussed later in this chapter, and touch up those areas.

7. Merge the blurred layer with the underlying layer; see Chapter 6 for details.

These steps assume that you want a consistent blur over the entire selected area. For an easy way to produce a varied blur, check out the next section.

Creating a Gradual Blurring Effect

The garden image featured in the preceding section presents a pretty easy example of how to shorten depth of field. All the leaves in the background are about the

Figure 11.14: Use a fading selection outline to increase the strength of the blur in areas farther from the focusing point.

same distance from the subject, so you can apply the blur consistently throughout the selected area.

Suppose, though, that the background contains objects at varying distances from the area that you want to keep in sharp focus, as in the Lavender.jpg example image shown in Figure 11.14. To realistically mimic the effect of shortened depth of field, the blur needs to become stronger as the distance from that focusing point increases.

If you want the effect to fade out around the entire perimeter of an area, you can create your selection outline using a feathered selection, as explained in Chapter 5. But to limit the fade to one direction, as I did in Figure 11.14, a little trickery is needed. Here's the secret:

1. Duplicate the Background layer.

Just drag the layer to the New Layer icon in the Layers palette. Or, if no selection outline is active, press CTRL-J (Windows) or ⌘-J (Mac). This step assumes that your image contains just one layer; if not, copy the layer that contains the area you want to blur.

2. Select the Gradient tool, shown in Figure 11.15.

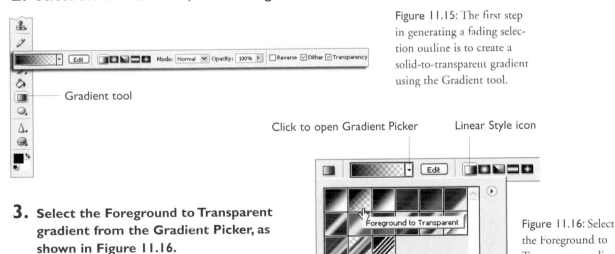

Gradient tool

Figure 11.15: The first step in generating a fading selection outline is to create a solid-to-transparent gradient using the Gradient tool.

Click to open Gradient Picker   Linear Style icon

3. Select the Foreground to Transparent gradient from the Gradient Picker, as shown in Figure 11.16.

Foreground to Transparent

Figure 11.16: Select the Foreground to Transparent gradient and click the Linear Style icon.

Select the Linear Style icon, as shown in the figure, and then set the other tool options as shown in Figure 11.15. Make sure that the Transparency check box is selected. Also note that the icon in the Gradient Picker will fade from the current foreground color to transparency; in the figure, the color was black, but you can use any color.

4. **Create a new empty layer above the layer you want to blur.**
Do the job quickly by clicking the New Layer icon in the Layers palette, shown in Figure 11.17.

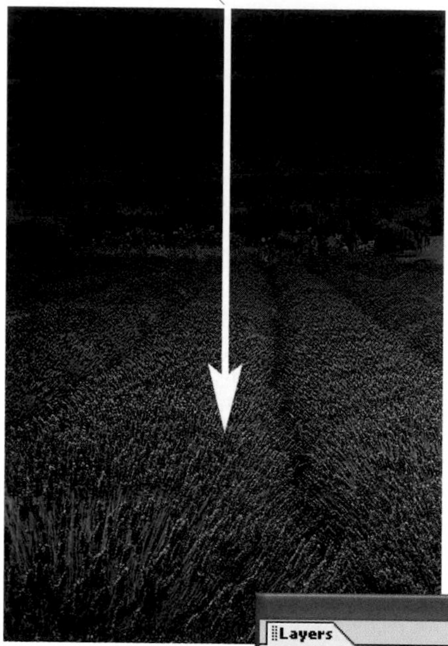

Start of drag

5. **Drag to produce a gradient on the new layer.**
Start your drag at the spot where you want the blur to be at full intensity and release the mouse at the point where you want no blur effect. For the sample image, drag from the top of the image to the position indicated by the white arrow in Figure 11.17. After you release the mouse button, a fading gradient appears over your image, as shown in the figure. Where the layer contains paint, the image will receive the blur; where the layer is transparent, no blur will occur. In the translucent areas, the blur will be applied at varying intensities, with darker areas getting a heavier impact. You can get a better idea of the placement of the transparency by looking at the Layers palette; remember, the checkerboard pattern indicates transparent pixels.

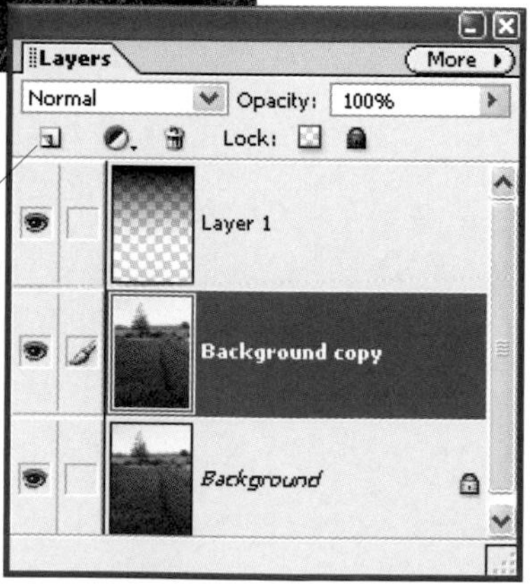

6. **CTRL-click (Windows) or ⌘-click (Mac) the gradient layer in the Layers palette.**
This step selects all non-transparent areas of the layer. Note that the selection outline doesn't accurately reflect the extent of the selection, so don't worry that it doesn't appear to encompass areas that are translucent in the gradient layer.

New Layer icon

Figure 11.17: Draw your gradient on a new layer, ending your drag at the point where you want the blur effect to fade completely.

7. **Hide the gradient layer by clicking its eyeball icon in the Layers palette.**

8. **In the Layers palette, click the duplicate layer that you created in Step 1.**

For the sample image, this layer is named Background Copy.

9. **Choose Filter | Blur | Gaussian Blur to open the Gaussian Blur dialog box.**

You can see the dialog box in the preceding section, in Figure 11.13. Turn on the Preview check box so that you can preview the results of the blur. Raise the Radius value as needed to produce the maximum amount of blur you want. For the sample image, set the value to 1.0 (or whatever looks good to you) and then click OK to close the dialog box. To compare the blurred and original image easily, just click the eyeball icon for the blur layer on and off.

If some areas didn't blur enough, try using the Blur tool, explained next, to strengthen the effect in those regions. Use the Eraser to remove or lessen the blur in areas that became too soft. You also can reduce the opacity of the blur layer to lessen the effect throughout the entire image, of course.

10. **When you're satisfied with the blur, get rid of the selection outline by pressing CTRL-D (Windows) or ⌘-D (Mac).**

11. **Delete the gradient layer and then merge the blur layer and underlying layer, as discussed in Chapter 6.**

Softening Focus with the Blur Tool

When you click or drag with the Blur tool, you blur pixels underneath your cursor. Use this tool for making focus adjustments to small areas or when applying a blur filter would require lots of intricate selection work. For example, on the right side of Figure 11.18, I dragged over the trees to make them less distracting. Notice how blurring the background makes the foreground appear sharper by comparison, too.

The following steps show you how to use this tool. To work along with the steps, open the sample image Statue.jpg.

Figure 11.18:
Dragging over the
trees with the Blur
tool softened their
impact on the
composition.

1. Create a new layer by clicking the New Layer icon in the Layers palette.

I named this layer "Blur Layer" for the purposes of illustration; you can stick with the default layer name, Layer 1.

Figure 11.19: Create a
new, empty layer to hold
the blurred pixels.

2. Select the Blur tool, shown in Figure 11.19.

The tool shares a flyout menu with the Sharpen and Smudge tools.

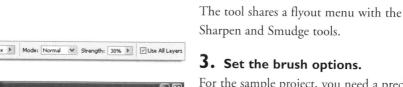

Blur tool

New Layer icon

3. Set the brush options.

For the sample project, you need a precise edge between the blurred and sharp areas, so select a hard brush. If you want the blur to fade at the edges of your strokes, however, use a softer brush. (For this tool, as with the Sharpen tool, you don't get a precise Hardness control, but you can press SHIFT-] to raise the Hardness by 25 percent. Or press SHIFT-[to reduce the hardness by 25 percent.)

4. Set the Mode option to Normal and set the Strength value to 30 percent.

The Strength value determines how much change you produce with each click or drag. Start low—you can always apply the tool multiple times to the same pixels if needed.

5. Turn on the Use All Layers check box.

This option enables the Blur tool to see through your new layer, which will hold the blur information, and access pixels on underlying layers.

6. Click on or drag over the pixels you want to blur, as shown in Figure 11.20.

It's a good idea to zoom in to a close-up view when you're working on the borders of the areas you want to blur. Press CTRL-+ (Windows) or ⌘-+ (Mac) to zoom in quickly; press CTRL or ⌘ with the minus key to zoom out.

As you work, adjust the Strength value as needed to create more or less blurring with each swipe of the tool. To reduce the blur effect throughout the entire image, reduce the opacity of the blur layer.

Remember

If you mess up while performing any change to a photo, press CTRL-Z (Windows) or ⌘-Z (Mac) to undo your last edit. See Chapter 3 for tips on undoing a series of editing blunders.

Figure 11.20: The Blur tool softens pixels under your cursor.

Tool Tricks

To quickly adjust the Strength value for the Sharpen and Blur tools, press the number keys. Press 0 for 100 percent, 9 for 90 percent, 85 for 85 percent, and so on.

7. **When you finish blurring, merge the blur layer with the underlying image as discussed in Chapter 6.**

In addition to creating depth-of-field effects, you can use the Blur tool to soften small image defects such as digital camera noise, film grain, or compression artifacts. (See the next section for more tips on that subject.) The Blur tool also acts as a great wrinkle-reducer when you're retouching portraits. For that use, try changing the Mode control to Darken or Lighten:

Figure 11.21: To try digital wrinkle-removal, open the sample image Eyes2.jpg.

- Use the Darken mode to soften light creases amid darker skin.
- Use the Lighten mode to reduce dark lines amid paler skin.

Try it out using the sample image Eyes2.jpg, shown in Figure 11.21. As with the statue example, create a new layer to hold your blurring strokes. Then, for the sake of experimentation, set the tool Mode Control to Normal and dab at the laugh lines near the left eye. You merely get blurrier lines, not less noticeable lines, as shown on the left in Figure 11.22. Now switch to Lighten mode and work on the right eye, keeping in mind that your goal is simply to *soften* the lines, not to create an unnatural, plastic look.

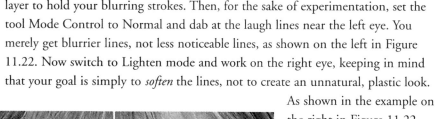

Figure 11.22: In Lighten mode, the Blur tool does a better job of softening dark wrinkles in light skin.

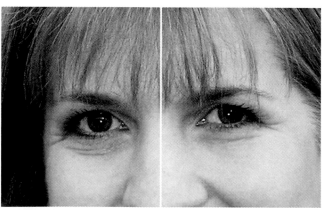

Normal mode   Lighten mode

As shown in the example on the right in Figure 11.22, this mode does a much more capable job of fading dark lines in light skin. (Again, use the Darken mode if the lines are lighter than the surrounding skin.) The same trick works for removing dust, scratches, and other small defects.

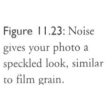

Figure 11.23: Noise gives your photo a speckled look, similar to film grain.

Softening Noise, Grain, and Compression Artifacts

Noise refers to a defect that sometimes occurs when you shoot with a digital camera in low light or at a very high ISO setting. Noise makes an image look as though it has been dusted with colored sand, as shown in Figure 11.23. The effect is similar to excess grain in a film print or slide.

Although you usually can't completely eradicate the level of noise found in the example picture, you can soften it by either applying the new Reduce Noise filter or simply applying a blur effect. These techniques also can reduce film grain or compression artifacts, a defect caused by too much JPEG compression. (Chapter 13 details this problem.)

First, give the Reduce Noise filter a whirl, working with the sample image Noise.jpg, featured in Figure 11.23.

1. Select and copy the noisy areas to a new layer.

For the sample image, copy the entire image by dragging the Background layer to the New Layer icon in the Layers palette (refer to Figure 11.19.) To copy just part of your image, create your selection outline and then press CTRL-J (Windows) or ⌘-J (Mac).

2. **Choose Filter | Noise | Reduce Noise to display the Reduce Noise dialog box, shown in Figure 11.24.**

If needed, you can click the plus and minus signs under the dialog box preview to zoom in or out on your image. Drag in the preview area to scroll the display. If you select the Preview check box, you can also preview the filter effects in the image window, although the dialog box itself may obscure most of the window.

Figure 11.24: The Reduce Noise filter can soften both luminance noise and color noise.

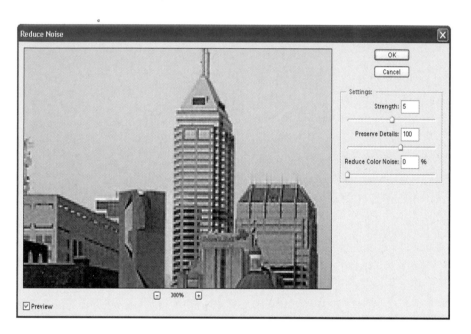

3. **Adjust the three dialog box sliders as needed to soften the image noise.**

The options work as follows:

■ **Strength** This slider affects so-called luminance noise, which refers to unwanted brightness variations. As you raise the value, Elements blurs pixels in a way that just affects their relative brightness.

- **Preserve Details**   As you lower this value, Elements becomes less discriminating about what it considers noise. At a very low value, details get blurry along with noise.
- **Reduce Color Noise**   This option is designed to remove color noise, which refers to unwanted, stray colored pixels. When Elements finds pixels that it thinks are color noise, it attempts to blend them with the surrounding pixels.

The proper settings depend on your photo. As you experiment with the sliders, keep an eye out for excessive blurring when you work with the Strength and Preserve Details sliders and too much loss of color detail when you adjust the Reduce Color Noise slider. (If you can't see your image clearly in the image window, you can click on the preview area inside the dialog box to toggle between the "before" and "after" views.)

4. Click OK to apply the filter.

If necessary, you can use the Eraser to rub out areas on the filtered layer that lost too much detail due to the Reduce Noise settings. Or lower the filtered layer's Opacity value to lessen the filter's effect throughout the entire layer.

5. Merge the corrected layer with the underlying layer using the techniques covered in Chapter 6.

In addition to the Reduce Noise filter, you can try these additional noise-removal tools:

- For light, overall noise or grain, try the Despeckle filter (Filter | Noise | Despeckle). This filter looks for edges—areas where significant color changes occur—and then blurs everything but those edges. The effect is subtle, and you don't get any control over the intensity of the blur. Apply the filter to a duplicate layer, just as when using the Reduce Noise filter.
- You also can manually blur problem areas with the Gaussian Blur filter or Blur tool, both explained earlier in this chapter. Again, do this work on a duplicate layer.

The problem, of course, is that any process that involves blurring pixels—which includes all the aforementioned remedies—also sacrifices image details, so you have to find a balance between removing the defect and retaining details. Fortunately, noise, grain, and artifacts usually are most noticeable in areas that don't contain much detail, such as the sky in the sample image. You can prevent the detail areas from being affected by creating a selection outline before tackling the noise problem.

As you blur, keep the final output size of the image in mind; you need to blur more or less depending on the print or display size. In fact, you may want to set the final output size and resolution, as explained in Chapter 13, before you tackle noise removal.

In most cases, you need to use a combination of these approaches to adequately conquer noise. For the improved image shown in Figure 11.25, for example, I applied the Reduce Noise filter first at the settings shown in Figure 11.24, which cleaned up the sky without doing too much damage to details in the foreground. Then I followed up with the Blur tool to soften noise in some areas in the buildings where the problem was most noticeable. The noise isn't completely gone, but the photo is much improved.

Figure 11.25: After a pass through the Remove Noise filter and some touch-ups with the Blur tool, the most noticeable noise is significantly softened.

One final tip: When working with the Despeckle filter, Blur tool, or Gaussian Blur, changing the blending mode of the blurred layer from Normal to Color can produce better results. In this mode, only color transitions are blurred, and the original luminosity details are retained.

Color Management Demystified

If you've read Chapter 1, you may recall that digital cameras, scanners, and monitors can generate colors beyond the printable spectrum, which is one reason why printed colors rarely match on-screen colors. To complicate matters, each monitor and printer puts its own spin on color. Display the same photo on 10 monitors, and you'll see 10 different renditions. Feed the same image to several printers, and no two prints will be exactly alike.

All this color confusion creates a dilemma: How do you make reasonable decisions when retouching your pictures if their appearance is subject to the whims of the output device? Keeping in mind that perfection isn't possible, you can improve color consistency significantly by following the steps outlined in this chapter.

Getting a Grip on Color Management

As discussed in Chapter 1, every color in a digital photo is represented by a numeric value. The actual hue, saturation, and brightness you get from a particular value, however, depend on the device—monitor, printer, scanner, or digital camera. Each device has different capabilities, so the same value can produce a variety of colors. For example, the two images in Figure 12.1 offer an approximation of how colors shift when they move from my monitor to my inkjet printer.

Figure 12.1: On-screen colors (left) usually appear more vivid than printed colors (right).

Although exact color matching between devices is impossible—especially between monitor and printer—you can achieve better color consistency by implementing a *color management system,* or CMS. A color management system involves two main components:

- **Color Profiles** A color profile is a data file that describes the color characteristics of a device, using a universally accepted color reference standard. The International Color Consortium developed the standard, which is why profiles are known as *ICC profiles*.
- **Color Engine** Sometimes referred to as the *color management module,* or CMM, the color engine serves as the color translator. When an image moves from one device to another, the color engine looks at the profiles for both devices. Then it decides the best way to translate the values from the first device to the second.

Remember

With personal photo printers, severe color problems may indicate a depleted ink supply, clogged print heads, or incorrect printer settings.

Although Elements doesn't offer all the color management features found in its higher-priced sibling, Photoshop, it does provide the basics. To implement the system, you first create or install color profiles for every device in your imaging chain. Next, you tell Elements how to deal with those profiles when opening your images. Finally, when printing, you specify the current image profile and the printer profile so that Elements knows how to translate the colors from screen to paper.

Don't worry if all this seems a little fuzzy right now. The rest of this chapter provides the specifics you need to set up your color management system, and the next chapter details the related steps to take when printing your photos.

Before I give you those details, however, you should know that entire books have been written on this subject. The information in this chapter is designed to give you a foothold from which you can explore more of the color management landscape. If you're interested in color science or continue to have serious color problems even after working your way through this chapter, I recommend studying the many other resources available, including those Adobe offers in the support area of its Web site. Just be prepared for your head to spin around its axis and perhaps twist clean off your neck. Yes, color can be that complex—who'd a thunk?

Enabling Color Management

To start taking advantage of color management in Elements, choose Edit | Color Settings if you're a Windows user. On a Mac, choose Color Settings from the Photoshop Elements menu. You then see the Color Settings dialog box, shown in Figure 12.2.

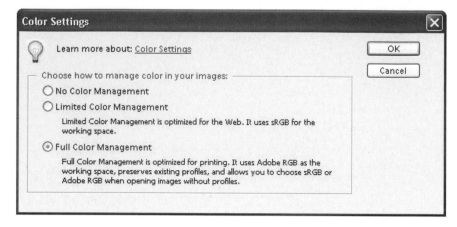

Figure 12.2: Select the Full Color Management button to take advantage of features that can improve screen-to-print color matching.

The choice you make in the Color Settings dialog box determines how Elements interprets the color values in the image files that you open in the program, as follows:

- **No Color Management** If you choose this option, Elements acts as if it doesn't have any color-management savvy at all. It tosses out existing image profiles and renders your image according to your monitor profile, which is what other programs that don't support color management do. Disabling color management simplifies your life in that you don't have to deal with some issues that crop up when you enable Full Color Management. So if you're happy with your photo colors and the way they translate to print, feel free to go the No Color Management route. Do still profile your monitor, however, as explained in the upcoming section, so that you're starting from a neutral canvas.

- **Limited Color Management** When you select this option, Elements interprets color data according to a profile known as sRGB. This profile is based on a limited color palette that can (theoretically) be reproduced by all devices and so should result in more consistent color. The problem is that because sRGB has a smaller range of colors—it even excludes some printable hues—your images may not be as rich or vibrant as they could be. Adobe provides this option mainly for Web artists who want to improve the chances that most people who view the images will see similar colors. If you want access to the broadest spectrum of colors, don't choose this option.

■ **Full Color Management** This option is best if you're picky about color. When you open an image, Elements retains the current profile, if one has been assigned—either by the device used to create the image or by you, when you previously saved the file, as explained later in this chapter. If the image hasn't been tagged with a profile, you see the dialog box shown in Figure 12.3, where you can choose between sRGB or Adobe RGB, a profile that encompasses a broader spectrum of colors than sRGB. If you choose the Leave It As It Is option, Elements doesn't color manage the image, so ignore this option if you want to take advantage of the improved printer-to-screen color consistency you get via color management.

Figure 12.3: When full color management is enabled, you can specify Adobe RGB or sRGB when you open an image that has no color profile.

To give you a better idea of the impact of choosing sRGB or Adobe RGB, Figure 12.4 shows the same image as it appears when opened using both profiles. The image on the left is the Adobe RGB version; the image on the right, sRGB. Of course, the differences you will see depend on the original subject colors. But my advice is to always use Adobe RGB when opening unprofiled images to give yourself access to the broadest range of colors. You can always make a Web copy of the final image using the sRGB profile if you want.

Figure 12.4: Adobe RGB (left) typically results in a richer color spectrum than sRGB (right).

Creating a Monitor Profile

Take a look at the background of the Elements program window. It's supposed to be neutral gray. But your monitor may be adding a tint to that gray—and to everything else on the screen. Figure 12.5, for example, shows a display with a serious blue bias. Unless you neutralize the monitor color cast, not only are you setting yourself up for color-matching problems when you print your photo, you're also editing the colors in your photo based on faulty information.

Most monitors don't allow you to tweak the machine

Figure 12.5: This screen shot was taken on a monitor that displays a blue tint.

itself to remove a color cast from the screen. Instead, you use a special tool to create a monitor profile. Elements uses the profile to automatically adjust on-screen colors to neutralize monitor-related tints. Figure 12.6 shows the neutralized version of the screen from Figure 12.5.

Figure 12.6: Profiling the monitor allows Elements to produce a neutral display.

Monitor profiling is quick and easy—what's more, a free profiling tool is available. For Windows users, Elements provides a tool called Adobe Gamma. On the Mac side, the operating system itself includes a profiling feature called the Display Calibrator Assistant.

These tools provide on-screen instructions for getting the job done, so I won't insult your intelligence by plodding through the process click by click. You do need to take one important preliminary step, however: Allow your monitor to warm up for at least 30 minutes. In addition, if your monitor allows you to change the White Point setting—which determines whether the monitor displays a "cool" (bluish) or "warm" (yellowish) white—choose either 5000 or 6500. This setting tends to produce better print color matching. Then start the profiling process as follows:

- **Windows XP (Adobe Gamma)** Adobe Gamma is installed in the Windows Control Panel when you install Elements. To run Adobe Gamma, open the Control Panel and then double-click the Adobe Gamma icon. You see the screen shown in Figure 12.7. Click Step By Step and then click Next.

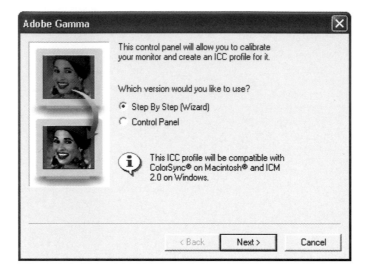

Figure 12.7: Windows users can use the Adobe Gamma utility, launched via the Windows Control Panel, to create a monitor profile.

■ **Mac OS X** Click the Apple menu and then click System Preferences. In the resulting dialog box, click the Displays icon and then click the Color button to display the options shown in Figure 12.8. To simplify things, check the Show Profiles for This Display Only option. Then click the Calibrate button to launch the Display Calibrator Assistant.

Figure 12.8: In OS X, the System Preferences dialog box houses the profiling tool.

The drawback to these free utilities is that they depend on your eyes to make color, contrast, and brightness judgments during the profiling process. For a less subjective approach, you can purchase a device known as a *colorimeter,* which analyzes the display for you. Figure 12.9 shows a colorimeter from ColorVision (www.colorvision.com).

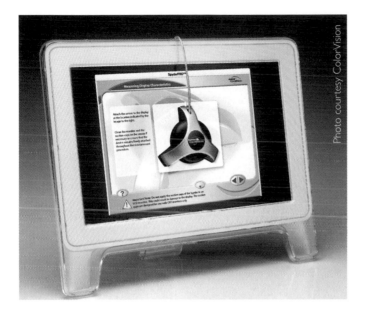

Photo courtesy ColorVision

Figure 12.9: A colorimeter offers a more precise approach to monitor calibration.

Colorimeters start at about $150. In addition to ColorVision, other respected manufacturers include X-Rite (www.xrite.com) and GretagMacbeth (www.i1color.com).

Watch Out!

Whichever calibration route you choose, repeat the process once a month. Displays drift over time, so your monitor profile can quickly become inaccurate. Also, if you build a Windows monitor profile with a colorimeter, consult the product manual to determine whether you should disable Adobe Gamma.

Profiling Your Printer

When you print an image, specifying a printer profile lets Photoshop best translate the image color information to the printer. Photoshop provides profiles for dozens of common printers, and many new printers add profiles when you install the printer software.

To see what profiles are installed on your system, choose File | Print to display the Print dialog box. Select the Show More Options box and then open the Print Space list, as shown in Figure 12.10.

Figure 12.10: Ideally, you should install printer profiles for each type of paper you use.

Depending on your printer, you may see several profiles, each specific to a type of paper (glossy, semigloss, watercolor, and so on). The paper stock impacts printed colors, so having paper-specific profiles is a good idea.

If you don't see profiles for your printer, you have several options:

- Check the printer manufacturer's Web site to see whether any profiles are available for download. In addition, some companies that sell photo paper make profiles available for using their products on certain printers. Follow the instructions on the Web sites for installing these profiles.
- Scout around on the Web for profiles sold by third-party companies. You can buy a collection of generic profiles for popular printer and paper combinations, or you can have custom profiles created just for your equipment. You also may be able to track down fellow digital-printing enthusiasts who are willing to share profiles they've created.
- If you're having your photo commercially printed, ask the company whether it provides profiles for its printer or press.

- Buy a profiling product such as Monaco EZColor, from Monaco Systems, or PrintFIX, from ColorVision. Although expensive—expect to pay $300 and up—these products enable you to create custom profiles, which usually provide more reliable results than the generic profiles from equipment manufacturers. For a little more cash, you can buy profiling products bundled with a colorimeter.

The next chapter explains all the Print dialog box options in detail. For now, just click Cancel to close the dialog box.

Profiling Your Scanner or Camera

If your digital darkroom includes a scanner, digital camera, or both, expert color management requires profiling them as well as your monitor and printer. Many scanner and camera manufacturers don't provide profiles, however, so if you want a profile specific to your equipment, you'll have to purchase a profiling system such as those mentioned in the preceding section.

As an alternative, you can simply rely on the two generic RGB profiles mentioned earlier—sRGB or Adobe RGB. Some cameras and scanners automatically tag image files with one of these profiles; if your equipment doesn't, you can simply specify the profile when you open the file in Elements, as discussed earlier.

Watch Out!

One caveat regarding digital camera profiles: As I mentioned in Chapter 2, many digital camera manufacturers include a color profile tag in the image metadata, sometimes referred to as EXIF metadata. Photoshop can read this tag when you open the image file. Unfortunately, the metadata tag sometimes *does not* reflect the actual color profile used by the camera—many manufacturers just assign the generic sRGB tag. (There are technical reasons for this; manufacturers aren't purposely trying to screw you up.) So unless you're certain that the metadata tag is accurate, see Chapter 2 to find out how to tell Photoshop to ignore the tag. Then you can choose a profile when you open the file.

Embedding Profiles

When you save photos in certain file formats, including PSD, TIFF, and JPEG, Elements enables you to include the color profile data in the image file. This is known as *embedding* the profile.

To embed a profile in Windows, simply check the ICC Profile box in the Save As dialog box, as shown in Figure 12.11. On a Mac, the option name is Embed Color Profile.

Figure 12.11:
You can embed a profile when saving an image.

Embedding profiles is most helpful when you're sharing files with others. Everyone who opens the file then can use the same profile, thereby maintaining color consistency. But this assumes that people open the file in a program that supports color management. If not, the profile is simply ignored.

Even if you're not sharing files, embedding profiles is usually a good idea, although not absolutely necessary. If you embed the file, you'll be able to open an image five years from now and know exactly what color profile you used to create the image.

There are some situations in which an embedded profile can screw up the works, however:

■ **Don't embed profiles in Web images. Profiles increase file size, and most browsers can't take advantage of them anyway.**

- If you're having your files commercially printed, ask the tech support contact whether or not to embed the file. This rule goes both for offset printers as well as for photo printers (such as a Fuji Pictography or Durst Lambda).

Print and Share Your Photos

13

For most of us, the real joy of photography comes from sharing pictures with others. And digital imaging makes it easier, cheaper, and faster than ever to get your photos out into the world. You can e-mail images to faraway clients or friends in minutes, and show off your favorite pictures at online photo-sharing sites. When you want prints to frame or sell, you can produce stunning results in your own studio or simply deliver your image files to a local lab for output. No more nasty darkroom fumes. No more wasting money on processing and printing those inevitable clunkers in every roll of film.

This chapter tells you everything you need to know to prepare your best images for their journey to print or the Web, from setting the picture size to choosing the right file format for the photo's final destination.

Making Beautiful Prints

Whether you print your own photos or hand the job to someone else, you need to take a few steps to prepare your image files. The next few sections give you the low-down. If you haven't read Chapter 12, explore it as well to find out how to achieve more accurate screen-to-print color matching.

Setting Print Size and Resolution

As explained in Chapter 1, print quality is greatly affected by output resolution, which is measured in pixels per inch (ppi). How many pixels you need for good prints depends on the printer.

- If you're using your own printer, check your printer manual or the manufacturer's Web site for recommendations. Most home and office printers do their best stuff with about 300 ppi; some Epson printers suggest 360 ppi, however. Note, too, that most printers don't demand that you be spot on with resolution; you probably won't notice much difference between 300 ppi and 280 ppi, for example.

- If you're taking your files to a lab, consult with the service rep. Some labs ask for only 200 ppi. Be sure to follow the lab guidelines, or your order may not be output correctly.

- If you're submitting files for use in a publication, get resolution guidelines from the production artist. The norm is 300 ppi, but as we both know, not everyone is normal. You may need to submit a particular photo size as well.

Figure 13.1: Turn off the Resample Image check box to avoid altering the pixel count.

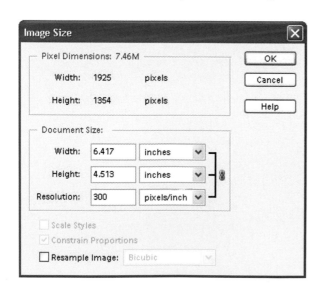

To establish output resolution and print dimensions, take these steps:

1. Choose Image | Resize | Image Size. You see the Image Size dialog box, shown in Figure 13.1.

2. Uncheck the Resample Image box at the bottom of the dialog box.

3. Enter the desired width in the Width box.

To retain the original proportions of your image, Elements automatically adjusts the Height value. You can alternatively enter the desired print height, in which case the Width value updates automatically.

The Resolution value also updates automatically to show you how many pixels per inch you'll get at the specified size. If the Resolution value is too low, you can either reduce the print dimensions or add pixels. Adding pixels won't improve print quality, however, and in fact may reduce it. See Chapter 1 for details.

If the Resolution value is too high, you can eliminate excess pixels—*downsampling,* in digital lingo—without doing much damage to the image. However, you may be able to skip this step if you're using your own printer; experiment to see whether print quality suffers noticeably when you send the printer an overage of pixels.

To adjust resolution by changing pixel count, select the Resample Image box, turn on the Constrain Proportions box and, if available, the Scale Styles box. If you're adding pixels, select Bicubic Smoother from the drop-down list next to the Resample Image box. If you're downsampling, select Bicubic. (Bicubic Sharper is also designed for downsampling, but because it sometimes oversharpens, I stick with plain old Bicubic.) Finally, type the new Resolution value.

4. **Click OK to close the dialog box.**

Printing from Elements

After setting the picture size and output resolution, load the photo paper you want to use into your printer. Then follow these steps to transfer pixels to paper:

1. **Choose File | Print to display the Print Preview dialog box, shown in Figure 13.2.**

Initially, your dialog box may not show all the controls you see below the Show More Options box in the figure. To display those additional controls, click the Show More Options box.

PART V | PHOTOGRAPHER'S GUIDE TO OUTPUT

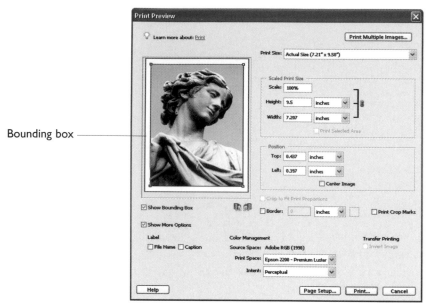

Bounding box ──────

Figure 13.2: Select your printer profile from the Print Space drop-down list.

2. Click the Page Setup button to open the Page Setup dialog box and set the paper size and orientation.

The dialog box differs depending on your operating system; you can see the Windows and Mac OS X versions in Figure 13.3. The options here also depend on your currently selected printer. In OS X, you can select a printer using the Format For drop-down list. In Windows, click the Printer button to select a different printer.

Regardless, you should be able to set the paper size and print orientation—Portrait (vertical) or Landscape (horizontal). On the Mac side, leave the Scale value at 100 percent.

Figure 13.3: Choose paper size and print orientation from the Page Setup dialog box, shown here for Windows XP (left) and OS X (right).

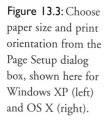
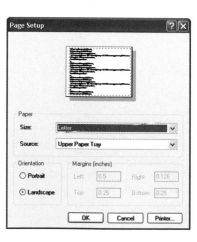

3. Click OK to close the Page Setup dialog box.

4. Set the Print Size option to Actual Size, as shown in Figure 13.2.

Other Print Size settings and those in the Scaled Print Size area enable you to adjust the print size for the current print job, which of course also adjusts the output resolution. You should instead set these values before heading to the Print Preview dialog box, as explained in the preceding section.

5. Use the Position controls to position the image on the paper.

If you deselect the Center Image check box, you can access the Top and Left boxes to position the image precisely. Alternatively, select the Show Bounding Box option to display an outline—called a *bounding box*—around your image, as shown in Figure 13.2. Then just drag the image to reposition the photo. But be careful not to drag a border of the bounding box, or you resize the image.

6. Specify a printer profile and intent.

Select a printer profile from the Print Space drop-down list. (See Chapter 12 to find out more about printer profiles. Choose Perceptual from the Intent drop-down list. This second option determines the formula Elements uses to translate the image colors to print; Perceptual is the best choice for most photographs. (But you may also want to experiment with Relative Colormetric.)

7. Click Print to display another Print dialog box.

Again, the dialog box depends on your operating system. Figure 13.4 shows the Windows XP version; Figure 13.5 shows the Mac OS X version.

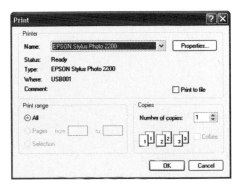

Figure 13.4: In Windows, click the Properties button to access printer-specific options.

Figure 13.5: In OS X, click the Copies & Pages drop-down list to access additional printer options.

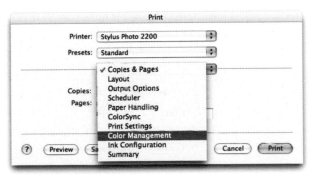

8. **Specify your printer options.**

In Windows, access these options by clicking the Properties button. On a Mac, open the third drop-down list—it should show the Copies & Pages item when you first open the dialog box. Then select a category of options from the list, as shown in Figure 13.5.

Every printer offers different options, so consult your manual to find out what each setting does and experiment to see what combination of options provides the best results. Figure 13.6 shows the multitude of controls available for an Epson 2200 as they appear in Windows. (Note that with this printer, you must click the Advanced button to display these options; other printers may similarly require you to switch to advanced mode to access the full options buffet.)

Figure 13.6: Turn off printer color management and let Elements handle the job.

Watch Out!

Two warnings apply regardless of your printer model:

■ Turn printer color management *off*, if that control is available. Otherwise, both Elements and the printer try to manage the image color, which can lead to problems. Again, you may need to access your printer's advanced options to turn off printer color management.

■ Select the media setting that matches your paper stock. Most printers adjust printing based on that setting, and a mismatch usually leads to improper colors or saturation.

9. In Windows, click **OK** to close the **Properties** dialog box.

10. Click **Print** to send the image file to the printer.

One more note about the Print Preview dialog box: The Border option allows you to add a solid border around the image for the current print job. But when you add a border this way, Elements doesn't simply increase the final print size to accommodate the border. Instead, it reduces the size of your image as necessary to retain the original print dimensions. In addition, the border affects your current print job only.

To add a permanent border, cancel out of the Print Preview dialog box and use this method instead: Choose Image | Resize | Canvas Size. Select the Relative check box and then enter the border thickness, times two, into the Width and Height boxes. For example, if you want a 1-inch border all around, enter 2 into both boxes. Click the center Anchor square and then use the Canvas Extension Color option to choose the border color. Click OK to complete the process. This technique does increase your picture dimensions, however. So if you're after a particular output size, you either need to first crop the image to accommodate the border or use the Image Size command to reset the print dimensions after adding the border. See Chapter 3 for more information about the Canvas Size dialog box.

Preparing Files for Commercial Printing

Before sending your photos to a lab or commercial printer, ask the service rep the following questions so that you can properly prepare your files:

- **What resolution (ppi) should I use?** Set the resolution and print dimensions as explained in the first section of this chapter.
- **Is an RGB file okay?** Most photo labs request RGB, but for commercial presses, you may need to supply your file in the CMYK color model. If the printer wants CMYK, ask for guidelines in doing the conversion—and find a friend who owns Photoshop to do the job for you, because you can't accomplish this step in Elements. For black-and-white printing, Grayscale may be the order of the day. See Chapter 1 for more about RGB, CMYK, and Grayscale.
- **What file formats can you accept?** Some printers accept Elements (PSD) files, but the most commonly used print format is TIFF. See the next section to find out how to save a TIFF version of your image.
- **Should I embed color profiles?** Some printers don't like profiles; others are happy to get them. (Head to Chapter 12 for details about color profiles.)

Finally, if you have a decent photo printer, it's a good idea to print a proof of your photo to give the printer a better idea of the colors you're after. Keep in mind that you shouldn't expect a perfect color match, however.

Saving TIFF Files for Publishing Use

Preparing a photo for publication in a newsletter, book, ad, or other document?
You need to save the file in a format that's recognized by the program used to put
the piece together. A few programs can work with the Elements (PSD) format, but
TIFF is the safest bet. Even word processing programs accept TIFF files.

Watch Out!

The following steps show you how to save a TIFF copy of your photo. If your photo
contains layers and you haven't yet saved the image in the PSD format, do so *before* you
create your TIFF file. Choose File | Save As and select PSD as the file format. Be sure to
select the Layers option in the Save As dialog box. (See Chapter 3 for details about the
other options in the Save As dialog box.)

With your PSD copy preserved, take these steps:

1. Choose File | Save As to display the Save As dialog box.
Figure 13.7 shows the Windows version of the dialog box. The Mac version contains the same basic options. (For details, see Chapter 3.)

Figure 13.7: To ensure
compatibility with other
programs, turn off Layers
when saving TIFF files.

**2. Choose TIFF
from the
Format drop-
down list and
give the file
a name.**

**3. Specify the
other
file-saving
options.**

Only a few pro-
grams—notably,
those from Adobe—
can work with files
that contain layers.
Presumably, you
took my advice at
the start of the steps

and saved a PSD copy of the file that will preserve those features, so disable the Layers option here if it's available. The As a Copy box then automatically becomes selected. Elements displays yellow warning triangles to remind you not to turn off that As a Copy box.

I'll leave the choice to embed the color profile up to you; for help in making the decision, read Chapter 12. (Some professional publishing applications can read profiles; most consumer programs can't.) Chapter 3 details the remaining Save As options.

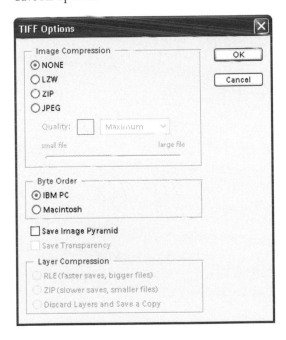

Figure 13.8: Use these options for maximum compatibility for images that will be used in a Windows-based publishing program.

4. **Click Save to display the TIFF Options dialog box, shown in Figure 13.8.**

Set the options as follows:

- **Image Compression** These options *compress* the image —which means to eliminate some data in order to shrink the image file. LZW compresses the file without harming image quality, but some programs gag on files that use this option. For maximum compatibility, choose None. (ZIP and JPEG aren't good choices in any circumstance.)

- **Byte Order**   Don't worry about what this one means—just choose IBM PC unless you know that you'll be using your photos only on a Mac. Most programs can open files saved in either byte order, but Windows programs seem to be more picky than Mac programs about this issue.
- **Save Image Pyramid**   This option stores the image in several resolutions within the same file. Turn it off; it's designed for pros distributing TIFF files via Web servers.

5. Click OK.

Elements creates the TIFF version of your file. If you saved the file with the As a Copy option enabled, the PSD version of the file remains open and the TIFF file is stored in the folder you specified in Step 3.

Preparing Photos for the Web

To prepare an image for a Web page or any other on-screen use, don't follow the same approach as for printed pictures. You must set the image size differently and save the file in the JPEG format, not TIFF or PSD. The rest of this chapter walks you through the necessary screen-prep steps.

Setting the Display Size

Output resolution—ppi—is irrelevant for screen pictures. For reasons detailed in Chapter 1, the size at which a picture appears on-screen depends only on the image pixel dimensions and the monitor resolution. For example, at a monitor resolution of 800 × 600, an 800 × 600–pixel image fills the screen. You get the *exact same display size* whether ppi is 72 or 300 or 3000.

If you shot or scanned your photo at a high resolution, it will have way too many pixels for screen use. So you need to *downsample* the image—a fancy way of saying dumping excess pixels. Walk this way:

1. Save a copy of the image in the PSD format.

Watch Out!

Don't skip this step! You may need all your original pixels back some day. If your image contains layers, enable the Layers check box in the Save As dialog box when you save your PSD file. Later you'll need to save your file in the JPEG format, which can't retain layers.

2. Choose Image | Resize | Image Size to display the Image Size dialog box.

3. Select the Resample Image check box, as shown in Figure 13.9.

4. Choose Bicubic from the adjacent drop-down menu.

This option determines the formula that Elements uses when downsampling the image. Bicubic typically produces the best results. Elements also offers Bicubic Sharper, which is designed to deliver a sharper downsampled image. The problem is that some areas may appear oversharpened.

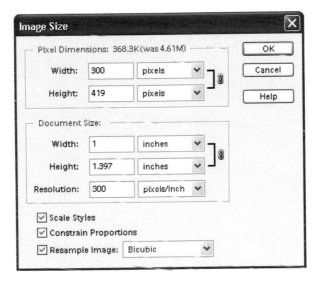

PART V | PHOTOGRAPHER'S GUIDE TO OUTPUT

Figure 13.9: For screen pictures, set the image size in pixels.

I usually stick with Bicubic and then apply the Unsharp Mask filter after setting the image size if needed. Chapter 11 discusses sharpening.

5. Select the Constrain Proportions box and the Scale Styles box, if it's not dimmed.

6. Enter the new pixel dimensions.

Use the top pair of Width and Height controls, in the Pixel Dimensions area at the top of the dialog box. If you're preparing a file for the Web or e-mail, keep in mind when setting the display size that the browser or e-mail program window will occupy a percentage of the available screen space. So for e-mail images, I typically use a maximum height of 300 pixels and a maximum width of 400 pixels. For a multimedia presentation, however, you may want the image to fill the entire screen—in which case, you just match the image width and height to the resolution of the display device.

7. Click OK.

After setting the image size, choose View | Actual Pixels to view the photo at the size it will appear on a screen that's using your same monitor resolution.

Time Saver

When you explore the next section, you'll discover that you can also change the pixel dimensions inside the Save for Web dialog box. This feature enables you to set the image size and save the file in the JPEG format (the Web format) in one step. The downside is that you don't then have the opportunity to apply the Unsharp Mask filter before saving the image. For important images, I set the display size with Image Size, sharpen with Unsharp Mask, and then use Save for Web to save the file. But for casual work, feel free to save a few seconds and do everything with Save for Web.

Saving JPEG Files

Save images headed for the Web in the JPEG format; browsers and e-mail programs can't open TIFF or PSD files. Also go JPEG for pictures that you plan to use in multimedia presentations.

JPEG earned its status as the leading online photo format because it produces smaller files than TIFF, PSD, and many other formats. To shrink files, JPEG applies *compression,* a process that eliminates some image data.

Compression comes in two forms:

- *Lossless compression* dumps only redundant image data and so does no visible harm to picture quality. LZW compression, available when you save in the TIFF format, is a lossless compression scheme.
- *Lossy compression* is less discriminating and can lead to a loss of image detail. JPEG uses this type of compression.

Watch Out!

When you save a JPEG file, you can specify how much compression you want to apply. The greater the compression, the more your image quality suffers. An overly compressed photo has a blocky look and is littered with *artifacts*—color defects that are most noticeable in areas of flat color.

Figure 13.10 compares an image saved with minimum JPEG compression to one saved with maximum compression. Both images contain the same number of pixels; the quality and file size differences here are due only to compression. The highly compressed version has a much smaller file size—always a goal for Web images—but the photo looks awful. Figure 13.11 shows a close-up segment of both examples.

Figure 13.10: Lightly compressed JPEGs (left) look fine; heavy compression destroys image quality.

Minimum compression, 140K

Maximum compression, 11K

 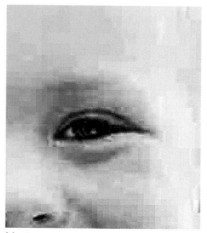

Figure 13.11: Overly compressed images have a "tiled" look.

Minimum compression   Maximum compression

Remember

You may be able to soften the impact of JPEG artifacts by using the blurring techniques discussed in Chapter 11.

As the photographer, you'll have to decide how much quality you're willing to trade for smaller files. Fortunately, Elements provides a *JPEG optimization tool* that helps you find the right balance. Take advantage of it as follows:

1. **With your image open, choose File | Save for Web to open the Save for Web dialog box, shown in Figure 13.12.**

Hand tool

Zoom tool

JPEG Options

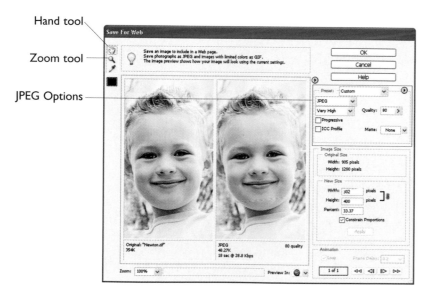

Figure 13.12: Save for Web enables you to see how your image will appear at various compression amounts.

The dialog box contains two previews: On the left, you see your original image; on the right, you can see how the picture will look at your chosen compression setting.

2. **Use the Zoom and Hand tools to adjust the area shown in the previews if needed.**

Figure 13.12 labels these tools. Click a preview with the Zoom tool to zoom in; ALT-click (Windows) or OPTION-click (Mac) to zoom out. Drag in the preview with the Hand tool to scroll the image.

3. **Open the Preview menu, labeled in Figure 13.13, and choose a modem speed.**

Underneath each preview, Elements shows you both the estimated file size and the download speed at the selected compression setting. Download speed is based on the option you select from the Preview menu. Choose 28.8 Kbps Modem, as shown in the figure—this is the slowest speed at which most people access the Web today. Prepare images with this lowest common denominator in mind.

Click to open Preview menu

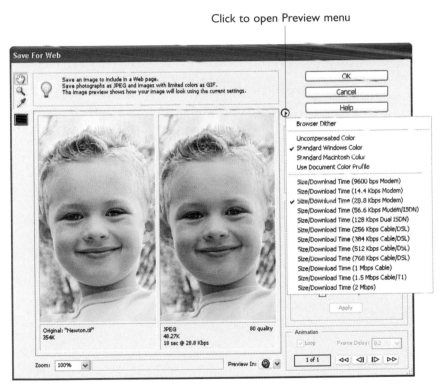

Figure 13.13: Select 28.8 Kbps Modem to see how long your file will take to download over a slow dial-up modem.

4. **Select a Color option from the Preview menu.**

These four color options enable you to preview the image as it will display under various monitor conditions. The Standard Windows Color and Standard Macintosh Color options display the image as it will appear on the average Windows or Macintosh monitor, respectively. Check the photo using both options because images typically appear darker on a PC than a Mac. If the image appears significantly dark with the PC preview or very light with the Mac preview, you may want to cancel out of the dialog box and adjust image brightness accordingly.

The Uncompensated Color option uses your specific monitor profile to display the image, which isn't much use for Web imagery. Neither is the Use Document Color Profile option very helpful: It displays the file as it would appear if you embedded a color profile (which adds to file size and increases download time) *and* displayed the photo in a program that could read the profiles, which excludes most browsers and e-mail programs.

Remember that these options adjust the display you see in the Save for Web dialog box *only.* They don't affect how Elements actually saves your file.

5. **Choose JPEG from the Format menu.**

Look for this menu in the area of the dialog box labeled JPEG Options in Figure 13.12. An enlarged view appears in Figure 13.14.

Format ——————

Quality options ——————

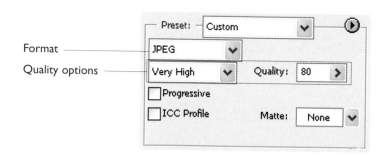

Figure 13.14: These options control the file format and compression amount.

6. **Use the Quality settings to specify the compression amount.**

Pay attention here: The higher the Quality setting, the less compression you apply—because less compression means a better image. Quality settings range from 100 (least compression, largest files, best images) to 0 (maximum compression, smallest files, stinky images). Either specify an exact value using the Quality option or choose one of the quality ranges from the drop-down list to the left (Very High is selected in Figure 13.14).

As you change the settings, the right image preview will update. Play with the Quality settings until you find a good balance between file size, download time, and image quality.

7. Disable the other JPEG options.

Turn off the Progressive option, which can cause conflicts with some older browsers. Enable the ICC Profile option *only* if you are preparing the file for a program that can take advantage of profiles—otherwise, you're only increasing file size needlessly. Again, most Web browsers and e-mail programs can't read profiles.

The Matte option comes into play only if the bottom layer of your image contains transparent pixels. Those pixels will become the matte color that you select. If you choose None, they become white. (Experienced Web designers sometimes set the matte color to match the Web page background so that the areas of the photo that were transparent appear to be part of that background.)

8. Click OK.

You're whisked to the Save Optimized As dialog box, a variation of the standard Save As dialog box. The dialog box design depends on your computer operating system; Figure 13.15 shows the Windows variety. On a Mac, you may need to click the arrow at the end of the Save As box to expand the dialog box and display additional options. Name the file and select the save location as usual. (Ignore the Save as Type option in Windows; you only get one choice.)

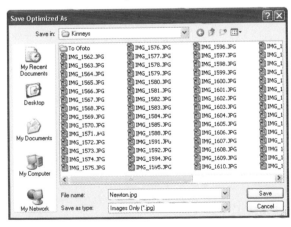

Figure 13.15: Web images should always be saved in the JPEG format.

Watch Out!

If you started out with a JPEG file, be sure to give this file a new name! Otherwise, you'll overwrite the original.

9. Click Save.

Elements creates and saves the JPEG version of your file. The file does not appear on-screen; if you want to see it, open it in the usual way. Your original image remains open.

Time Saver

Using the controls in the Image Size area of the Save for Web dialog box, you can specify the pixel dimensions of the image at the same time you save the photo. (Refer to Figure 13.12.) As mentioned earlier, I don't recommend this option for important photos because you lose the chance to sharpen images after the resampling, but for quick projects, it's fine. Be sure to select Constrain Proportions and click Apply after you enter the new pixel dimensions.

You also can save to the JPEG format via the regular File | Save As command. You get access to the same options as in Save for Web, but without the advantage of the side-by-side image previews or the option to change the image pixel dimensions. If your computer takes a long time to generate the Save for Web previews,

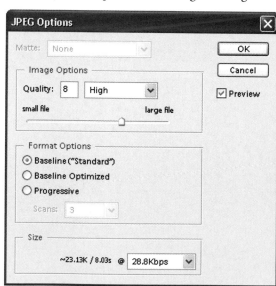

you may be able to save some time by using Save As to create your JPEG copies. When you go this route, specify whether or not to embed a color profile in the Save As dialog box. After you click Save, you see the JPEG Options dialog box, shown in Figure 13.16. Set the Format Options control to Baseline ("Standard"), which gives you the same results as turning off the

Figure 13.16: When you save to JPEG via the Save As dialog box, set the Format Options control to Baseline ("Standard").

Progressive Option in the Save for Web dialog box. The numbers in the Size area show you the approximate file size and the download time for the modem speed you select from the drop-down list. By turning on the Preview box, you can see how your chosen settings will affect the image. Click the box on and off to toggle between the original and compressed versions of the photo.

Watch Out!

Every time you edit and save a file in the JPEG format, it gets compressed again, resulting in more image damage. So never save works-in-progress in this format—always work in PSD Save the JPEG version only when the file is finished and ready for its screen debut.

INDEX

C

color spaces, 8. See also color models

color tints, 164

Color Variations dialog box, 160

Color Variations filter, 158–161

color wheel, 9, 158, 170

colorimeter, 246–247, 249

Colorize option, 185, 187–188

ColorVision colorimeters, 247

commercial printers, 251, 259

compression

    artifacts, 233–237, 264, 266

    described, 264

    JPEG, 261, 264–271

    lossless, 264

    lossy, 264

    LZW, 261, 264

    Quality settings, 268–269

    TIFF options, 261

    types of, 264

    ZIP, 261

Contiguous option, 95–96

Contract command, 103

contrast, 93, 138–140, 142

convergence, 65–69

Cookie Cutter tool, 74–79

cooling filters, 174–176

Copy command, 117

copying

    adjustment layers, 129

    images, 116–117

    layer selections, 126, 137

    photos, 116–117

    resolution and, 116–117

crop boundary, 70–72

Crop command, 72–73

Crop tool, 50–51, 70–73

cropping

    to aspect ratio, 72–73

    canvas, 50–51, 74

    image borders and, 259

    images, 64, 69–79

    to irregular shapes, 74–79

    methods for, 69–79

    photos, 69–79

    with precision, 74

    to specific size, 72–73

crosshair cursor, 20, 193, 201

Current Color swatch, 37

cursors

    Brush Size, 20

    brush styles, 19–20

    crosshair, 20, 193, 201

    customizing appearance of, 19–20

    non-brush tools, 20

    Outline Move, 101

    painting, 19

    Precise, 20

    preferences, 19

    rotate, 64

    source, 193, 201

    Standard, 20

    tool, 201

custom swatches, 39

D

Darken mode, 232

Default Colors control, 35

Delete Selection command, 107

deleting

    adjustment layers, 129

    color swatches, 39

    layer elements, 112

    layers, 113

INTERNATIONAL CONTACT INFORMATION

AUSTRALIA
McGraw-Hill Book Company
Australia Pty. Ltd.
TEL +61-2-9900-1800
FAX +61-2-9878-8881
http://www.mcgraw-hill.com.au
books-it_sydney@mcgraw-hill.com

CANADA
McGraw-Hill Ryerson Ltd.
TEL +905-430-5000
FAX +905-430-5020
http://www.mcgraw-hill.ca

GREECE, MIDDLE EAST, & AFRICA
(Excluding South Africa)
McGraw-Hill Hellas
TEL +30-210-6560-990
TEL +30-210-6560-993
TEL +30-210-6560-994
FAX +30-210-6545-525

MEXICO (Also serving Latin America)
McGraw-Hill Interamericana Editores
S.A. de C.V.
TEL +525-1500-5108
FAX +525 117 1589
http://www.mcgraw-hill.com.mx
carlos_ruiz@mcgraw-hill.com

SINGAPORE (Serving Asia)
McGraw-Hill Book Company
TEL +65-6863-1580
FAX +65-6862-3354
http://www.mcgraw-hill.com.sg
mghasia@mcgraw-hill.com

SOUTH AFRICA
McGraw-Hill South Africa
TEL +27-11-622-7512
FAX +27-11-622-9045
robyn_swanepoel@mcgraw-hill.com

SPAIN
McGraw-Hill/
Interamericana de España, S.A.U.
TEL +34-91-180-3000
FAX +34-91-372-8513
http://www.mcgraw-hill.es
professional@mcgraw-hill.es

UNITED KINGDOM, NORTHERN, EASTERN, & CENTRAL EUROPE
McGraw-Hill Education Europe
TEL +44-1-628-502500
FAX +44-1-628-770224
http://www.mcgraw-hill.co.uk
emea_queries@mcgraw-hill.com

ALL OTHER INQUIRIES Contact:
McGraw-Hill/Osborne
TEL +1-510-420-7700
FAX +1-510-420-7703
http://www.osborne.com
omg_international@mcgraw-hill.com

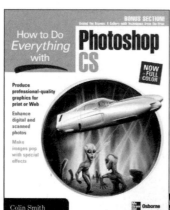